TORCH BIBLE
COMMENTARIES

General Editors

THE REV. JOHN MARSH, D.PHIL.
Principal of Mansfield College, Oxford

THE VERY REV. ALAN RICHARDSON, D.D.
Dean of York

FOREWORD TO SERIES

The aim of this series of commentaries on books of the Bible is to provide the general reader with the soundest possible assistance in understanding the message of each book considered as a whole and as a part of the Bible.

The findings and views of modern critical scholarship on the text of the Bible have been taken fully into account; but we have asked the writers to remember that the Bible is more than a quarry for the practice of erudition; that it contains the message of the living God.

We hope that intelligent people of varying interests will find that these commentaries, while not ignoring the surface difficulties, are able to concentrate the mind on the essential gospel contained in the various books of the Bible.

ISAIAH 1-39

JOHN MAUCHLINE

*Professor of Old Testament Language and Literature
in the University of Glasgow*

SCM PRESS LTD

BLOOMSBURY STREET LONDON

334 00684 8

First published 1962
by SCM Press Ltd
56 Bloomsbury Street London WC1
Second impression 1966
Third impression 1970
Fourth impression 1972

© SCM Press Ltd 1962

Reprinted in Great Britain by
Lewis Reprints Ltd
member of Brown Knight & Truscott Group
London and Tonbridge

CONTENTS

5

COMMENTARY

SERMONS OF ISAIAH'S EARLY PERIOD

1.1–6.13

THE RAVAGES OF WAR AND THE WAY OF PEACE

7.1–12.6

UTTERANCES AGAINST FOREIGN NATIONS

13.1–23.18

YAHWEH'S WORLD JUDGMENT

24.1–27.13

THE RULE OF GOD AND THE PLANS OF MEN

28.1–32.20

PRESENT DISTRESS AND FUTURE BLESSEDNESS

33.1–35.10

A HISTORICAL RECORD

36.1–39.8

PREFACE

Most modern scholars hold the view that chs. 40-66 of the Book of Isaiah belong to a period much later than the lifetime of the prophet Isaiah; but I have assumed that, since my commission is to write a commentary upon chs. 1-39 only, I am not expected to discuss the unity of the Book of Isaiah as a whole.

In writing this book I have tried to avoid discussing subjects in the Introduction which may be deemed to be adequately covered in the Commentary; but a certain amount of overlapping is unavoidable. In cases where detailed historical or literary problems are discussed in the commentary, the results are assumed in the introduction.

In using this book the reader is invited to have a copy of the RSV at hand. Where the differences between the renderings of a verse in AV and RSV are great, it has sometimes been possible to write an appropriate note; but lack of available space has sometimes ruled this out and the bald statement that the RSV gives a better rendering has to suffice.

For the understanding of some historical events of the time of Isaiah, help is available from some extra-biblical sources. The reader's attention is drawn to these by means of references to a recently published volume which is now widely used, viz, D. Winton Thomas (ed.), *Documents from Old Testament Times*. For topographical questions, reference is made to L. H. Grollenberg, *Shorter Atlas of the Bible*.

It is often said in commentaries that any utterance in Isa. 1-39 which is universalist in theological outlook, or expects a return to their native land of the Jews of the Diaspora, or looks forward to the new age of prosperity and peace, is much too developed in standpoint for the prophet's own day and must be referred to a later time, exilic or post-exilic. But out of his

9

own experience, Hosea, a prophet of the same period as Isaiah, came to have hope for his people; the fact that that hope is expressed in chs. 1-3 and 14, and little if at all in 4-13, does not make us deny it to Hosea. Rather do we say that his message developed with his experience. As I studied again Isa. 1-39, I became persuaded, more strongly than ever before, that an analogous development took place in the teaching of Isaiah, although it arose out of quite different circumstances. In particular, I became persuaded that various passages within chs. 1-39 which speak of the new age could, in respect of the terms in which they are expressed, have arisen more easily and more suitably out of the circumstances of Isaiah's time than out of any later period. There is ample evidence that the remarkable deliverance of Jerusalem from grave danger in 701 BC, when the might of the greatest power of that time was arrayed against it, was interpreted as an act of God and had a tremendous effect on Isaiah's preaching. For this reason I have argued for the authenticity of many passages which are often regarded as in origin later than the time of Isaiah; that means that this has been done, not by the compulsion of a conservative outlook which sought to save as much as possible for the prophet, but by letting the evidence be heard and by giving it due weight.

Any scholar, whatever may be his field, is debtor to many. Known debts he acknowledges explicitly, by footnote or otherwise; but less specific borrowings and deeper and more generalized influences become absorbed into his own ideas and attitudes, without his being mindful, and sometimes without his ever having been clearly aware, of the source of them. That sense of indebtedness I fully acknowledge.

The University   JOHN MAUCHLINE
Glasgow
December 1960

BIBLIOGRAPHY

The following books may be consulted:

COMMENTARIES

J. Skinner, *The Book of the Prophet Isaiah, Chs. I-XXXIX*
(Cambridge Bible for Schools and Colleges), Cambridge
University Press, 1896.

Owen C. Whitehouse, *Isaiah I-XXXIX* (The Century Bible),
T. C. & E. C. Jack, 1905.

G. W. Wade, *The Book of the Prophet Isaiah* (Westminster
Commentary), Methuen, 1911.

G. B. Gray, *A Critical and Exegetical Commentary on the
Book of Isaiah:* Vol. I, Chs. I-XXVII (International Critical Commentary), T. & T. Clark, 1912

R. B. Y. Scott, 'Isaiah 1-39, Introduction and Exegesis', *The
Interpreter's Bible*, Vol. V, Nelson, 1956.

J. Kissane, *The Book of Isaiah*, Vol. I, Browne & Nolan,
Dublin, 1941.

D. Otto Procksch, *Jesaia* I (Sellin's Kommentar zum Alten
Testament), A. Deichertsche Verlagsbuchhandlung, Leip-
zig, 1930.

V. Herntrich, *Der Prophet Jesaia, Chs. 1-12* (Das Alte Testament Deutsch, Vol. 17), 3rd ed., Vandenhoeck & Ruprecht,
Göttingen, 1957.

EXPOSITION

George Adam Smith, *The Book of Isaiah, Chs. I-XXXIX* (The
Expositor's Bible), Hodder and Stoughton, 1896.

GENERAL WORKS

H. Wheeler Robinson, *The Religious Ideas of the Old Testament*, Duckworth, 1913.

T. H. Robinson, *Prophecy and the Prophets*, Duckworth, 1923.

N. H. Snaith, *The Distinctive Ideas of the Old Testament*, Epworth Press, 1944.

C. R. North, *The Old Testament Interpretation of History*, Epworth Press, 1946.

John Paterson, *The Goodly Fellowship of the Prophets*, Scribner's Sons, New York, 1948.

E. W. Heaton, *The Old Testament Prophets* (Pelican), 1958.

L. C. Grollenberg, *Shorter Atlas of the Bible*, Nelson, 1959.

D. Winton Thomas (ed), *Documents from Old Testament Times*, Nelson, 1958.

E. W. Heaton, *Everyday Life in Old Testament Times*, Batsford, 1956.

INTRODUCTION

SIGNIFICANT FACTORS IN THE HISTORICAL SETTING

Isaiah's prophetic activity took place during the last forty years of the eighth century BC; it may have continued into the seventh. In a way not paralleled in the activity of the other great prophets of that century whose utterances have a place in the Old Testament canon, Isaiah took a very prominent part in the national crises of the days through which he lived, so that, before we begin to outline his life and to pick out the significant elements in his message, it is necessary to understand the general situation in which the prophet lived. About that situation several factors should be carefully noted:

(a) Before the time of Omri and Ahab, kings of Israel about a century before Isaiah received his call to be a prophet, the history of the two kingdoms of Israel and Judah after the death of Solomon had been an unimpressive record of petty squabbles, and events of very local significance. But these two kings saw the folly of such behaviour on the part of two politically weak kingdoms, which, in face of an aggressive policy by a great power such as Assyria or Egypt, could hope to survive only by the combined military resources of an alliance of western states, in which they had a part. Towards this end they made a compact of peaceful co-operation (although Israel was obviously the dominant partner); and Israel ceased, at least temporarily, her warrings with Syria and established a trading arrangement, while with Phoenicia she had a close association which was celebrated by the marriage of Ahab to Jezebel, daughter of a king of Sidon. That Israel

13

could enter into such an agreement with her northern neighbours means that her political power was recognized by these
neighbours, because in every age political and commercial
bargaining is most successfully done from a position of
strength. The effects of such agreements upon Israel, however,
were important and not wholly salutary. First, they meant a
considerable increase in national wealth owing to the opening
up of profitable avenues of trade, a development which, in
turn, widened the social gap between the wealthy, upper class
in Israelite society and the poor peasants. Secondly, they
meant, according to the customs of the times, a certain recog-
nition in Samaria, the capital of Israel, of the gods of the
allied peoples. This was particularly so in the case of Phoenicia,
a temple to Melkart being built in the capital (I Kings 16.31 f.)
and the attempt being made by Jezebel to make the worship
of the Phoenician god the national worship of Israel. This fact,
together with the attitude shown by Jezebel in the king's negotiations with Naboth for the acquisition of his vineyard which
lay close by the royal palace (I Kings 21.1-14), makes it clear
that at this time there was a very real danger that Phoenician
culture might become dominant in Israel. Such a situation was
liable to recur whenever Israel entered into a close relationship
of association with, or, even more, of dependence on, a people
greater in power than itself, and it was the main reason for the
warning which the prophets repeatedly gave against any policy
which encouraged or relied upon such relationships.

(*b*) The next factor of great political significance for the
period was the rise and westward expansion of the Assyrian
Empire which began when Tiglath Pileser became its ruler in
745 BC. By 721 Samaria, the capital of Israel, had been captured and that little kingdom had become an Assyrian province. Before that time Judah, by seeking Assyrian help during
a time of national crisis, had reduced herself to a like condition, but in the very troubled conditions at the end of the eighth
century, of which more will be said later in this Introduction,
while Judah was devastated by an Assyrian army, Jerusalem

was not captured. The greatest range of the Assyrian empire was not attained until after the death of Isaiah, Egypt being conquered in 672.

(c) Israel, by reason of its geographical position close to Phoenicia on the one hand and Syria on the other, had opportunities to become involved in profitable trading enterprises and so enjoyed an increase in wealth and in prestige. During the middle period of the eighth century, when Jeroboam II was king of Israel and Uzziah was king of Judah, Judah also enjoyed a comparable prosperity, had trade by sea with south Arabia and used the revenues to develop the natural resources of the country and to strengthen its military power (II Chron. 26.1-15). In this way there arose in both kingdoms a wealthy commercial class who seem to have had little sense of social obligation towards their less fortunate brethren. Amos and Isaiah in particular sharply rebuke the oppression, injustice and corruption which were rampant, and the evils of which there was apparently no redress to be had by means of the normal processes of the law. The law, as it was codified and administered, prescribed penalties for offences against persons and against property by violence and by deceit, but not against the subtler methods of extortion and injustice which were now practised in Israel and in Judah. Where the law was silent, the prophets had a word to speak and they claimed that they were simply applying the fundamental principles of the law to the changed human situation.

(d) Another point of significance must be noted. We have seen that until the fall of Samaria, the kingdom of Israel occupied a much more important position among the peoples of neighbouring lands than did Judah. With the fall of Samaria, the position of Judah became notably changed. She could no longer hope to remain in comparative isolation among her hills, uninvolved in any turmoil of events which enveloped her neighbours. She would not be allowed so to remain, but would find herself more and more committed, even against her will. That very issue comes up very sharply on two important occasions during the ministry of Isaiah and he took a very firm and unpopular stand (cf. pp. 35 ff.).

THE PROPHET ISAIAH AND THE RECORD OF HIS LIFE AND WORK

The Prophet Himself

According to 1.1 Isaiah exercised his prophetic ministry during the reigns of Uzziah (783-742 BC), Jotham (742-735, although he had been regent from 750 until the date of his accession), Ahaz (735-715) and Hezekiah (715-687)—the dates being according to the chronology of W. F. Albright.[1] But if we accept the common view that the vision which is recorded in ch. 6 was the one which constituted the call of Isaiah to be a prophet, his prophetic career began in the year when Uzziah died. His home was the city of Jerusalem; he was married and had at least two children (cf. 7.3; 8.3). The name of the prophet's father, Amoz (1.1), bears no resemblance in the original Hebrew to that of the prophet Amos. It has sometimes been said that Isaiah must have belonged to the aristocracy of the capital because he knew the ways of the court and had ready access to the presence of the king when he had need. Such a conclusion is not at all necessary, for in a city of the very limited extent which it had at that time, a prophet of the stature of Isaiah must soon have made himself a well-known member of the Jerusalem community and one whose words were treated with very great respect.

His Call to be a Prophet

The vision which is recorded in ch. 6 bears all the marks of being the one which laid a sense of compulsion upon Isaiah to be a prophet of Yahweh. The backcloth to the vision, if we may so describe it, was the Jerusalem temple; the occasion

[1] 'The Chronology of the Divided Monarchy of Israel', *Bulletin of the American Schools of Oriental Research* 100, Dec. 1945, p. 22.

seems to have been soon after the death of King Uzziah (Aza-riah) who, according to II Kings 15.2, reigned for fifty-two years. Whether the precise occasion was a celebration of the New Year Festival or not cannot be affirmed with any cer-tainty; but it is abundantly clear that Isaiah's thoughts at the time were centred, not only upon the end of a great king's reign, but upon the unending reign of a much greater King who had not received in Judah, and was not receiving, the obedience and loyalty to which he was entitled. When in vision he saw this King, enthroned in glory and exalted, he bowed down with an overwhelming sense of his own creatureliness and profane-ness. All his people stood in a like judgment; yet his eyes had seen the King. It was a lesson in the holiness of God and in his condescension and self-revelation to man which constituted thereafter an important and integral part of Isaiah's religious belief and therefore of the doctrine which he preached. A statement of what the experience meant for Isaiah can be found at greater length in the commentary *in loco*. But it must be said here and now that it induced in him a searching, deeply-moving, spiritual experience, in which he had an awareness of being cleansed and purified as by fire, became cognizant of the demand which was now laid upon him to commit himself to the service of this God, and knew, apparently from the begin-ning, that it was a hard, unremitting task to which he was being sent.

Isaiah 1-39: An Analysis of its Contents

The record of the utterances of Isaiah and of the autobio-graphical and biographical material concerning him is con-tained within chs. 1-39 of the book which bears his name. As will be learned from the notes which are written in the Com-mentary to some sections within these chapters, not all that they contain has been accepted by scholars as genuinely Isaianic material; but the tendency today is to find more authentic material within them than was the case in the quite recent past. There are certain clues which have led to the conclusion that the record which we now have before us was composed from earlier collections of material. For example, there are three separate titles in the book (1.1; 2.1; 13.1); and there are references to two occasions when Isaiah himself caused a collection of his utterances to be made for record purposes. The first (cf. 8.16) was during, or soon after, a great national crisis in 735 BC, when his advice to the king of Judah of that time, Ahaz, was entirely disregarded; as a consequence he had his words committed to writing and withdrew from public ministry for a period. The other (cf. 30.8) was much later, in the reign of Hezekiah, and again the purpose was that a written record might be preserved for the future. The first of these probably contained the bulk of what now stands within chs. 1-12, the exact amount of it being open to question; the latter may have contained chs. 28-32, the section of the Book of Isaiah within which the verse 30.8 stands.

It has sometimes been held that we may distinguish three periods of prophetic activity, the first from the death of King Uzziah to the beginning of the reign of Ahaz in 735 BC, the second the period immediately following that date when the Syro-Ephramitic war took place (cf. II Kings 16.5-20), and the third the time of Assyrian activity in Palestine which culminated in the invasion of Sennacherib in 701 BC. Since, however, there are not a few utterances which cannot easily be referred to a particular date with any assurance, it is probably wiser to say that these were the principal periods of the prophet's activity.

An analysis of chs. 1-39 may suggest that the material may be conveniently divided into the following main sections:

(i) *Chs. 1-6.* These chapters contain most of the material we possess which may be attributed to the first period of the prophet's activity. The central portion, chs. 2-4, contains in 2.6–4.1 typical utterances of that time, in which Isaiah calls upon his people to walk humbly and purely before God and to do justly and to love mercy in the community of men (cf.

Micah 6.6). The remaining parts of these three chapters, viz. 2.2-4 and 4.2-6, belong to a later date; they speak of the coming day of restoration and blessedness. Many scholars are unable to regard them as authentic utterances of Isaiah, although an argument for their authenticity is presented in the Commentary. Ch. 1 gives the impression of having been given the form which it has to enable it to serve as an introduction to at least the section of the book at the head of which it stands, so that it may be later in date; but in content it is so closely related to chs. 2-4 that it may be taken in association with them. Likewise in association with these chapters we should take 5.1-23, but the remainder of that chapter is to be conjoined with 9.8-10.4, a poem with recurring refrain, of which 5.24 f., may be a displaced stanza and to which 5.26-30 may be suitably attached as a sequel. Ch. 6, the record of the call of Isaiah, may be as easily attached to what follows it in the book as to what precedes; the fact that it is placed here and not at the beginning of the book in ch. 1 has suggested to some scholars that it may once have served as the introduction to a small collection of utterances and biographical passages (such as 6.1-9.7) but that is not a necessary conclusion (cf. Amos. 7.14-16).

(ii) *Chs. 7-12.* The remarkable poem contained in 9.8-10.4, together with 5.24 f., may very well belong to the early period of Isaiah's ministry before 735 BC. It describes the rampant wickedness and pride of Israel. No misfortune or disaster can destroy their self-assurance, no loss of leaders can arouse apprehension or fears for their security, no threats from Syrians or Philistines are ever interpreted as a warning sent by God. But the axe will not vaunt over the master who wields it; judgment will come upon such a wicked people. 7.1-9.1 describes a great national crisis during the second main period of Isaiah's prophetic activity, when Rezin, king of Syria, and Pekah, king of Ephraim, marched against Jerusalem because Ahaz, king of Judah, would not join them in revolt against

Assyria. Ahaz, setting aside Isaiah's counsel, appealed to Assyria for help against his antagonists and was roundly condemned by the prophet for such an ill-advised policy. The rest of 7.1–9.1 describes the condition in Judah at the time and the conditions which will ensue. 10.28-34, descriptive of the Assyrian invasion of Palestine, may, like 5.26-30, be attributed to the period around 735 BC, but the list of places named supports its reference to the campaign of Sennacherib in 701. To this date also should be referred 10.5-27 which speaks of the coming judgment upon Judah (cf. vv. 9-12). With respect to the passages which promise deliverance, 9.2-7 and 11.1-9, which are often attributed to a date long after the time of Isaiah, an argument is presented in the Commentary for the view that they are most fitly regarded as spoken by Isaiah with reference to the wonderful deliverance of Jerusalem from Sennacherib's besieging army. It is probable, but by no means certain, that 11.10-16 should be associated with the same occasion; but ch. 12, composed of what may be considered two separate psalms, is almost certainly later than Isaiah and was inserted as a suitable conclusion to a small collection of Isaiah's utterances.

(iii) *Chs. 13-23.* The contents of these chapters are mostly utterances against foreign nations, but ch. 20 relates a symbolic action on the part of Isaiah, while 22.15-25 tells of the overweening presumption and ostentation of a certain Shebna who was the royal treasurer and master of the household. The dating of many of the passages in this section of the book is particularly open to debate; as far as is possible within the limits of this book, the question of the most likely date is discussed in each case in the Commentary. In what is said here, therefore, the conclusions reached in the Commentary are assumed.

It is generally agreed that 17.1-14 belongs clearly to the time when Ephraim was still a kingdom and was in alliance with Syria, so that it must belong to the earliest period of Isaiah's

ministry (i.e. before 735 BC). Again, there is a group of passages which may, assuredly in some cases, plausibly in others,
be referred for occasion to the campaigns of Sargon against
Ashdod and other cities during the last ten years of his reign
(he died in 705 BC). The elegy on Moab in 15.1-8 and 16.8-11,
which shows decided Moabite sympathies, may have come
from a Moabite source, and it is possible that the related
poem in 16.1-7 comes from the same source; both were taken
over by Isaiah who added the parts which now appear as 15.9
and 16.12. The occasion may well have been Sargon's campaign of 715 BC which he conducted against certain north
Arabian tribes and for which his route may well have passed
through Moab, which he devastated. The same occasion may
be given for the utterance against Edom in 21.11-12 and that
against the Arabian steppe in 21.13-17. The symbolic action
of Isaiah related in ch. 20 took place at the time of Sargon's
campaign into Palestine in 711 BC, while 14.28-32 may belong
to the year of Sargon's death. The date of the utterance against
Tyre is highly problematical; it may belong to the reign of
Shalmaneser V (727-22) when Phoenicia was conquered and
Tyre was besieged for three years, or to the end of the eighth
century when Sennacherib devastated Phoenicia and captured
Sidon.

Another group of passages may be related to the time of
Sennacherib's invasion. 13.2-16 is a doubtful example; it
speaks of the gathering of many peoples for conflict and of
natural convulsions which represent this as the day of the
Lord. Such passages as Joel 2.1-11, Zeph. 1.14-18 appear to be
close parallels to what is found here and may imply for this
passage a date much later than the days of Isaiah. But Amos
speaks of the day of the Lord in terms at least somewhat analogous (5.18-20; 8.9), so that it seems quite possible to contend
that, in terms of such teaching on the part of Amos and in
view of the experiences through which Isaiah lived c. 701 BC,
such a passage on a great judgment of the peoples may have
come to us from him. Likewise, 22.1-14, in which the contrast

is sharply made between the carefree, heedless attitude of the
people of Jerusalem who put their trust in material possessions
and the prophet's sorrow over their unrepentant sinfulness and
his sense of a great judgment impending, may be attributed
to the period after the surrender of Jerusalem to Sennacherib
(cf. II Kings 18.13-16) and before the later threat to the safety
of the city (II Kings 18.17 ff.). Again, in terms of 36.3, 22 and
37.2 (cf. II Kings 18.18, 37) the condemnation of Shebna the
royal steward (22.15-25) belongs to the same period. The passage 19.16-25 has commonly been attributed to a period much
later than Isaiah's time; but the probability that these verses
come from Isaiah after the departure of the Assyrian army
from Jerusalem in 701 BC, without having captured the city,
must be seriously considered. That deliverance of Jerusalem,
not achieved by military power or by human resources, must
have been interpreted as a triumph of Yahweh, God of Judah.
over the gods of Assyria. That circumstance may well have
made Judah a terror to the defeated Egypt (v. 17; cf. p. 159).
The resultant respect for Yahweh may have had the effects
mentioned in 19.18-22. The Jews will now be received in
Egypt and will name one of their cities as City of Righteousness (cf. 1.26); the Egyptians, having seen the power of Yahweh, will now have an altar for his worship within their land
and a stone pillar to his honour on their border. And in this
day, when great Egypt had been defeated by Assyria, and Assyria had been forced to retreat empty-handed from Jerusalem
in what was virtual, if not actual, defeat, was there not an
occasion, such as was not to occur in parallel circumstances
again in Judah's history, for the vision and the expectation of
a highway from Egypt to Assyria and the bond of friendship
between these two and Judah, all now reconciled to one
another and united in the worship of Yahweh? And is this not
a universalizing of religious thinking which emerged out of the
stress of this great national crisis in Judah? Further, if such
thinking did emerge out of this time which was so conspicuous-
ly suitable to evoke it, 14.24-27, which speaks of a world

judgment, cannot brusquely be denied to Isaiah because it is adjudged that his thought could not have reached out to such an idea.

But some passages remain which seem to demand a later date than the time of Isaiah. For example, 13.17-22, with its reference to Babylon as the glory of kingdoms, the splendour and pride of the Chaldeans, cannot be regarded as a fit description of the Babylon of the second half of the eighth century BC, no matter what importance we attribute to the figure of Merodach Baladan (cf. ch. 39). The absence of reference to the Assyrians and the specific reference to the Medes in the passage confirms the impression that it must have arisen out of the circumstances of the sixth century BC and of the Jewish exile in Babylon. To the same period, it would appear, we must consign 21.1-10, the oracle upon the so-called wilderness of the sea. 14.4b-21, in consideration of the way it speaks of the condition of the departed in Sheol, seems in this respect to represent beliefs which are otherwise unknown in Isaiah's day and belong to a later time.

(iv) *Chs. 24-27*. These chapters are usually considered to form a separate section of the Book of Isaiah; but there is a certain fitness in their position following chs. 13-23. The day of the Lord has come; there is a world judgment. It is possible to discern in these chapters signs of the transition from prophecy to apocalyptic. Condemnation of certain peoples for specific sins passes into a condemnation of men for their depravity and transgression; a judgment announced as about to take place in the near future in specified historical circumstances gives way now to one of all peoples in the undefined future ' in that day '. The question which is very much open to debate is whether we can say that all this is but an extension of Isaiah's thought occasioned by the catastrophic experiences through which he and his people lived, or whether the differences are so great that Isaianic authorship of the passages in which these ideas are to be found cannot be maintained. A state-

ment on this subject may be found in this section of the
Commentary; only a summary can be given here. 24.1-20 describes the disorder and confusion in the earth and its return to
the primeval disorder which existed before God gave order to
all creation. The disconsolate and miserable remnant of people
which survives gives thanks for its blessings, but is contradicted
by the prophet who sees further sufferings in store. Whatever
date this passage may be given—and there are no determinative criteria—the time after 734 BC, when Jerusalem had survived the hazards of the Syro-Ephraimitic war, is certainly
fitting. Again, in 25.6-26.19 the three small passages within
26.7-19 can without difficulty be regarded as genuine, although
little which is specific can be said for or against Isaianic authorship with regard to them. 25.10-12, with its reference to Moab,
may be accepted as an authentic utterance of Isaiah in view
of the evidence of 15.9 and 16.12-14. 26.1-6, which speaks of
the strong city of the righteous and the downfall of a high and
lofty city, may belong to the period of the deliverance of
Jerusalem in 701 BC, and 25.6-8, which speaks of the great feast
for all peoples, to the same occasion, on the ground that it may
have given rise to the belief of victory over death for the faithful. 27.2-6, 7-9 may also be genuine utterances of the prophet,
the former being related in content to 5.1-5.

But 25.1-5 seems to demand a date later than Isaiah;
27.10-11, in which Jerusalem is spoken of as in ruins, must be
referred to the sixth century BC; and the date when the hope of
the resurrection expressed in 26.19 became alive cannot be
stated with assurance. It can easily be adjudged too high doctrine for Isaiah's days; but the question as to whether it was
too high doctrine for Isaiah is a different question and one
which is not so easily answered.

(v) *Chs. 28-32.* It seems clear beyond any reasonable doubt
that these chapters are concerned with events in Ephraim and
in Judah during the final quarter of the eighth century BC.
They reveal the conflicting plans and activities of these critical

years and give us some insight into the difficult task which confronted Isaiah in his attempt to turn the leaders of the people from relying for safety upon help from fickle, ineffective Egypt to trust in the living God, whose ways are not spectacular and do not necessarily appear wise to men but are for man's spiritual welfare. Judgment and promise are intermingled in these chapters, sometimes strangely intermingled; so does the prophet seek to convey the truth that the God who judges wills to save, and he who hurts is ready to bind up the wound.

28.1-4, with its picture of the degeneracy and debauchery of Ephraim, may well belong to the period in that country's history immediately before the fall of Samaria in 721 BC. The remainder of the chapter which concerns Judah may belong to that period also, but is more suitably related to the end of the eighth century, to the period around 701. The fuddled, besotted leaders of Judah mock at what they regard as Isaiah's childish patter and are told that kindergarten instruction in the ways of God is all that they are capable of understanding; even that may be too much for them. These scoffers, it is said (28.14-22), have made a covenant with death, i.e. moral corruption and idolatry; but their refuge in lies will be swept away and their covenant with death will be annulled. When Yahweh establishes his kingdom of righteousness and trust in Jerusalem, they will be punished for their faithlessness. But the punishment will not be indiscriminate; it will be ordered in such a way that it may produce a harvest of good grain.

Ch. 29 also speaks of judgment. Jerusalem is to be offered as on an altar hearth (vv. 1-14); the people will suffer their doom in a condition of spiritual stupefaction. But in due course the enemy will depart and be remembered only as a bad dream. In vv. 15-24 another common subject of these chapters is introduced; those who lay their plots with Egypt for help in their need cannot hope to escape the notice of Yahweh or to avoid punishment; but those who survive will rejoice in him. 30.1-5 continues the same subject; such overtures for help to

Egypt are wholly useless and are a sign of lack of faith in
Yahweh (vv. 6-11). The downfall and ruin of those who follow
this policy are near (12-14); but vv. 15-17 call to them to put
their trust in Yahweh and not in Egyptian chariots. God is
waiting to be gracious; he is always near at hand to guide the
erring and to prompt them from behind with the word they
need. When the people so return, they will prosper and be
happy again and nature will share in man's revival (18-26). But
against the Assyrian God will act with indignation and flaming
fire, and judge them with the sieve of annihilation (27-33).

The beginning of ch. 31 follows the same line as ch. 30. It
reminds the people that the Egyptians are men, not God (1-3);
they cannot overthrow the plans of the Almighty. They are
utterly unable to deliver Jerusalem from the Assyrian lion but
Yahweh will save his city (4 f.), not by the sword of man but
with his own weapons of deliverance (6-9). Ch. 32 makes a
notable finish to the section. Verses 1-8 speak of righteousness
enthroned and of the dethronement of fools and knaves. After
a scathing condemnation of the ease-loving, fastidious women
of Jerusalem (9-14), the chapter closes with a description of
the effect of the rule of the spirit of God in the new age (15-20).

(vi) *Chs. 33-35.* Ch. 33 speaks of the destroyer who will be
destroyed and of the deceiver who will be deceived (1-6). That
is followed by a celebration of the God who delivers his people
and is exalted in power and glory. Therefore, righteousness
alone will be the stability of Judah's life, since Yahweh is
their only Saviour. Verses 7-9 tell of the desolation wrought in
the land by the enemy and vv. 10-12 tell of their destruction.

God is a consuming fire. Who can stand before him? Those
whose hands are clean and whose heart is pure and who keep
themselves from evil (vv. 13-16). The enemy will pass away, the
glory of Jerusalem will be restored, and from it rivers of refreshing will go out, not to be means of trade and commerce, but
to bring life to the peoples (vv. 17-24). The date of this chapter
is uncertain. The fact that Sennacherib, a destroyer of nations,

may be deemed to have acted deceitfully by demanding again the surrender of Jerusalem after its surrender had recently been made (II Kings 18.13 ff.), and that he was himself, according to II Chron. 32.21, put to death at a later time by some of his own family, makes it possible that the chapter refers to him; but it is unlikely that the prophet Isaiah was still alive at the time of Sennacherib's death.

Ch. 34 is a summons to nations and peoples to listen to the Lord's indictment of all peoples. In vv. 5 f., Edom is specified as a doomed people; the rest of the chapter describes desolation, dereliction and forsaken dwellings. The hostility between Judah and Edom was very deep-rooted (cf. the story of Jacob and Esau in Gen. 27), and it is probable that Edom here typifies Judah's enemies in general. The style of this chapter is not Isaiah's, as we know it, and it is probable that it belongs to the sixth century BC (cf. Isa. 63).

Ch. 35 describes the renewed fertility and beauty of the land of Palestine and the renewed sense of personal and social well-being among the people. A highway shall be there, free from hazards, untrodden by fool or knave, but reserved for the redeemed of Yahweh's people when they return to Zion with joy and gladness. The returning people might, of course, be those who were removed from the northern kingdom after the fall of Samaria in 721 BC; but the parallelism of thought and language between this chapter and parts of Isa. 40-55 make a date in the sixth century more probable.

(vii) *Chs. 36-39.* These chapters describe the part played by the prophet Isaiah in certain great national crises of his time. Chs. 36-37 are closely paralleled in II Kings 18.13–19.37, and are taken from that source. They give an account of Sennacherib's invasion of Judah in 701 BC and his threat against Jerusalem, giving prominence to the bombastic claims of the Assyrian Rabshakeh in the hearing of the citizens of the capital. No place is given to the account of the surrender of the city which is to be found in II Kings 18.14-16, but that is probably because Isaiah had no part in the negotiations which took place on that occasion. It is not easy to determine the exact course of events in Judah at this time; this matter is discussed in the Commentary and the likely sequence of events is outlined. It is notable that the Assyria which Isaiah could describe in 10.5 as the rod of Yahweh's anger and the rod by which he expressed his indignation is now mocked and scorned and accused of arrogance (cf. 37.22 f., 28 f.).

Ch. 38 tells of an illness of king Hezekiah and of his subsequent recovery. The record of the event in II Kings 20.1-11 gives warrant for reading 38.21-22 after v. 6, where doubtless they have their proper place in the narrative; II Kings 20 does not contain the psalm of thanksgiving which is found here in vv. 9-20. Whereas at first Isaiah tells the king that his illness will be fatal and that he must prepare to die (v. 1), he later receives a word from God to the effect that his life will be spared and that he will be given fifteen years more in which to live.

Ch. 39 describes a visit of Merodach Baladan, king of Babylon, to Jerusalem. We know that he was king for twelve years during the reign of Sargon of Assyria, viz. 721-709 BC, and for a period of six months at the beginning of the reign of Sargon's successor, Sennacherib. This visit probably took place during Merodach Baladan's long period of power, when he may have looked like a serious threat to the imperial rule of Assyria. It probably requires such a reading of the circumstances of the times to explain why Hezekiah should have shown to him all the wealth of his kingdom. Unless we can make this estimate of the stature in which Merodach Baladan appeared to his contemporaries, it is necessary to consider that the statement attributed to Isaiah that some of Hezekiah's sons would be removed to servitude in Babylon and all the wealth of the kingdom would be taken also, must be attributed to a much later period, probably c. 600 BC.

THE THEOLOGICAL VALUE OF THE CALL
OF ISAIAH

A detailed examination of the narrative of the call of Isaiah is given in the Commentary, and there is no need or occasion to do that here. But in the narrative there are expressed theological truths which remained basic in all his later work, and conceptions of his responsibility which he may well have grasped thus early, even if it was only afterwards that their full implications were realized in the school of hard experience. In the forefront must be placed the truth of the sovereignty of God, who rules without ceasing and whose kingdom endures for ever. Ephraim and, to a much lesser extent, Judah, had learned, by the time of Isaiah, the contentions and warring factions which can be associated with dynastic rule, and they had seen how often the issue had been decided by force of arms, to usher in an ensuing period of uneasy peace. In the full acknowledgment of the rule of God, he became convinced, lay the only road to a stable peace, for then the king himself would be an anointed servant under vow to do God's will.

But Isaiah's vision meant a new sense of the holiness of God. As had been seen in the instance of Uzzah, careful for the safety of the Ark of the Covenant though he had been (II Sam. 6.6-8), holiness could be a destructive power against anyone who intruded rashly into the realm of the holy; but here was something very different. By the touch of a glowing coal from the altar the power of the holy had come upon the prophet and by it he had been consecrated to his holy task. The gulf between God the holy and man the unclean and profane had been bridged by the cleansing and enabling grace of God; thus the conception of a holy people came to have meaning and the very word 'holy' was transformed in connotation.

The result of this experience for Isaiah was twofold. He had a sense of sins forgiven (6.7) and he became aware that the responsibility had been laid upon him to do God's will as he

came to know it and to lead others to the same experience as
he had had. But soon the conviction arose in the mind of
Isaiah that his task would be hard and exhausting because men
as a whole are so enslaved by practices which range from the
self-centred to the wilfully pernicious, and so materialistic in
their outlook, that they will not listen to any prophet who calls
them to the austere joys of righteousness and justice and love
of their fellow-men, and who bids them put their trust in God
for security and well-being. And with that came the conviction
that for such faithlessness and wickedness the people would
come under judgment (6.11). Sometimes the prophet was so
overburdened with his tasks in later days that he almost lost
patience with his people and was ready to say that they did
not deserve forgiveness (cf. 2.9, 22). And, indeed, it would
appear that after 734 BC, when his advice had been completely
disregarded by King Ahaz, he retired from public ministry as
a prophet (cf. 8.16-18); and some scholars are inclined to
believe that he did not resume until after the death of Ahaz
twenty years later.

ISAIAH'S INDICTMENT OF THE PEOPLE

Religious Apostasy and Moral Weakness and Wickedness
In Isaiah's indictment of his people, as it is contained in
chs. 2-5 and the early portions of chs. 6-12 (see pp. 18 ff. above),
he makes charges similar to those which are made in the Books
of Amos and Micah. They are, on the one hand, concerned
with the application to the circumstances of a new age of the
demand expressed in the first commandment that the people
of Yahweh must have no other God in his presence. On the
other hand they take account of the fact that the laws concerning crimes of violence against person and property codified
in the Book of the Covenant, for instance (Ex. 20.22–23.33),
have relevance for a simple form of agricultural economy, but
not for the more complex and more covert forms of oppression,

extortion and injustice which were now possible and were practised in the wealthy, commercialized civilization of Isaiah's day. The condemnation of injustices, false weights and measures, oppression and inhumanity comes into the Law only at a later stage (cf. Lev. 19.15-18, 35-36; Deut. 25. 13-15; cf. Prov. 16.27-30; 18.5; 19.5, 9; 20.10, 14, 23). These crimes were not yet on the statute book and prophetic exhortations had to take the place of legal demand. Isaiah sees his people now as rebellious children who have forsaken God and as a sinful nation laden with iniquity (1.2-4). The whole body is corrupt and the festering wounds are not being healed (1.5 f.). The people have become appetitive, aggressive and pitiless; no man spares his brother (9.18-21).

But Isaiah lays emphasis upon certain aspects of his people's unfaithfulness and wickedness, and this remains as a continuing, characteristic aspect of his preaching. For instance, the people were dull, unresponsive and case-hardened (cf. 6.9 f.); they almost appeared stupefied, drunk but not with wine; sometimes in their stubborn obtuseness they even mocked the prophet for having the effrontery to teach them what were but nursery rhymes fit for the kindergarten, not proper instruction for men of experience (28.9-13; 29.9 f.). Clearly the possession of wealth accentuated this attitude of callous indifference; finding the conditions of life congenial, they had no time for Isaiah's dismal drolleries; finding profit from their fellow-men's misfortunes, they gave no heed to his idealistic call for justice and mercy (2.7; 3.16 ff.; 22.13-16; 28.1-4, 7 f.). The verses just quoted from ch. 28 show how wealth opens the way to drunkenness and debauchery (cf. also 5.11 f.; 24.7-11). The result is that moral standards are dishonoured and neighbourly obligations are treated with contempt; murder, thieving, bribery, extortion and injustice abound (1.21-23; 5.8 ff.). The women are swept along by the same currents as the men and they show as little resistance (3.16–4.1; 32.9-14).

The leaders of the people are severely condemned; elders and princes alike are blameworthy (3.14 f.); there is a flight from responsibility on the part of those who might be expected to be leaders, and the most inexperienced and the most unfit find themselves thrust into positions of trust and importance (3.4-7; 9.13-17).

But the whole situation is summed up in the fact that the people are estranged from Yahweh and no longer honour his law (1.4b, 29). They have lost any spiritual knowledge and insight which they ever had, and, in the spiritual twilight in which they now live, they resort to old superstitions and outworn practices, to diviners and soothsayers, to wizards and necromancers, hoping that they may receive from them a word of guidance. And they turn to fertility rites and to gardens of Adonis that they may preserve to themselves the bounties of nature (1.29 f.; 2.6; 3.2; 8.19; 17.10 f.; 19.3; 28.15; 29.4).

Yet the traditional forms of religious life are preserved. The altar sacrifices are faithfully offered, the great festivals are kept, and many prayers are made (1.11-15). In this way conventions are observed, and in some of the people the illusion is encouraged that they are fulfilling their obligations toward God, even when they are wholly neglecting their duty toward their fellow-men (29.13).

A Day of Judgment

It is Isaiah's conviction that for all this sinfulness a day of judgment is coming. God is not mocked; men cannot disobey his will with impunity. The land will be desolated, Lebanon will become a heath, fruitful places like Carmel and Sharon will become a wilderness, men and cattle will be few (1.7 f.; 2.10 f.; 7.21-25). It is the Day of the Lord of which Amos had spoken (Amos 5.18 ff.), a day against every form of man's pride, against strong towers and fortified walls, and against all idolatry (2.12 ff.; 10.20-27; 13.1-16; etc.) Time after time Assyria is specified as the instrument by which the judgment will be accomplished (cf. 7.17-20; 8.1-8; 10.5-11; 5.25-30; 10.28-34; 31). In these passages Assyria is spoken of as an instrument in the hands of Yahweh who uses it for his own purposes, as a hired razor, with which Yahweh will scrape his land bare. The theological importance of this conception will be considered later, when we come to take note of the full teaching Isaiah had to give on the subject of Assyria and Egypt as factors in the life of the people of Judah.

It is significant and typical of Old Testament teaching on the subject that in this judgment all nature is involved. The whole land becomes withered and waste, the harvest fails; the moon, the stars and the constellations will not give their light, and the sun will be dark at its rising (5.9 f.; 13.10, 13; 24.1-13). Thus the whole of creation is thought of as an organic unity, so that the judgment which is occasioned by man's sinfulness affects all creation. The corollary of this, viz. nature's renewal in the new day, will be found at a later stage in Isaiah's ministry.

A Remnant Will Survive

There are certain other notes in the prophet's teaching which must be taken account of at this point:

(i) In spite of the fact that the judgment is spoken of as if it were inevitable, that does not exclude from Isaiah's preaching the note of pleading and entreaty calling upon the people to return (cf. Hos. 14.1 ff.; Amos. 5.14 f.); this is found several times in ch. 1 (5, 16 f., 18 f.). The people are called upon not to be carried away by every plot and conspiracy which is advocated enthusiastically among them by its supporters; let their fear be of God alone and let their trust be in him. Indeed, the people who have no faith in God can have no confidence for facing the hard experiences and crises of life (7.9; 8.12-15; 28.16; 30.15 f.).

(ii) Again, Isaiah often declares his confidence that, however devastating the judgment may be, a remnant of the people will survive. Out of the stump of the tree new life will come. The glory will have departed, the comeliness will have perished, the new shoot will be a miracle of renewed life; but therein is

C

the hope of the people and therein lies the possibility of the continuance of their work and witness. That conviction on the part of Isaiah may be related to the fact that even in human relations a complete obliteration of an individual or a people was guarded against with very great care (cf. Deut. 25.5; Ruth 4.10 f.; Amos 1.6, 9). But if man refrained from such a total obliteration of a people as might seem to be a gross inter-ference with the order of creation, surely God himself could not turn against, or utterly forsake, the creatures whom he had made or the people whom he had chosen (cf. 1.9; 4.2-4; 7.3; 10.20-27; 24.13 f.; etc.)

(iii) This doctrine of the surviving remnant in turn is related to the fact that whereas the prophet can speak in terms of a judgment upon the whole people, he can, at the same time and without any sense of contradiction, speak of a discriminating judgment in which a distinction will be made between the righteous and the wicked (1.27 f.; 3.10 f.; cf. 28.23-29). Also it may be noted at this point that Isaiah thought of the neces-sary cleansing of the peoples as consisting substantially of restoring in them a former righteousness and purity which had become corrupted; he comes near to describing it as a renewal of the wilderness ideal (cf. Hos. 2.14 f., 19 f.). But the possi-bility of such renewal depends upon the grace of God who is waiting to be gracious and who answers the cry of his people; and his voice is heard as a gentle prompting, a voice from behind, saying: 'This is the way, walk in it' (cf. 30.18-21).

YAHWEH'S JUDGMENT ON THE NATIONS

There are to be found in chs. 13-23 utterances against foreign nations. It may be right to see an early form of such utterances against neighbouring nations in the story of the prophet Balaam (Num. 22-24). He was summoned by Balak, king of Moab, to curse the Israelites who were threatening to take complete pos-

session of his land. the belief of the king obviously being that a
great prophet like Balaam could lay on the Israelites a great
curse and that he would do it if he were suitably rewarded. In
fact Balaam made it plain that his services could not be bought
in this mercenary fashion, and that he could speak in blessing
or in curse only as he was directed by God. A prophet like
Amos or Isaiah, in the judgments he uttered against the nations
which were neighbours to Israel, was in the line of Balaam;
his utterances against these nations could not be bought or
commanded by the people. But it must be noted that these
nations are not described specifically as Israel's enemies and
they are not judged for actions against Israel, the chosen people
of Yahweh; they are judged for their offences against the moral
law and against neighbourly obligations as they knew them.
And they are judged in the name of Yahweh the God of Israel.
That is a fact of very great significance, although it is clear that
the full theological implications of it were not as yet wholly
appreciated by the prophet himself.

Two Great National Crises

But it is quite apparent that Isaiah's chief concern in this
regard was with Assyria and Egypt, the two great powers of his
day; and it is now necessary to consider the part which Isaiah
played in two great national crises in which he took a con-
spicuous part.

(i) *Pekah and Rezin against Jerusalem in 735 BC.*

The first of these was the threat to the safety of Jerusalem
which was occasioned by the march of Rezin of Syria and
Pekah of Ephraim against it in 735 BC (cf. chs. 7-8; II Kings
16.5-9). The king took practical measures for the safety of the
city (7.3) and in the end, against Isaiah's explicit advice,
applied to Assyria for help against his adversaries, not trust-
ing in the waters of Shiloah which go softly but in the mighty
river of Assyria (8.5-8; II Kings 16.7). We may say that Ahaz
took the only practical way to meet the emergency with which

he was faced; there were risks involved in it, but these, he believed, he had to take. Isaiah affirmed that the danger would soon pass (an assessment of the situation which must have seemed unduly optimistic to the king), offered the king the sign of the child Immanuel to show that he was a genuine prophet giving God's word, and told Ahaz to have faith in God and not to involve the country in that corrupting religious syncretism which would be the result of the subjection to Assyria which would follow upon the acceptance of Assyrian help. The king took his own way; the prophet must have seen that it is one thing to call a man to trust in God in his own personal life, but another to expect a king to take that way to secure or maintain the welfare of his country. A similar situation has been seen many times since then.

But one thing has to be added. Isaiah did regard Assyria, not as help to meet this emergency, but as a scourge to punish his people for their wickedness (10.5 ff.); yet he became convinced that Assyria's attitude was such that she too must be punished. It was not simply that she planned destruction without a thought of the will of God or of any other being, but that she so boasted of her power and of her achievements that she was plainly arrogant and impious and must be humbled (10.12-19).

(ii) *Sennacherib of Assyria against Jerusalem in 701 BC.*

The other national crisis is dealt with in chs. 36-37 (cf. II Kings 18.13–19.37), and it is the view expressed in the Commentary that not a few passages in Isaiah 1-39 arose out of the circumstances of this time. According to the interpretation of the course of events which is given in the note on chs. 36-37, a surrender of Jerusalem was made when Sennacherib made his first assault upon it (II Kings 18.14-16); it is not said that Isaiah had any part in the consultations or negotiations on this occasion. But when the Rabshakeh later appeared outside the walls of the city and arrogantly demanded its surrender, Isaiah told the king that Sennacherib would return to his own land without having taken the city (37.6 f.). 37.22-29 gives a more elaborate answer, stating that all the Assyrian conquests had been in accordance wtih God's will and that the Assyrian would now be humiliated for his arrogance (cf. 10.7-11, 12-14, 15-19, 25-27; 14.24-27; 30.29-33; 31.8 f.).

In this crisis the people had hoped for much from Egyptian help but unfortunately for their hopes the Egyptian army was defeated by the Assyrians at Eltekeh. Such reliance upon Egyptian aid was scoffed at by Isaiah; 'the Egyptians are men, and not God; their horses are flesh and not spirit' (31.3); 'Egypt's help is worthless and empty, therefore I have named her: Rahab who sits still' (30.7); and the Assyrian Rabshakeh could scoff at them in the same way (36.9).

As Isaiah Saw Them

Thus these two great national crises evoked from Isaiah a clear and emphatic enunciation of certain of his fundamental theological positions:

God rules, and his purposes are not frustrated by the plannings and achievements of men. In this Isaiah amplified a lesson he had learned at the beginning of his career in his inaugural vision. Since God rules and is not mocked or frustrated, political alliances are useless and, indeed, harmful improvisations to meet crises which ought to throw men back on trust in God as the only saviour and deliverer. Such trust in God may not bring the expected escape from the temporary emergency or the expected deliverance in it; but it will bring a continuance of the national life with the people's faith unimpaired, albeit with their economic and political life changed in a way which may not be pleasant. This was hard doctrine for a people to receive, and it is as hard today. Judah had a spiritual office, a faith to commend, a moral law to honour; that could be done only in spiritual purity and in moral integrity. But then, as now, only a small proportion of the people held such high doctrine concerning their life as a people; in most cases their standards of conduct tended to conform to the prevailing pattern. And that, said Isaiah, was the way in which most surely they would cease to be an elect people. Our wonder is not that the kings and people of Judah of Isaiah's day found this doctrine too hard for them; rather it is that Isaiah had the vision and the insight to preach it (22.9-11; 30.15 f.).

THE EFFECTS OF THE DELIVERANCE OF JERUSALEM IN 701 BC

That Sennacherib and his army left Jerusalem without having captured the city is an undisputed historical fact. Likewise it is undisputed that the Assyrian *débâcle* was not due to any defeat in battle. Isa. 37.7 says that a rumour of trouble at home caused the abandonment of the siege; but Isa. 37.36 and II Kings 19.35 agree in saying that it was because the angel of the Lord passed through the Assyrian camp and destroyed a huge number of the army. That is commonly interpreted as meaning that plague broke out and speedily worked havoc. The account of the event given by Herodotus affords in its own way support for this interpretation (cf. the Commentary on chs. 36-37). In other words, the fact that Jerusalem survived this crisis inviolate was an act of God, and, as such, a wonderful demonstration of his power against the might of Assyria (cf. 31.8); and, at the same time, it was a vindication of the preaching of Isaiah that the people of Judah should trust in God as their saviour and deliverer; his rule does not end and his power is not mocked. The effects of this event are to be found in several different ways:

Jerusalem Sacrosanct

There arose a belief in the inviolability and the sacrosanctity of Jerusalem, as is shown in the reference to 'an immovable tent whose stakes will never be plucked up, nor will any of its cords be broken' (33.20; cf. 33.16). This was a belief which Jeremiah had to combat strongly (7.1-4; 21.13-14; 26.6-9).

The Rule of Yahweh

Isaiah emphasized the truth of the rule of Yahweh (e.g. 14.24-27; 24.23; 37.26-29). In him alone should men trust (10.20).

Yahweh alone is God

If the impotence and untrustworthiness of Egypt had been demonstrated in this crisis and the might of Assyria had been humiliated before the power of Yahweh, then there was no other god who could vie with him or pretend to share his supremacy. Out of such a situation there must have arisen the belief that Yahweh was the only God, whether that belief was expressed in clearly monotheistic terms or not. That being so, it can readily be understood how a prophet who lived through such a time should now see this great God Yahweh entering into a judgment of all the nations. In view of the judgments already expressed by Isaiah against some of the neighbouring peoples as they are contained in chs. 13-23 and the judgment against Egypt and Assyria which was involved in the events around 701 BC, it was a small step in thought to a world judgment (cf. 11.13-15; 17.12-14; 18.3-6; 24; 29.7 f.; 34.1-4). This will be a day of bloodshed and destruction, of tumult and confusion, of hunger and suffering and social disorder; and it will bring a doom which will be inescapable. It is notable that in 24.21-23 it is said that the punishment will extend to the host of heaven, presumably the angelic host, the principalities and powers which had not acknowledged the rule of Yahweh.

The Remnant of the Nations

But it is of great importance to note that, just as Isaiah speaks of a remnant of his own people which will survive, so he foresees a similar remnant among the nations. 24.13 speaks of them as like the few berries which remain in their place when an olive tree is shaken. Such a remnant is spoken of in the case of Assyria (10.19), Syria (17.3), Egypt (19.16-22) and

Kedar (21.17 f.); the reference to the remnant of Tyre in
23.15-18 is possibly later than Isaiah.

Marks of the New Age

It would be difficult to believe that there did not arise out of
the circumstances of this time a hope that the new age would
now arise. God will now raise his standard, it is said, the only
one in which his people can triumph (11.12; 13.2; 18.3 ff.). His
people scattered abroad in many lands, will be gathered
home (11.11 f., 16; 27.12 f.; etc). Prosperity and peace will
come again (e.g. 11.14 f.; 30.23-26); the hostilities among the
beasts of the field will cease and the light of the sun and the
moon will shine more brightly, so that, just as, in the time of
God's displeasure, the whole of creation came under the consequences of it, so, when his favour returns, nature will be
renewed, order displacing disorder (11.6-9; 30.26).

Righteousness Enthroned

In this new age righteousness will be enthroned; or, to put it
otherwise, Yahweh will be enthroned in righteousness (1.26 f.;
26.7-9; 28.17 f.; 32; 33.5 f.). The qualities of the righteous
man who will be found in the new age are characterized in
33.14-16. There will now be so keen a sense of social responsibility that men will no longer be deaf to the cry of need nor
will they shut their eyes to the situation which requires a
saviour or a healer (29.17-19; 32.3). As in former days it was
the leaders of the community in Ephraim and in Judah who
led the people astray, in the new age a king will reign in righteousness (32.1). It is probable that the child to be named
Immanuel (7.14) is not to be thought of as the coming prince
who will deliver and rule his people, but as one who will bear
a name which will betoken the fact that by the time he is born
the danger, in the presence of which the prophet Isaiah fore-
told this name for him, will have passed completely away. But
in 9.2-7 the qualities of this ruler are made plain; the seven-
fold gift of God's spirit will be upon him so that he will be

dedicated to his task and will be obedient to God's will. And
there are passages in which it is made clear that the expectation was that this ruler would be a member of the house of
David (7.2, 13; 9.6 ff.; 11.1; 22.22).

Yahweh Worshipped among the Nations
   It is in line with all this that there should be taught the
doctrine that if Yahweh judged and punished all the nations,
yet so that a remnant survived on the basis of which they
might rise again, these nations should now worship Yahweh.
Thus we are told of the river which goes forth from Jerusalem
—surely if that city is a place of broad rivers and streams, they
must flow out into the surrounding country, like Ezekiel's
river (33.21; cf. Ezek. 47). 18.7 speaks of service paid to Yahweh by a people tall and smooth, the Ethiopians, presumably
when they learned of the humiliation of the Assyrians (cf. 37.9);
19.18 speaks of five cities in Egypt which swear allegiance to
Yahweh and 19.19 of an altar to him in the midst of the land.
Even more important are the words of 19.21 which say that
Yahweh will make himself known to the Egyptians and they
will know him and worship him, and the words in 19.25:
' Blessed be Egypt, my people, Assyria the work of my hands,
and Israel my heritage.' At what other time in the history of
Israel and Judah was there an occasion for a prophecy such
as this, and for that of the highway from Assyria to Egypt
(19.23)? The next occasion when the doings and, as in 701 BC,
the defeat, of Egypt were of significance to Judah was in 605
BC, when the victory over her was won by Babylon; but by
that time Assyria had ceased to be a great power. And there
was no occasion after that until the time of the Ptolemies when
Egyptian interests and fortunes were at all closely knit with
those of Judah. Therefore, the argument for the authenticity
of 19.16-25 is very strong; the verses arose out of a situation
in 701 BC such as was without parallel in exilic or post-exilic
times. The greatest passage of all, probably, 2.2-4, which cannot with assurance be attributed to Isaiah (see the Commen-

tary) fits this situation also, speaking as it does both of the
incoming of the peoples to Jerusalem and of the going forth
of the law from that city.

Signs of Apocalyptic

It has been said incidentally already that a passage such as
30.25 f., which is commonly described as apocalyptic and is
attributed to a date much later than that of Isaiah, is to be
understood as saying that in the new age the whole creation
will be transformed and restored to order, thus bringing to an
end that state of confusion and chaos which, according to ch.
23, had come to the earth through man's sinfulness and rebelliousness. We may see in the words used in 30.25 f., a step in
the transition from prophecy to apocalyptic, without our feeling any necessity to deny these verses to Isaiah.

Victory Over Death

But death had been one of the penalties of the disordered
order brought upon the earth by man's sinfulness (cf. Gen.
3.19). In the new day, a day of rejoicing, God will remove the
mourning garb from all peoples and will swallow up death in
victory (30.19; 25.7 f.). This does not mean that men by their
nature are immortal, but that among the cleansed and redeemed peoples of the new age God will have swallowed up
death, that death with which they had made a covenant (28.15,
17 f.), and they will now live the life of righteousness and truth.

The Resurrection of the Dead?

But 26.19 is a more difficult problem. The preceding vv. 17 f.,
seem to say that Yahweh's people had not gathered other
people to his allegiance, under the figure that they had not
brought any children to the birth as his children. Then comes
the sudden and, it must be admitted, unexpected contrast:
'Thy dead shall live, their bodies shall rise.' The first phrase
might mean that Yahweh's sinful children will rise to newness
of life, being delivered from the covenant of death; but the

following phrase is much more difficult to interpret. Is this a doctrine of the resurrection of the body after death? That is most unlikely. Is it simply an alternative, parallel way of saying that they will find the life of the new age? That is the likely interpretation; but an assured interpretation is not possible.

If the contentions in favour of the authenticity of several debated passages, which are presented in this Introduction and Commentary, are sustained, Isaiah stands forth in even greater stature than has sometimes been allowed to him. He appears as a prophet of noble vision and penetrating insight, a great man living in great times, one who entered into the place of God's counsel and who had clear-sightedness and understanding which enabled him to read the pattern of the days in which he lived. He has a grandeur of utterance beyond that of the other canonical prophets of the eighth century BC; he is a poet who can express his thought in haunting and in memorable form. More obviously than Amos, his work was both to break down and to build up, both to judge the present and to hope and prepare for the future. He may not have some of the tender notes of Hosea, but compassion in large measure he certainly had; and he obviously rejoiced to tell of the joy and peace of the new age which he saw in store for the redeemed and righteous people. 'Except you have faith, you can have no confidence'—that may fitly be his final word.

SERMONS OF ISAIAH'S EARLY PERIOD

1.1–6.13

ISRAEL'S INDICTMENT

1.1-31

After the first verse, which is introductory, the chapter appears to be divisible into three parallel sections (vv. 2-9, 10-17, 18-31). each of which contains a call or summons, an indictment, and a final word of comfort or hope. Between adjacent sections there are connections of thought and what may have been intended as key words (e.g. SODOM and GOMORRAH in v. 9, and RULERS OF SODOM and PEOPLES OF GOMORRAH in v. 10, YOUR HANDS ARE FULL OF BLOOD, WASH YOURSELVES, MAKE YOUR-SELVES CLEAN in vv. 15 f., and the phrases AS WHITE AS SNOW and LIKE WOOL in v. 18). Within the sections too there is often a clear sequence of thought; for example, in the first section, the indictment of Israel (vv. 2 f.) is followed by a statement of the resultant estrangement from Yahweh (v. 4), of the suffering of the sinful people (vv. 5 f.) and of the devastation of their land (vv. 7 f.), while in the third the faithful city which became idolatrous and wayward (v. 21) will once again be given its fair name (v. 26), and the genuine metal which became dross (v. 22) will in the end become cleansed of its impurities (v. 25). Therefore, the conclusion seems justified that, whether or not the sections which now make up this chapter were uttered by the prophet on one occasion as a connected discourse or be-

longed to various phases of his prophetic career, they form a
most fitting introduction to the book and present in sharp outline and in impressive language the tenor of an important part
of Isaiah's teaching.

The movement of thought within the chapter may be briefly
outlined in this way. In the first section (vv. 2-9) a great protestation, addressed to heaven and earth as witnesses, laments,
not people who have disobeyed the law or who have rejected
the testimony of God's saving work in history, but sons who
have rejected a father's love and care and left home to go their
own rebellious way. This is followed by the indictment, whose
fourfold address reaches its climax in the phrase 'sons who
act corruptly' (v. 4). Wonder is expressed at such continued
rebelliousness, and such inability to learn from repeated suffering (vv. 5-8); but not all is lost, for by the mercy of God a few
survivors remain (v. 9). In the second section (vv. 10-17), the
unfaithful and sorely punished Israelites are called a Gomorrah
people (v. 10), i.e. a morally corrupt people; from such a
people altar sacrifices offered in worship of Yahweh are mean-
ingless and useless, and they are detested and loathsome in the
eyes of God (vv. 12-15). The people must be cleansed from
every evil pollution, and then, turning from evil, must do what
is right according to Yahweh's law. In the third section (vv.
18-31) Yahweh makes his plea to his people to return to him,
or they will suffer the extreme of punishment. Thereupon the
indictment is directed against Yahweh's city, Jerusalem, the
faithful city become infidel, the genuine metal become base,
the pure wine become adulterated. But even yet there is hope;
the metal may be made pure again and Israel become once
more as she was in the days of her pure espousals in the
wilderness (vv. 21-26). Only God's justice and righteousness
can bring this about; but man must respond to the grace and
love of God which are manifested in this way. Those who
refuse will by their refusal deny themselves that life and
vitality which can come to men only from fellowship with God;
they will become withered and dry as dead wood, fit only to

be burned in a fire beyond any man's ability to extinguish (vv. 27-31).

The only section of the chapter which may be referred to a specific period in the prophet's career is vv. 7 f. Some scholars have adjudged the threat to Jerusalem and Judah by Pekah of Ephraim and Rezin (Rezon) of Syria in 735-34 BC to be the occasion (cf. Isa. 7.1 f.). The perturbation within the city then was certainly great, and much fear was felt for its safety (cf. Isa. 7.3); but it is improbable that Judah, south of Jerusalem, was devastated. The invasion of Sennacherib of Assyria in 701 BC certainly involved a serious devastation of Judah and a siege of Jerusalem, so that this would seem to have been a crisis of much greater importance and of much more serious effect; it is likely that it gave occasion to the words recorded in vv. 7 f. The trampling of the Temple courts by eager worshippers (v. 12) need not refer exclusively to this occasion, but may describe the zeal of the worshippers in Isaiah's day; and the other sections in the chapter, describing likewise prevailing attitudes and practices, cannot be referred to any particular phase in the prophet's career. At many points parallels with the thought of Hosea can be discerned and these are mentioned in the Commentary.

1. Title

This verse begins, not with 'The word of God which came to Isaiah . . .', but THE VISION OF ISAIAH . . . WHICH HE SAW (cf. Nahum 1.1; Hab. 1.1). Often the noun for 'vision' which is used here and its related verb 'to see a vision' are found in conjunction with terms signifying divination and soothsaying (cf. Micah 3.6; Jer. 14.14; Ezek. 12.24, etc.), and in Amos 7.12 'visionary' is used as a term of contempt; but the words are also found without such associations, in such a use as is exemplified here (cf. Hos. 12.10; Hab. 2.2 f.; Ezek. 7.13, etc.)

It will be observed that a shorter, and somewhat different form of title is found in 2.1, in which no reference is made to the kings of Judah in whose reigns Isaiah exercised his ministry; but such a reference is proper and common (cf. Jer. 1.1-3, Ezek. 1.1 f., etc.) in the case of a title at the beginning of a book. Two observations may be made: (*a*) It has sometimes been said by scholars that the phrase KINGS OF JUDAH, which seems tautologous at the end of 1.1, was probably added later by an editor when the utterances of Isaiah and the narratives about him were gathered together. That may be so, but there are parallels in the titles of the Books of Jeremiah, Hosea, Amos, Micah; (*b*) The title which occurs in 2.1 (cf. also 13.1) shows that there were probably several collections of the prophet's utterances in circulation before these were incorporated into the book as we now have it. The fact that chs. 13-23 contain utterances against foreign nations makes it probable that the title in 1.1, which refers to what Isaiah saw concerning Judah and Jerusalem only, was attached originally to one of these early collections.

The name of Isaiah's father, Amoz, is quite different in form from that of Amos the prophet, so that the question of whether Amos the prophet could have been Isaiah's father does not arise.

2-3. Renegade Israel

Heaven and earth are called to bear witness to Yahweh's indictment of his people. It is a most impressive and significant beginning. It implies, first of all, that Israel must not imagine that they sin to themselves alone or that they can say: 'We will choose our own way, and if we suffer, we suffer.' No man or people lives in such isolation; all are involved inescapably and responsibly in the context of human society. If Israel fails to do God's will, such failure brings penalties upon themselves and upon others; its effects are much more widespread than they can discern; for the penalties upon others mean, not only what they may directly suffer, but what they may continue to lack or not enjoy.

But the call to heaven and earth means more than that. Yahweh, against whom they have offended, is not only their

God, but is the God whose glory fills heaven and earth (cf.
6.1-3; Amos 4.13; 5.8 f.; 9.5 f.), and who acts with saving
power in history to accomplish his sovereign will (cf. 10.5;
Amos 1-2; Micah 4.11-13). The Israelites in Isaiah's time, and
later, were not monotheists in the strict philosophical sense, in
that they recognized that other peoples had their gods (cf.
Amos 5.26; Hos. 14.3; Jer. 32.35; 48.7, 13; 49.1; 50.2); but that
did not prevent them from considering their God to be the
only true God, the God of heaven and earth. Now this God
had, at the Creation, established an order in the universe (Gen.
1). Every created thing has its part to play. Inanimate nature
is content to play its part (cf. Jer. 18.14); the beasts of the field
do not rebel. It is man, made in the image of God, the sentient
being called to choose between good and evil (cf. Deut. 30.15
ff.), who is guilty of rebellion (cf. Gen. 3; Jer. 2.9-13; etc.). Yet
this rebellion takes place in spite of God's love and care for
man, and Israel had experienced his love and care in abundant
measure (cf. Amos 2.9-11; 3.2; Hos. 11.3 f.; 10.11; Isa. 57.
15-19). If they had been given the law at Sinai and had been
left unaided to be obedient to it, there might have been some
excuse for such rebellion; but they had never been so forsaken.
Thus in that rebellion there were mingled together ingratitude
and wilfulness, disregard of past benefits and favours and
sheer obtuseness; the result now was that they could no longer
distinguish between good and evil (cf. 5.20). The bond between
the father God and the sons he had nurtured and tended had
been broken.

3. This verse contrasts the ignorance and rebelliousness of
Israel with the docility of dumb, driven cattle. Domestic animals which work for man and serve his need and receive some
nourishment and care from their owner, show an attachment
to him and to the crib where they feed; they have no inclination to forsake their way of life. Israel's response to the love
and care shown to them is in sharp contrast. The phrase BUT
ISRAEL DOES NOT KNOW does not mean in this context simply

that they are ignorant and brutish, but that they do not know
their master and do not recognize his solicitude for their welfare. The verb 'know' is one of the key-words of the Bible.
Adam knew his wife (Gen. 4.1), and man is called to know
God (Ex. 6.7; Isa. 43.10; John 17.3; II Tim. 1.12; etc.); the
reference in each case is to intimate fellowship and loyal love.
Israel does not now know God in this way, nor do they ever
give a thought to the situation which has arisen because of
their rebelliousness. They have no understanding or insight;
they are spiritually immature, 'God's grown-up children'.[1]

4. This verse stands by itself. In the four nouns used to describe the people in the first part of the verse there is probably
to be seen a crescendo of condemnation moving in rhythm with
the increasingly nearer definition of the kin relationship between Yahweh and Israel. The NATIONS surrounded Israel;
they were ignorant of Yahweh's law. The term 'sinful nation'
means that by their sinfulness Israel has become as one of them
in Yahweh's eyes. PEOPLE at once suggests the chosen people
(Amos 3.2; Ex. 19.5; Deut. 14.2; etc.); it had been chosen for
good, now it is burdened with iniquity. But this iniquity is not
a new development; Hosea traces it back to the early days in
Moab or Palestine (Hos. 9.9, 10, 15; 10.9). SEED may suggest
'seed of Abraham' (cf. Isa. 41.8; Jer. 33.26; John 8.33; etc.).
Thus it is an evil inheritance in which they live and which they
perpetuate. It is when the word SONS is used that the greatness
of the iniquity is revealed (cf. v. 2).

The second part of the verse describes Israel's sin in a twofold manner, as neglect, remissness, ingratitude, failure before
God—negative categories signifying sins of omission—and as
despising him, showing active hostility towards him, or even
contumaciously disregarding his existence.

The title THE HOLY ONE OF ISRAEL occurs frequently (5.19, 24;
10.20; 12.6; 17.7; 30.11 f.; etc.) as a name of Israel's God.
Holiness means separateness, and denotes the glory and

[1] G. Adam Smith, *The Book of Isaiah*, I, p. 6.

D

majesty of God, before which, as revealed in heaven and earth
and in mighty acts of deliverance as at the Red Sea, man, the
finite creature, must bow down in reverence and godly fear.
Since God is thus apart and separate, man himself can never,
by searching, find him (cf. Job 11.7); but God has revealed
himself. Since he is thus holy, man can never invade God's
sphere (cf. Gen. 3); he is human, and even the king in Israel
was never regarded as the son of God (as was the Pharaoh in
Egypt); he was a son only by adoption (cf. Ps. 2.7).

Israel through their sinfulness had become a people
ESTRANGED. They had been called to be the holy people of the
holy God; now they were involved in evil, and apart from
God. The covenant relationship had been broken; they who
had been God's people were no longer his people (cf. Hos.
1.9; 2.23). Certain versions indeed have the reading THEY
HAVE TURNED AWAY BACKWARD (so AV; cf. Isa. 42.17) instead of THEY HAVE BECOME ESTRANGED (so RSV); but
probably the latter, as the more difficult reading, should be
retained.

5-9. Israel sick and derelict

The first part of v. 5 may be interpreted in several ways. The
first phrase has sometimes been rendered: 'On what [part of
the body] will you be smitten further?' That suggests a slave
who has been beaten so much by his master that his body is
full of wounds and weals, and the master wonders what more
punishment he can inflict on a body so wounded. That is
possible, but the common rendering 'Why' instead of 'On
what' is surely to be preferred. But in RSV the second clause,
THAT YOU CONTINUE TO REBEL, is closely joined to the first
which suggests that further suffering will only harden Israel's
rebellious attitude and will not prove remedial. AV gives
generally the same interpretation, but makes the second clause
independent: YE WILL REVOLT MORE AND MORE. But parallelism
might suggest that the two clauses be rendered as parallel
questions, both introduced by the initial 'why':

Why should you be smitten still more?
[Why] should you persist in your rebelliousness?
Surely they had had enough of the penalties of such obduracy? The whole body had been bruised and the heart made
sick. Into the midst of all that suffering there had come neither
comfort nor relief, because they had despised God, the source
of comfort; so their body had become a mass of wounds and
bruises unmollified, uncleansed and unbandaged. The tragedy
was that it was self-intensified suffering; there could have been
relief if Israel had repented, but they would not. Ezekiel's
words come to mind: 'As I live, saith the Lord Yahweh, I have
no delight in the death of the wicked, but rather that he should
turn from his way and live. Turn back, turn back from your
evil ways, for why will you die, O house of Israel?' (33.11; cf.
18.31 f.).

7-8. These verses tell how the land has been ravaged and desolated. This may suggest that the occasion of this punishment
was Sennacherib's invasion in 701 BC, when he claims to have
destroyed forty-six walled cities and unwalled villages without
number, and to have taken a heavy load of booty.[1] The Syro-
Ephraimitic war of 735-4 seems a less suitable occasion (see
pp. 35 f. above). But an element of disgrace has been added to
this national disaster. The Israelites held the land of Palestine
as tenants for Yahweh (cf. I Kings 21; Lev. 25.25 f., 33; Ruth
4.4, 6) and they have failed to honour their obligations. Aliens
have devastated the land which is Yahweh's portion; it is dese-
cration. The last phrase of v. 7 has sometimes been rendered
'like the overthrow of Sodom' or, as we might say, 'a Sodom-
like disaster'. But the other reading (as in AV and RSV)
should be retained. The comparison with the fate of Sodom
comes in v. 10, and the phrase AS OVERTHROWN BY STRANGERS
means that the land had been devastated in a way in which
only strangers, who had no interest whatever in it, would in-
dulge.

[1] Cf. D. Winton Thomas, *Documents from Old Testament Times*, p. 67.

52   ISAIAH 1.7-8

THE DAUGHTER OF ZION (sometimes 'the virgin daughter of
Zion') is a common term for Jerusalem. The name does not
mean daughter of, belonging to, Zion, but daughter-Zion, the
two nouns being in apposition. The name Zion was originally
applied to David's city on the eastern ridge of the site on the
west side of the Kedron which was more fully occupied by
the later city; and it remained in use. To compare Jerusalem in
its desolate isolation with A BOOTH IN A VINEYARD or A LODGE IN
A CUCUMBER FIELD does not seem very suitable, since both
these shelters are set in pleasant surroundings. Jeremiah's wayfarer's lodge in the wilderness might have been thought of as
a better parallel (9.2). But doubtless both booth and lodge
suggested loneliness to Isaiah, since they were away, sometimes
remotely, from other houses. The final descriptive parallel, a
besieged city, is much more apposite. On the occasion of Sennacherib's invasion Jerusalem was besieged but was not taken
(II Kings 19.35); the Assyrian record just referred to does not
claim its capture.

Had it not been for God's mercy, the destruction would have
been utter (v. 9), like that of Sodom, without survivor. The
words in the original text which are rendered by VERY SMALL
in AV and A FEW in RSV are not found in several important
ancient versions, and their omission would not alter the sense
of the verse. This is an example of Isaiah's teaching concerning the remnant of Israel which will survive (cf. 4.2; 10.19-23;
17.6; 28.5 f.; and the name of the prophet's first child given in
7.3 as Shear-jashub, 'a remnant shall return'). It should be
observed that total destruction is sometimes condemned in
the Old Testament as if it were an excess (cf. Amos 1.6, 9);
King David, in his harsh reprisals on Moab, did not wholly
blot out the population (II Sam. 8.2). Therefore, the sentence of
Jer. 13.19 that Judah would be wholly taken captive must have
sounded extreme. But the doctrine of the remnant here has
another basis, not any clemency on the part of man, but mercy
on the part of God. The sinful people deserve only destruction;
but God, being God, cannot cease to love, cannot forsake his

people, cannot abandon them to destruction (cf. Gen. 9.12-17; Isa. 57.16; Hos. 11.8 f.).

The term 'Lord of Hosts' was sometimes used in the sense of Lord of the war hosts, Lord of battle (cf. Ex. 17.15; I Sam. 17.45); that interpretation possibly fell out of use after the capture of the ark by the Philistines at the battle of Aphek (I Sam. 4.1-11). But, from an early period, the term was also used with the meaning of Lord of the heavenly hosts (cf. Judg. 5.20; II Kings 6.17) and later came to mean Lord of heaven and earth (cf. Amos 4.13; Isa. 54.5; Jer. 31.35).

10-17. Religion and life

Verse 10 is a call to the RULERS OF SODOM and the PEOPLE OF GOMORRAH to listen to teaching of God which they have so long disregarded. But the following verses do not seem to express that teaching directly; we have to wait until vv. 16 f., for it. Rather in vv. 13-15 is there a condemnation, not of the wickedness they have done, but of the worship they have rendered Yahweh, under the illusion that in this way they were doing his will. Altar sacrifices offered by a faithful people may be an expression of their faith and of their desire to live in fellowship with God; but, offered by a Gomorrah people, they are an empty form and may be a deceptive practice. In the same way the great festivals and popular religious assemblies are condemned. Such forms of worship, in so far as they were taken seriously by the Israelites, were regarded as means by which the beneficial rhythm of nature might be maintained for their own interests and advantage rather than as tribute rendered to God and acknowledgment of his rule and bounty. Many appear to have been very assiduous in this way (v. 11; cf. Amos 4.4 f.); the phrases THE MULTITUDE OF YOUR SACRIFICES and I AM FULL make that clear. But God loathes the whole, empty show; he hates it. Bigger and costlier sacrifices will not meet the need. What is required is something quite different and for it what they are now offering can be no proper substitute (cf. Micah 6.6-8).

12. The first clause in the Greek is attached to the preceding verse; such a rearrangement makes no appreciable difference in the sense. The original form of it was undoubtedly ' when you come to see me ' (cf. I Sam. 1.22; Ex. 34.23; Deut. 16.16; 31.11; Pss. 42.2; 84.7). But when the belief developed that no man can see God and live (Gen. 32.30; Ex. 33.20; Deut. 5.24-26; Judg. 6.22 f.; Isa. 6.5; Rev. 1.16 f.), the verb ' see ' was read as passive, i.e. to be seen, to appear before.

The question propounded in v. 12, ' Who has required such altar offerings and such frequenting of the temple courts? ' reminds us at once of two verses which are often quoted as implying complete condemnation of such forms of worship (Amos 5.25; Jer. 7.22); but rather do they say that what was distinctive in the law of Sinai belonged to another sphere, namely, the observance of moral obligations within Yahweh's community.

13. OFFERINGS here seems to mean quite generally gifts; but the same word is used later to mean unbloody offerings, cereal offerings; the word rendered INCENSE can also mean ' offerings consumed in smoke ', i.e. by fire.

15. Of long prayers also from such a people there is utter condemnation. The hands which are blood-stained with crimes committed against God's children cannot be raised acceptably in entreaty before God and cannot expect to gain his favour. (It is notable that at the end of v. 15 the Dead Sea Scroll of Isaiah, 1Q Isaᵃ, adds ' and your fingers with iniquity ' which is a suitable parallel to the preceding phrase.)

16-17. These verses make the positive demand for cleansing and state what Yahweh requires from his people. Ritual cleansing the priests practised, that they might fulfil their office acceptably (cf. Ex. 29.4; 30.19 ff.; Lev. 14.8; cf. II Kings 5.10, 12); but inward cleansing is needed that man may be pure in heart and, in consequence, clean of hand (cf. Ps. 24.3-5; John

13.6-10). That means not blood, rapine, injustice and oppression as a way of life, but justice, righteousness, mercy and compassionate concern for the needy and the helpless (v. 17).

18-20. Stating the case

The introductory words, COME NOW AND LET US REASON TO-GETHER, give the clear impression that a case is about to be stated in support of Israel's obligation to obey and serve Yahweh in righteousness and truth. That may be considered to be stated in vv. 19 f., which set down antithetically the consequences of obedience and rebelliousness.

But v. 18 does not seem to fit in; its two parallel clauses affirm that the people's sins, though they are blood-red, shall become as white as snow or as wool. Such a categorical statement, referring to all the people, seems quite out of place in a 'reasoning together'. To avoid this difficulty we may:

(a) regard the words as expressing the people's case for themselves, as spoken by God. They would then reveal an attitude of utter complacency or even hypocrisy.

(b) interpret the words as a challenge: ' . . . let them become white as snow; . . . let them become as wool.' But such an interpretation makes the sentence unsuitable as part of a 'reasoning together'.

(c) read the words as a statement by God of an open possibility, which can be translated into a reality only by the willing response of the people: ' . . . they may become white as snow; . . . they may become as wool.'

Only (c) fits the context, and fits very well.

21-23. The once faithful city

The faithful and loyal city, Jerusalem, has played truant and become wayward. Harlotry, a description of religious apostasy and unfaithfulness commonly used by Hosea (cf. 4.12; 5.4; 9.1), Jeremiah (3.1, 6, 8; etc.) and other prophets, is contrasted with the love and constancy which Israel owed to Yahweh to whom she, as a wife, was betrothed in the wilderness (Hos.

2.19 f.; Jer. 2.2; Isa. 62.4 f.); compare the figure of Jesus Christ and his bride the Church (Eph. 5.22-27; Rev. 21.2, 9). The corruption is shown in various forms: wilful violence and destruction, gross deterioration of inherent worth (silver turned into dross), pretence and deceit (wine adulterated with water), bribery and pursuit of selfish gain and total disregard of social obligation—a damning indictment.

24-26. Judgment and remedy

The solemnity of this judgment is deepened by the recital of the titles of the Judge (v. 24). Yahweh was often regarded as the new name given in the wilderness (cf. Ex. 3.14; 6.3), although it is found in some narratives in the Book of Genesis. The Lord of Hosts (cf. note on v. 9) had many associations for Israel, and the Mighty One of Israel was a title which went back to the days of the patriarchs (cf. Gen. 49.24; Isa. 49.26; 60.16; etc.). The enemies and foes mentioned in v. 24 may not mean Israel alone, but in v. 25 the narrower reference is made plain. Israel will be cleansed from all impurities and be made genuine metal again (contrast v. 22). Lye, an alkali, is usually mentioned as a cleansing agent in washing (cf. Jer. 2.22; Mal. 3.2), but here it must signify a cleansing agent which was used for smelting, for separating impurities from pure metal. A suggested alternative reading ' in the furnace ' instead of WITH LYE (RSV; AV, PURELY) gives excellent sense but is unsupported by mss or versions.

But that is not enough. The people's leaders had failed them (vv. 10, 23); therefore, rulers will be restored as they were in Israel's early days as a people (v. 26), as in the great days of King David or of the Judges of pre-monarchic times. When that happens, Jerusalem will regain her former prestige and glory; she will, once more, be the righteous city, the faithful city.

27-31. The two ways

Verse 27 is startlingly different from what has gone before, and that in two ways: it speaks of *redemption*, a word not elsewhere used in this chapter, and the verse seems to imply that the people are to *qualify for salvation* by their justice and righteousness. The act of redemption often involves the payment of a redemption price. The Israelites are said to have been redeemed from Egypt (cf. Deut. 7.8; 13.5); slaves had to be redeemed if they had not served their full time (cf. Ex. 21.2; Deut. 15.12; Jer. 34.14). At a later date the Jews were redeemed from exile in Babylon (cf. Jer. 31.11; Isa. 43.1; 44.22 f.; 48.20; 51.11; 63.4, 9); Isa 43.3 f. speaks of a redemption price being paid. But the verb rendered here as 'redeem' can mean simply 'save' or 'deliver' (cf. Pss. 25.22; 130.8; etc.) and that seems to be the sense which is required. But, secondly, the JUSTICE and RIGHTEOUSNESS spoken of are of God and not of men. It is by his steadfast purpose and in his mercy that the way of renewal for Israel is opened up. Verse 9 says that a few survivors of Israel will remain after God's judgment on the people; v. 27 implies that it is the repentant who will survive. Thus while this chapter as a whole speaks of the judgment upon Israel's sinfulness as a people, the statement here concerning the salvation of the repentant is a preparation for Jeremiah's (and Ezekiel's) doctrine of individual responsibility (Jer. 31.33-34; Ezek. 18; 33.10-20; 36. 22-27) and for that separation of the righteous from the wicked which is so prominent in the Books of Psalms and Job.

The change to the second person in vv. 29-31 from the third person of vv. 27 f. illustrates that fluidity of reference which is often exemplified in the prophetical books of the Old Testament, and does not necessarily mean that the two sections were originally unconnected. Much more notable in vv. 29-31 is the fact that, whereas the rest of the chapter speaks of Israel's rebelliousness in terms of transgression of the moral law and neglect of brotherly obligation, here it is religious apostasy which is spoken of and the practice of fertility cults. Such a section may have been added here to show, as Hosea does, that the people's rebelliousness had this double aspect. The

oaks (v. 29) are an allusion to illicit fertility cults practised
under every green tree (cf. I Kings 14.23; II Kings 16.4; 17.10;
Deut. 12.2; Hos. 4.13; Jer. 2.20; 3.6, 13; etc.); 'gardens' have
a similar reference. Actually such references to fertility practices and other rites in gardens are few in the Old Testament
(cf. Isa. 65.3), but that provides no warrant for assuming that
the cultic practices alluded to became common only at a later
date than Isaiah.

It is a fitting metaphor (v. 30) which describes the faithless
renegades, who worshipped under vigorous oaks and in luxuriant gardens, as themselves oaks which have lost all their vigour
and vitality and as waterless gardens, arid and dry, fit only to
provide fuel for devouring flames. In v. 31 neither the rendering of the AV nor that of the RSV satisfies; THE STRONG gives
no clear sense; indeed, in this passage it can refer only to the
oak, whereas the reference ought to be to the wicked who become like a withered oak. In addition 'the maker of it' (AV)
must be read as HIS WORK (so RSV) or something comparable.
The fact that the Dead Sea Scroll of Isaiah 1Q Isa[a] reads 'your
strength' for 'the strong one' gives some support for the following rendering which seems to meet the needs and suit the
context: 'His strength (i.e. the strength of the wicked man)
shall become tow, and his work (or produce, as from a garden)
shall become a spark,' and both of them shall perish. But it
must be admitted at once that the likening of his work to a
spark, rather than to dry, inflammable tinder, remains a difficulty. It was presumably this difficulty which gave rise to the
reading 'his maker' (i.e. his God) instead of HIS WORK, because God is appropriately the agent of destruction; but, just
as 9.18 describes man's wickedness as a consuming fire, it may
here be described as the spark which kindles the fire which
consumes both man and his work.

JERUSALEM NOW AND IN THE DAYS TO COME

2.1–4.6

These three chapters may be grouped together. The central portion 2.6–4.1, exemplifies the sermons which Isaiah preached early in his career. It is often said that these express a social gospel, but that is not all; he, equally with Micah, knew that man is required not only to do justly and to love mercy but to walk humbly and purely with God (Micah 6.6). While, as the Commentary will show, some of the allusions to prevailing modes and practices enable us to refer these sermons with confidence to the reign of Jotham, before the *débâcle* of 735-34 took place, the sermons themselves in turn enable us to understand more clearly the religious, social and economic situation in Judah at that time. Wealth abounded, a spirit of materialism was rampant, and an innocuous brand of formalism centred in fulfilling the sacrificial rites at the temple in Jerusalem encouraged the people in their own conceits by inducing them to believe that they were paying their debts to God and were free to enjoy themselves. Isaiah shatters this complacency by proclaiming the coming of the Day of Yahweh when he will judge his people. 2.6-22 condemns particularly religious unfaithfulness and idolatry on the one hand, and moral turpitude on the other, and tells the people to flee from the wrath to come. 3.1–4.1 continues in the same tenor and describes the state of sheer confusion and topsyturvydom which will ensue in the community when all the leaders are removed, all men of experience avoid any responsibility, and children are called upon to exercise authority and women to bear rule. The passage concludes with a particularly devastating arraignment of overdressed women who strut about like birds with fine feathers but who find their perfume turned to a stench and their beauty to shame.

But this central block, 2.6–4.1, is enclosed between two small

sections which tell of what shall be IN LATTER DAYS. These
passages are commonly termed eschatological in character and
their date has been much discussed. The first of them, 2.2–4(5),
if it has come to us from Isaiah, belongs to the late period of
his ministry; but by some scholars it has been attributed to a
much later date, to the sixth century BC, which saw the return
of Jewish exiles from Babylon. The second, 4.2-6, is composed
of two small sections, each of which speaks of the righteous
remnant which will survive in a land renewed in its fruitfulness and rid of all uncleanness, and vv. 5 f. tell of the return
of God's glory to Jerusalem in an encircling cloud and his continuing presence among his people, as he was among them in
former days in the wilderness.

THE HOUSE OF YAHWEH AND THE
HOUSE OF JACOB

2.1-22

Verse 1 is obviously a title (cf. note on 1.1). It was probably
the title of chs. 2-4, to which ch. 5 may have been appended,
although the limits of the collection of Isaianic material to
which it served as title cannot be defined with any degree of
assurance.

It has been noted that the title in 1.1 speaks of the vision
which Isaiah saw, and not of the word of God which came to
him. Here it is the word which he saw in vision which is mentioned. Isaiah, like, for instance, Ezekiel, had an inaugural
vision (ch. 6) at the beginning of his prophetic career, as distinct from Amos who became convinced of his call amidst the
recollections and musings which are the bliss of solitude (7.
14 f.; but his visions [7.1-9] may have come early in his
career), or Jeremiah who was aware of his call so early in his
life that he became persuaded that he was destined to be a
prophet even before his birth (1.5). In view of the fact that what

a prophet learned in a vision was the word of God to him,
there is no difficulty in understanding the phrase used here,
THE WORD WHICH ISAIAH *SAW* . . .

2-4. In the latter days

The description which these verses give of the exaltation of
the temple of Jerusalem IN THE LATTER DAYS is paralleled in
Micah 4.1-3; between the two forms of it thus recorded, the
only differences are minor ones (concerning chiefly the use of
the nouns PEOPLES and NATIONS and adjectives related to these
nouns, apart from the fact that in v. 3 Micah adds ' afar off ').
Therefore, it may be said at the outset that in respect of form
alone, it is impossible to say whether the passage comes from
Isaiah or Micah. In addition, Joel 3.10 shows a substantial
resemblance to Isa. 2.4 and Micah 4.3.

The hope for the future which these verses express is centred
around the mountain on which the temple is built. Quite a
small hill itself, it is to be raised above all the mountains and
hills in height. It may be remembered that it is said in I Kings
8.13 that Solomon, by building the temple, had made for Yahweh ' an exalted house ', a term which is found also in ancient
Near Eastern cultures on Israel's border.[1] Thus it is clear that
Yahweh is to have his exalted house on the highest mountain,
supreme above all gods. The fact that *all* the nations shall flow
to Yahweh's mountain, but *many* peoples will inquire of him
with a view to learning his ways and walking in his paths, can
be interpreted to mean that, while all are anxious to see this
wonderful thing which has taken place, not all make response
in mind and heart (cf. Zech. 8.23; Isa. 56.3-8). The fact that
Micah has simply ' peoples ' in place of ALL THE NATIONS leaves
room for the inference that some peoples will take no note at
all of the great event. The promise that the law shall go forth
out of Zion and the word of Yahweh from Jerusalem shows
that this hope of a new day is not for Israel only, but for all

[1] G. R. Driver, *Canaanite Myths and Legends*, T. and T. Clark, 1956,
pp. 44 f., 50 f., 78 f.

men. Yahweh, thus exalted and enthroned, will, by his law, judge the nations and admonish many peoples. The judges of ancient Israel were local rulers who, as prophet, priest and leader in battle, held their people together in a common loyalty; now Yahweh will rule the nations and unify them. The hostilities and bitternesses which provoke wars will cease and the weapons of war will be adapted to peaceful uses. Verse 5 is here additional but apposite; the way to be ready for a great day is not to wait for it but to prepare for it; Micah has quite a different and much less impressive epilogue (4.4).

This passage, 2.2-4, has sometimes been described as a 'floating oracle'; or it might be termed a prophetic broadsheet. The question of its source cannot be fully dealt with in the space available here. The one possibly related verse (3.10) in the Book of Joel, whose date is now commonly given as in the fifth century BC, gives little support to the view that that prophet was the author of the passage; and it is highly doubtful if a prophet of an earlier age than that of Isaiah could have attained to the width of vision and nobility of outlook to produce it. It may, of course, have come from some unknown, deeply spiritual author who exercised no prophetic ministry of which a record has come down to us, but left this one treasure, as an artist, otherwise unknown, might leave one great picture. That possibility apart, it seems most likely that the author was Isaiah or Micah, and when we think of the utterances of Isaiah, especially of ch. 11.1-9, the former seems the more probable source.

But it surely must be maintained that only some great experience, personal or, more likely, national, could have evoked such a vision. G. Adam Smith regards it as Isaiah's first great vision, when all things seemed possible and he believed himself able to lift the whole world at once.[1] It is very difficult to accept that view when we remember what intimation of the hardness of his task and the toughness of the opposition he would encounter was communicated to him at the beginning

[1] *Op. cit.*, p. 25.

of his prophetic ministry (cf. 6.9 ff.). But there were two great
occasions of wonderful deliverance in Jewish history which
come to mind and which might have made hope for the future
rise with a great upsurge. The one has been taken into the
reckoning by many scholars, the return of the Jews to their
own land from exile in Babylon (cf. Isa. 40.1-5; 44. 24-28;
45.1-7; etc.). That was not achieved by the Jews by force of
arms; it was the result of a decree of Cyrus who, all unwitting-
ly, was used by God for his gracious purposes; the glory of
Yahweh was revealed in the event; it was a second Exodus.
In terms, therefore, of the wonder of this event and such passages as Isa. 59.16 ff.; 60; 62; etc., many scholars believe that
this passage we are considering belongs to the sixth century
and, in consequence, is not Isaiah's.

The return of the Jews from exile in that century was a great
event, but we now know from the Cyrus Cylinder that when
that prince had gained possession of Babylon, he restored to
their own shrines the images which had been brought into
Babylon by its last king, Nabonidus, and he let the captives of
the downfallen empire go free,[1] so that deliverance and restoration did not come to the Jews alone.

Therefore, another great historical occasion must be considered, the wonderful deliverance of Jerusalem and its temple
from disaster in 701 BC, when the Assyrians had devastated
Judah and besieged the capital city. Samaria had fallen in 721
BC, so that the northern kingdom since then had been an Assyrian province; now the end of Judah seemed to have come.
But, in the event, the Assyrian army left the country without
having taken the city. Trouble at home may have forced Sennacherib to withdraw; there is evidence that a plague worked
havoc among his soldiery,[2] which may be compatible with the
statement in II Kings 19.35 that an angel struck down a huge
number of them. It was a momentous and memorable deliverance which the people of Jerusalem themselves had not

[1] D. Winton Thomas, op. cit., p. 93.
[2] Herodotus II 141.

achieved; it was Yahweh's doing. This deliverance gave rise to
a belief in the inviolability of the Jerusalem temple (cf. 33.20;
Jer. 7.4); and, since the deliverance was from the mighty Assyrians, it was evidence of the supremacy of Yahweh. That surely
must have given the Jews great hope for the future, and it may
have inspired Isaiah and have given him this great vision. If
so, then it occurred towards the end of his career, not at the
beginning.

If this view is accepted, it is not necessary to say, as Herntrich does in his recent commentary, that the statement that
wars will cease IN THE LATTER DAYS (v. 2) signifies that it will
not happen in the course of human history, but ' in God's time,
not in a distant future, but in another aeon which will come
into being when ours ceases to be '.[1] The vision, indeed, represents an eschatological expectation, but the Old Testament
teaching as a whole supports the view that the vision speaks of
the Day of the Lord within the course of human history, when,
after judgment (cf. 2.6 ff.), there will be blessing and peace, and
righteousness and justice will abide. The phrase IN THE LATTER
DAYS, as used here, does not say when the great Day will come,
soon or late.

6-22. God is not mocked

This passage contains some evidence that it may once have
been in three stanzas much more clearly than it is now. It may
be observed that vv. 10, 19 and 21 are substantially parallel,
as are vv. 11 and 17 in a different way, with v. 9 bearing a little
resemblance to them.

It will be wise, therefore, to take vv. 6-11 first. It is in two
parts, 6-8 being descriptive of *Israel's materialism and secular-
ism*, and 9-11 of the *anger of Yahweh* against such unfaith,
pride and presumption. Verses 6-8 speak of the practice of
divination and soothsaying (cf. 8.19; Ex. 22.18; I Sam. 28.9)
which ought to have had no place in the life of a people called
to obey Yahweh's law; of the foreign influence in Israel which

[1] *Der Prophet Jesaia, Kap. 1-12*, p. 28.

is indicated by such practices, and which must have been increased by commercial relationships ('the striking of hands', signifying the making of agreements) and political alliances; and of the material well-being and prosperity which resulted, and the use of horses and chariots such as had not been heard of since the days of Solomon (I Kings 9.17-19, 22; 10.26-29) but had come again in Uzziah's reign (II Kings 14.22; II Chron. 26.7 ff; cf. Isa. 31.1-3). In v. 6 a word like 'diviners' has obviously fallen out of the text inadvertently before the words FROM THE EAST, and the form of v. 7 may suggest that the first half of v. 8 may have read something like:

'Their land is filled with idols, and there is no end to their images.'

The beginning of vv. 9-11 is difficult. It may be that the first part of v. 9 is a comment upon the conduct of Israel which has just been described: (a) SO THE MAN OF LOW DEGREE BOWS DOWN AND THE MAN OF HIGH DEGREE ABASES HIMSELF (so AV; cf. Pss. 49.2; 62.9), or (b) SO HUMAN BEINGS BOW DOWN AND MEN ABASE THEMSELVES (so RSV); otherwise (c) it can be interpreted as referring to the future ('shall bow down', 'shall be abased') and be associated with v. 11. The final phrase of v. 9 is a greater difficulty; the words FORGIVE THEM NOT, addressed by the prophet either to God (cf. v. 6) or to the people who are willing and obedient (1.19) in respect of the wicked in Israel, come in very suddenly. If it is retained, the earlier part of the verse should be interpreted as in (a) or (b) above; but the form of vv. 11 and 17, to which this verse is partly parallel, rather suggests that the earlier part of the verse should be interpreted as in (c), and that this final clause should speak of the exaltation of God. Indeed the rendering 'but God shall be exalted to their downfall' (lit. 'to them') assumes a text very close to the accepted text.

It is not clear who are addressed in v. 10; probably it is the wicked who are told to hide themselves in caves to avoid the

E

coming judgment (cf. I Sam. 13.6; 22.1; I Kings 18.4) and to cover their heads with dust, as in mourning, or simply to hide themselves in the ground (cf. v. 19) that they may escape notice. Man's pride will be humbled in that day when the terrors of Yahweh's judgment are abroad in the earth. His law cannot be disregarded with impunity. Men who treat man-made laws with respect and know that, if they offend, they must pay the penalty, are tempted to think that they can sin against God and go unpunished. But God is not mocked; what a man sows he shall reap; to God belong the kingdom, the power and the glory.

12-19. The Day of Yahweh of Hosts

The Day of Yahweh was popularly conceived as the time when prosperity would return to Israel, all her enemies would be defeated and the people would enjoy Yahweh's blessing unmolested and in peace (cf. Amos 5.18). Amos taught that it was to be a day of darkness and not of light, and of inescapable judgment and punishment. It is this idea which is developed in other Old Testament passages also (cf. Isa. 13.6; Joel 1.15; 2.1, 11, 31; Zeph. 1.7, 14; Mal. 4.5; Zech. 14.1); the judgment became in later passages one not concerned with Israel alone, but with all the nations.

12. It is in consonance with what is said in vv. 6-22 as a whole that the proud should be spoken of first as coming under judgment. The last word of v. 12 means 'low' or 'lowly', and AV tries to get sense by translating it as AND HE SHALL BE BROUGHT LOW. Rather we should assume that the original was a word meaning 'exalted' or 'proud', a term parallel to the preceding LIFTED UP (so RSV).

13-16. When these verses say that Yahweh acts against the cedars and the oaks, the mountains and the hills, the towers and the fortified cities, and the ships of Tarshish and 'the beautiful forms', the meaning may simply be that he overturns everything which is strong, enduring and secure; in other words, the Day of Yahweh will be one of upheaval when the strong will be made to look weak and the firmly established will be overthrown (cf. I Cor. 1.27), and when accepted values will be revealed as worthless and not to be trusted. But there may be certain overtones also to be detected in the precise words used. The cedars of Lebanon represented man's vain-glory and his love of ostentation (cf. Isa. 9.10; Jer. 22.14 f.). The oaks, of course, symbolized strength (cf. Isa. 44.14; Amos 2.9), but the name may also have suggested the worship which the Israelites practised under green and shady trees (cf. Isa. 1.29 f.; Hos. 4.13; Isa. 57.5). The high mountains must have seemed immovable; to overturn them required more than human strength, and meant cosmic upheaval and the over-throw of the pattern of creation; but they may also have sug-gested the cultic rites which were practised in Israel on the hill-tops. The high towers and fortified cities typified man-made defences and armaments of war (cf. 2.7), in which men often seek salvation when they should trust in the living God (see 7.3-13). The ships of Tarshish represented in the popular mind the wealth and prosperity of the days of Solomon and Jehosha-phat, kings of Judah, who built fleets for trading voyages from Ezion-geber at the northern end of the Red Sea. The oppor-tunity for such enterprise had come again in Isaiah's day (cf. I Kings 9.26-28; 10.22; II Chron. 20.36 f.). Tarshish or Tartes-sus was a Phoenician colony in southern Spain (although it is now sometimes located in Sardinia) so that ' a ship of Tarshish ' thus designates a long-distance ship, like an Indiaman of a much later date. But evidence has now come to hand that there was a Phoenician word ' tarshish ' meaning a mine or a smelt-ing plant, so that ' a ship of Tarshish ' was a heavy ore-carrying vessel.[1] In each case the significance of the term is the same. The translation PLEASANT PICTURES (v. 16 AV) is uncertain; BEAUTIFUL CRAFT (RSV) is based on a different text, suggested

[1] See W. F. Albright, ' New Light on the Early History of the Phoenician Colonization ', *Bulletin of the American Schools of Oriental Research* 83, Oct. 1941, pp. 21 f.

by the need to find an appropriate parallel to SHIPS OF TAR-
SHISH. But there is another possibility; 'beautiful forms',
which is a literal translation, may mean 'beautiful temple
vessels' or 'beautiful images' made with the gold and silver
which the ships brought to Palestine from distant lands (v. 20;
cf. I Kings 10.22).

17-19. These verses are comparable to vv. 11 and 10 in that
order. Here man, seeking an escape, is not said to hide in the
dust (v. 10) but in holes in the ground, i.e. in storage-pits and
cisterns and natural cavities; but there is no essential difference
in meaning. Verse 18 seems to be an interpolation which breaks
the connection between vv. 17 and 19 and is read by some
scholars in the first stanza, following v. 9; it is similar in content to v. 20 in the final section of the chapter.

20-22. This final section or stanza has little distinctive to add.
There is missing from it, as it stands, a verse like 11 and 17
in the preceding sections; and there is the additional point that
when the people escape to their places of refuge, they throw
away their precious idols to the moles and the bats which haunt
the clefts and the caves to which they resort, for they are
worthless at such a time. Their own hands made them (cf. Isa.
40.18-20; 41.6 f.; 44.9-17; Jer. 10.3-5); how can such things,
which have no life-force or power, save them now?

22 remains a questionable finish to the chapter, because it
has no place in the Greek version. It resembles v. 9 to some
extent, and may be an appeal by the prophet to the Israelites,
before the day of judgment comes, to cease to trust in man-
made things such as idols, or in man himself; for man is a
fragile being, whose days are as grass and the breath in whose
nostrils is from the Lord, who giveth and taketh away (Job
1.21). Sometimes it has been suggested[1] that, since a verse
parallel to vv. 11 and 17 is notably absent in this final stanza,

[1] Cf. R. B. Y. Scott on this verse in *The Interpreter's Bible*.

it should be assumed that this v. 22 has suffered some corruption in transmission and was originally such a parallel verse—
an appropriate suggestion but difficult to sustain.

LAWLESS AND GRACELESS WANTONS

3.1–4.1

3.1-5. The day of judgment which is coming will be for Jerusalem and Judah a time of utter confusion and social anarchy.
The existing pattern of life will be completely overthrown and,
in the absence of all law and order, every man will fend for
himself with reckless abandon. It illustrates the truth which
during this century has often been illustrated under new
national régimes, in bombed cities, and in other circumstances
where the forces existing to preserve law and order cannot cope
during a crisis, that temporary disorder induces, and gives
opportunity to, distressingly large numbers of people who,
law-abiding within an undisturbed order, quickly turn disorder
to their own advantage and make profit from a state of confusion without hesitation and without a qualm (cf. v. 5). It is
evidence that there is within most men an evil propensity and
selfish inclination which normally are confined within narrow
limits of activity because of respect for, or fear of, the controls
within the social situation and the sanctions which can be
applied, but which can break out into free expression when a
suitable opportunity of undetectable unlawful gain occurs.

The words THE STAY AND THE STAFF mean the supports or
pillars of the established order, in the same sense as we speak
today of certain people as 'pillars of the Church'. Who these
people are is stated in vv. 2-4. The clause which introduces the
list, THE WHOLE STAY OF BREAD AND THE WHOLE STAY OF WATER
seems to be so different from what immediately follows that it
has often been questioned whether it was part of the original
text of the passage. But there are at least two reasons for

accepting it as authentic: the first is that it would be difficult
to account for its later intrusion into a passage which, without
it, reads coherently and easily; and secondly, v. 7 supports what
is said here, that the land suffered from famine and dire want
as well as from social commotions.

The list of leaders in the community given in vv. 2-4 specifies
three types. First, the military leaders are mentioned; the fact
that they are given first place in v. 2 might be construed to
mean that they were regarded in Isaiah's time as the most important for the security and peace of the land; but a second
reference to them at the beginning of v. 3 makes that a somewhat uncertain conclusion. Secondly, there are the prophets,
the judges, the elders and the counsellors, those leaders of
whom we know most in ancient Israel. At their best they spoke
and acted as they believed they were directed by God to do,
but often they became mercenary, so that the prophets prophesied for gain, the judges could be bribed and the counsellors gave the pleasing answer (Micah 3.11; 7.3; Amos 5.12;
Jer. 6.13; Ezek. 22.12). Possibly we are surprised by the nature
of the third group; the DIVINER (cf. Num. 22.7; 23.23; II Kings
17.17; Micah 3.6 f.; Jer. 27.9; 29.8; Ezek. 13.9, 23; 21.29; etc.;
not PRUDENT as in AV), and two other classes which are described very differently in AV and RSV. THE CUNNING ARTIFI-
CER (AV) is a possible rendering, but a failure on such a man's
part would not mean the misguidance or corruption of the
community but its impoverishment. Nevertheless, that is suitable enough, since poverty and want are mentioned or implied
as part of what the community will experience (cf. v. 7). But
RSV has SKILFUL MAGICIAN, a rendering which is linguistically
well-supported, and is probably to be preferred, because the
following term, which appears in AV as ELOQUENT ORATOR is
certainly to be rendered, as in RSV, EXPERT IN CHARMS. These
magicians and charmers were common in ancient Egypt and
Babylon (cf. Gen. 41.8, 24; Ex. 7.11, 22; 8.7, 18 f.; Dan. 1.20;
2.2, 10, 27). The mention of such types among the supports of
the community obviously means that the people who forsook

the word of God had to find guidance from some other source and turned to outworn and discredited ways and to superstitious practices (cf. 8.19). When men forsake God, they turn to idols; when they will not drink from cisterns of living water, they will hew for themselves cisterns which cannot hold water (Jer. 2.13). As a modern writer says: 'A more searching and momentous challenge to Christianity than bleak irreligion is the tendency, so marked in the modern period, either deliberately to advocate, or apathetically to relapse into, some substitute form of religion. . . . In the last resort the choice of the modern world will lie not between Christianity and sheer unbelief, but between Christianity and some form of idolatry.'[1]

The absence of kings from the list of leaders has led some scholars to think that this utterance of Isaiah must belong to a time when the ruling king was very young, even a minor, so that he counted for little or nothing in the life of the community; and they find support for this in the reference to CHILDREN as ruling officials in the following verse. In particular, they believe that the early days of Ahaz must have been the occasion, since he began his reign at the age of twenty. But there is little doubt that the age of twenty in Isaiah's time was not considered so youthful an age as it is among us today; and when we note that the great Uzziah began to reign at the age of sixteen (II Kings. 15.2) and Jotham and Hezekiah at twenty-five (II Kings 15.32 f.; 18.2), the age of Ahaz at his accession (II Kings 16.2) cannot have appeared notably young. Besides, while it is true that kings have no place on the list, neither have priests. We must conclude that the list is not an exhaustive one and may not have been intended to be so.

One important point remains to be taken into account. The situation described in these verses is not simply a contingency of human history or an unfortunate, lamentable state of affairs such as, man being man, may be expected to occur periodically on this earth. Verse 1 states clearly that it was Yahweh who

---

[1] J. V. Langmead Casserley, *The Retreat from Christianity in the Modern World*, Longmans, 1952, pp. 42, 8.

removed all the supports of Jerusalem and Judah so that the situation which supervened was willed by him and was sent by him as a judgment. This illustrates the interpretation of history which is found time after time in the Old Testament; everything which happens has its co-ordinate place in God's plan for his people.

6-8. These verses speak of what may be described as a retreat from responsibility. All the leaders having been removed, only the young and the inexperienced are left (v. 4). But the pattern of human society, in which some have the responsibility of leadership and others are more or less content to be governed, is so dominant and long-established that even in the lawless situation just described there must be brought into being some appearance of order, however farcical it may be. In the poverty-stricken community one man is found who still possesses his outer garment and is, therefore, presentable; an attempt is made to thrust the leadership on him. At once he declines, saying that his household is as poverty-stricken as the rest; he will be neither butt nor scapegoat.

9-12. An interposed soliloquy
The first part of v. 9 is a continuation of the preceding verses. AV and RSV have different renderings of the first clause. The verb which is at the root of SHEW (AV) and PARTIALITY (RSV) means to observe, to regard, and can mean to regard with favour, to be partial. On the whole, the way in which the word THEIR is used leads to the conclusion that AV is nearer to the prophet's meaning, which appears to be that the ' expression of their face ' testifies against them. On a great occasion when Moses had been in communion with God, his face is said to have shone (Ex. 34.29); the opposite of that is intended here; the faces of the people were hard and crafty or weak and stupid, so that they bore the external marks of their inner attitudes and characteristics (Gal. 6.17).

ISAIAH 3.9-1573

9. WOE TO THEM! seems to begin a soliloquy, as the prophet stands back to reflect on it all, in much the same way as Abraham did over the destruction of Sodom and Gomorrah (Gen. 18.22 f.). Would nothing be salved from the ruin of Jerusalem and Judah? Would the righteous perish with the wicked? They had brought it all upon themselves; but would all equally bear the penalty, would none be exempt? Verses 10 f. give the answer; with the righteous it will be well in the day of judgment, but the wicked will receive the just reward of their deeds. Verse 12 concludes the soliloquy. The first part can be rendered: 'My people—oppressors glean them (i.e. take away the last straw) and exactors rule over them,' and that is certainly suitable in the context. But the statement that exactors 'rule' is not likely, so that the rendering in AV or RSV (which are very much alike) should be followed. The rule of the queen-mother had been experienced in Judah (cf. II Kings 11.1-16), and was not well-esteemed.

13-15. The hub of the situation

It may be justifiable to think that of all the supports of the community mentioned in vv. 2-4, those upon whom the welfare of the community most depended were the elders and the princes. If the former had remained men of integrity, giving just judgment and keeping themselves incorruptible, they would have done much to keep their fellow-men from evil; if the latter had not abandoned their responsibilities, the disorder would not have occurred. The greater the rock which comes hurtling down, the more stones and rubble it brings with it. Therefore, v. 14 says, Yahweh enters particularly into judgment with them; he does not stand up to plead, as AV says (v. 13), but to contend, for he has a controversy with his people (Hos. 4.1; Micah 6.2; Jer. 25.31). Isaiah reminds us in vv. 14 f. that, whereas in a time of disorder suffering and loss may be widespread, the suffering of the poor is the most tragic, because they lack the resources to make a speedy recovery and they can exert no influence in any claim for their rights.

3.16–4.1 Wanton women

A quick glance at these verses as they are printed in RSV shows 16 f. in poetic form, 18-23 in prose, and 24-26 again in poetic form with 4.1 as an epilogue. That has raised the question of the authenticity of vv. 18-23, which contain an amazing list of the fineries and ornaments which were available for the coquettes and the fine ladies of Isaiah's time; without these verses no hiatus between v. 17 and v. 24 would be felt. The question is not easily decided. Animus against wicked women is not peculiar to Isaiah among the prophets (cf. Amos 4.1-3; Jer. 44.15-30); but, if it is difficult to think that Isaiah interrupted a connected utterance to insert this catalogue, it is equally difficult to think that a later editor ever thought of doing so. Probably we should leave the verses where they are and believe that this whole passage deals with a subject upon which the prophet had very strong views.

The content of vv. 16 f. is clear in AV as in RSV, and the punishment in v. 17 is one which fits the crime. In vv. 18-23 the precise meaning of some of the terms is not certain, and the RSV is to be followed rather than AV; if this is done, a notable picture of material wealth and the ostentatious display of its products is to be found. Verses 24 f., like 17, describe the fate of the women; the terms ROTTENNESS, A ROPE, BALDNESS, SACKCLOTH mark the extent in the change of their fortunes. The last line of v. 24, INSTEAD OF BEAUTY, SHAME (RSV), has the support of one ms, as RSV notes; but it may be better to follow the line of AV and read: 'instead of beauty, a brand-mark' (lit. burning), and consider that the brand-mark may be a sign of slavery. Verse 25 adds another note to the judgment scene; the women have been thoroughly put to shame, stripped of all their finery and ornament, and reduced to a pitiful and even contemptible condition; now they are widowed and left desolate and bereft (cf. Ex. 22.24).

26, one presumes, must express a personification of Jerusalem, a city now of lamentation and mourning. She sits dumbfounded

and appalled by all that has befallen her; in the last clause
RSV reads RAVAGED and AV DESOLATE; the latter may give a
clearer idea of the meaning of the original word which could
mean 'cleaned out', and so derelict and desolate.

4.1, in a vivid way, gives an insight into the awful loss which
the city has suffered. Seven women, widowed (cf. 3.25) or now
without hope of marriage, entreat one man to receive them into
his household that they may be given his name. They will not
be a charge upon him for maintenance (cf. Ex. 21.10); they
simply ask that they receive his protection and the place in the
community which such an acceptance of them will bring them.
Whether, if the man had acceded to their request, the women
would have had full marriage rights is not clear and in this
context is not important.

THE NEW JERUSALEM

4.2-6

Verses 2-4 should be taken as a closely knit unit; its connection with vv. 5 f. must be discussed. The section obviously
speaks of a day of restoration and restitution in Jerusalem. The
great judgment described in the preceding chapter has taken
place. IN THAT DAY is, therefore, not the day mentioned in
2.12-20, but that which is referred to in 1.26 f. In v. 2 the main
question to be decided, if possible, is the significance of the
term rendered THE BRANCH OF YAHWEH. It is possible, of course,
to correlate its use here with its use in such passages as Jer.
23.5; 33.15; Zech. 3.8; 6.12, and to say that it is the Messiah
who is spoken of, the scion of the house of David. In this
interpretation the beauty and the glory (v. 2) belong to God;
the work of the Messiah is God's work, and the kingdom
which he establishes and rules in righteousness is God's kingdom. If we follow this line, we may then take the second half

of v. 2 to refer to the fruitfulness and the bounty of the earth
which constitute a token of this new day. Just as in a day of
wickedness and woe the earth is said to be parched and dry
or to mourn (cf. Amos 1.2; Jer. 4.28; Zech. 12.12; etc.), so now
it will be glad and rejoice with a new fruitfulness; it is as if
the joys of the garden of Eden before man's fall were to return.
This line of interpretation may be considered to find support
in 11.1 ff., 6 ff. (cf. Hos. 2.21 f.). But some scholars have ob-
jected that the parallelism which is characteristic of Hebrew
poetry requires that THE BRANCH OF THE LORD should be interpreted of nature's revival, as is THE FRUIT OF THE LAND in the
second clause; in consequence, they make it mean 'the new
growth of the Lord'. But it is impossible to believe that, had
this been the meaning the prophet wished to convey, he would
have done it by the use of this particular phrase.

But there is another line of interpretation related to the first
but not identical with it; it is to make the reference in THE
BRANCH OF THE LORD to the remnant which will survive the
judgment (cf. 1.9, 25 f.). Only by the mercy of Yahweh will
such a remnant survive; it will rise as a shoot or branch from
the stump of the tree which has been stripped to the ground
(cf. 6.13); it is evidence that there is still life in the tree and it
is the hope of the new day. That remnant will be BEAUTIFUL
AND GLORIOUS, because it is the righteous remnant and is of
God; and the fruit of the land which will spring up in this new
day will be their pride and glory. This meaning, it may be
maintained, finds support in v. 3 f. Now all the filth of Jerusalem has been washed away (v. 4; cf. 1.16) and the blood-
stains cleansed (1.15); therefore, those who remain will be a
holy remnant (Deut. 7.6). By the spirit of God they will be
kept from evil and will serve him with willing obedience
(1.19); they are recorded for life in Jerusalem, their names are
on the roll of the city (v. 3). In Ex. 32.32 f. there is reference
to the writing of the names of the righteous in God's book;
and other relevant passages are Dan. 12.1; Mal. 3.16; Pss.
69.28; 139.16; Rev. 3.5.

5-6 refer to the same great day of restoration and blessedness as the preceding vv. 2-4, but the description given is quite different. The main idea is that the blessedness of the wilderness fellowship between Yahweh and his people is now restored, his presence is among them as it was then. For just as in Ex. 13.21; 24.15-18; 33.9-11; etc., it is said that God came down on Sinai in fire enveloped in cloud, and on the Tent of Meeting in a pillar of cloud when Moses was communing with God, and was for the journeying Israelites a pillar of cloud by day and a pillar of fire by night, so now this tabernacling presence of God will be among his people again and will settle upon Mount Zion and all its assemblies. Thus, while these two verses describe the new day as bringing again the blessing of the wilderness period in Israel's history, the time of the pure espousals, vv. 2-4 speak of the restoration of the human community as it was before the Fall. It is notable that the Greek version has a form of text in v. 5 which is much nearer to the style of the wilderness narrative of Exodus: 'Then Yahweh will come upon every dwelling place on mount Zion and upon her assemblies as a cloud by day . . .'

The final phrase of v. 5 and the first part of v. 6 are difficult. The AV rendering has no intelligible meaning. RSV is possible but doubtful; it means that the glory of God will be shrouded or veiled by A CANOPY AND A PAVILION. But v. 6, as translated, would then mean that the glory of God, thus veiled, will be A SHADE and A SHELTER, a confused figure. It is probable that the following slightly modified rendering, which keeps close to the original text, may convey the meaning more clearly: 'And over all (i.e. everything) the glory of God will be a canopy and a covering, and will be a shade by day from the heat,' etc. This would mean that the figure of the cloud, as enshrouding God's mysterious presence and as indicating that presence, is now given a fuller application, for the glory of God, thus represented, will be a shelter from the heat and a refuge and shelter from the storm and rain, so that it is not

simply God's presence but his protective and saving activity
among his people which are described.

It seems necessary to conclude that, if vv. 5 f., come to us
from Isaiah, they must belong to a different occasion from
vv. 2-4 with which they appear now in close association. Indeed the thought forms used in vv. 5 f. are so unlike those
used by the prophet that it must remain doubtful whether they
are authentic; they may be a fragment which was incorporated
later into a collection of the prophet's utterances.

SOWING WILD GRAPES AND
HARVESTING WOE

5.1-30

This chapter, which, as has been said already, is to be
regarded as attached to chs. 2-4, is composed of three sections.
Verses 1-7 contain the great parable of the vineyard which, in
spite of all the attention given to it and care taken to secure
its welfare, produced bad grapes. All care of that vineyard is
to cease and it is to be destroyed. The second section, vv. 8-24,
contains a series of judgments or woes, in which prevalent
social vices are condemned. The woes are not arranged in
regular sections; the three in vv. 20-23 are very briefly expressed, whereas vv. 11-17 form a seemingly composite section,
in which vv. 13-17 do not appear to be in all parts closely
related to the woe pronounced on drunkards in vv. 11 f.
Finally, the section 25-30, has two notable features; it begins
with ' Therefore ', as if implying the precedence of some verses
no longer extant; and, secondly, it contains in the final part of
v. 25 a form of words found four times as a refrain in the
section 9.8–10.4. These two features have raised the question
whether this section, 5.25-30, may not be part of a long, connected poem, of which the major part is preserved in 9.8–10.4.

The middle section might belong to any part of Isaiah's
career, and the same might be said of the first; the final one

obviously belongs to a time when the Assyrian danger had
become serious. That means not earlier than 735, when Assyrian help was invoked by Ahaz (II Kings 16.7-9), but soon
after that date would be suitable (see the Commentary on the
chapter).

1-7. The parable of the vineyard

This is unfolded with great skill. Verses 1 f., in a few
graphic phrases, describe the vineyard; they combine to show
that it had every chance to become luxuriant and fruitful.
Occupying an excellent position on a hill with rich, fertile soil
which had been well cultivated and cleared of stones, the vineyard had been planted with choice vines. Beyond that, a watchtower had been built in it so that marauding invaders and
despoilers might be driven off and the plants be kept from
injury and violent stripping. But the disappointing result was
that, whereas a vineyard so cared for should have produced
excellent grapes, it produced very bad ones.

Doubtless some kind of blight must have attacked the vines
and wasted them. They had not been from the beginning a
degenerate stock; their environment had been excellent; they
had never lacked care. Yet something had gone wrong. Not a
hint so far has been given of the underlying significance of this
LOVE SONG (v. 1; or SONG OF MY BELOVED AV), nor has an
interpretation of the term MY BELOVED been given. The most
notable fact is that the love song finishes in a note of disappointment, if not of disillusionment.

3-4 contain the next movement. It is an appeal to the people
of Jerusalem and Judah for a verdict of 'not guilty' upon any
charge of negligence against the keeper of the vineyard. The
term 'beloved' is not now found; it is simply 'I and my vineyard'. It is affirmed that nothing had been left undone which
could have been done for the good of the vineyard. Why,
then, this corruption of good plants and waste of good husbandry?

5-6 continue the use of the first personal pronoun. The love-song is finished; the vineyard is to be abandoned, left to become wild and overgrown again. Its protective hedge is to be pulled down, and its surrounding wall broken; the vineyard will be open to all kinds of invaders and marauders and will be trampled down and ruined. No pruning and hoeing will be done; it will receive no care or attention at all. Briers and thorns will soon occupy it as their own; and the command is given that no refreshing and life-giving rain is to fall on it. Here at last the interpretation of the parable begins to become plain. Until the withholding of the rain is mentioned, no clue had been given; the description of the vineyard being left to go to ruin could mean simply human neglect. But only God can withhold the rain.

7 states the interpretation explicitly. The beloved who planted the vineyard is God; the vineyard is the house of Israel. The parable, therefore, is more or less parallel in teaching to those passages (e.g. 1.21-23, 26; 4.2-6) which idealize Israel's life in the wilderness and speak of the evil which infected Israel's life thereafter until it became utterly and irremediably corrupt. The second part of v. 7 expresses briefly and memorably the grievous disappointment God experienced because of Israel's failure; he looked for justice between man and man, i.e. a healthy, wholesome social life free from evil and corruption, but, behold, bloodshed (1.15); he looked for right dealing, honesty and moral integrity and, instead, there was the outcry of the suffering against injustice and oppression. There is an assonance in the words in the original language which must have made them easily remembered; it is extremely difficult to find a similar mode of expression in English which sufficiently accurately conveys the sense. We might, in free translation, say: 'He looked for right and behold might; for law-abiding and behold law-deriding'; but that is heavy and lacks the crispness of the original form.

8-24. Woe upon woe

There are signs that this passage, which obviously consists of a series of woe passages, has suffered some disarrangement in transmission. The introductory word WOE is found six times (vv. 8, 11, 18, 20, 21, 22); the considerable gap between the second and the third occurrences suggests either that there was an intervening woe passage of which parts may remain before us, or that some of the material in the intervening verses may originally have been associated with the last three woes which are very briefly expressed. The passage condemns some of the social evils prevalent in Judah and it is notable that drunkenness, which is the subject of the second, is also the subject of the last, although the vices and failures to which it gives rise are different in the two cases.

8-10. Big estates and fine houses

Palestine is often described in the Old Testament as Yahweh's portion or inheritance, and his people hold it in fee as his tenants. Therefore, they are as stewards of it, obliged to care for it and to keep it within their possession, as a family inheritance and as Yahweh's land. The fact that land which had to be sold by reason of economic need was offered first to a kinsman shows one way by which the attempt was made to honour this obligation (Ruth 4.3 ff.). And when Ahab was told by Naboth that he could not have the vineyard close by his palace which he so much desired because it was a family inheritance, he did not try to force the situation; he knew how zealously a true Israelite tried to keep intact the family property. (It was Jezebel, brought up in a different tradition, who had no compunction about telling the king to exercise his royal authority and to take what he wanted; cf. I Kings 21.) Apparently in Isaiah's time the land question was critical. We must assume that there was much economic hardship, so that many were forced to sell their lands and houses in order to pay their debts and to escape becoming enslaved to their creditors; and we must assume that often there was no kins-

F

man who was able to buy the land or the house and so keep it
in the family until the temporarily harassed owner was able
to recover possession of it. It is possible that the economic
situation was made more difficult at this time for people of
limited resources by the havoc which must have been caused
in at least part of the land of Judah by the threat to Jerusalem
in 735 BC by Pekah of Israel and Rezin of Syria. The result
was that a comparatively few men acquired field after field
and house after house, either because these had to be sold for
cash in order that debts might be paid or because they were
appropriated in respect of unpaid debts (cf. II Kings 4.1;
Micah 2.2). The result was an increase in the number of land-
less people, some to become hired labourers finding work as
opportunity offered, others to become slaves. It is interesting
that Hebrew law, as it developed (cf. Ex. 22.25 ff.; Deut. 23.19),
contained regulations to the effect that, if an Israelite gave a
loan of money to a fellow-Israelite, he was not to exact interest;
that was doubtless an effort made to ease the burden of the
poor and the temporarily harassed.

It seems fitting punishment for the land-grabbers and financial opportunists (whose counterparts exist in every age in
some shape or other) that, in the forthcoming devastation of
the land, the fine houses which they inhabited should become
desolate and the fields, of which they had gained possession,
should yield a wholly uneconomical return. The second part of
v. 10 says that a homer of seed would yield only one-tenth of
that quantity; and the first part says that the amount of land
which could be ploughed in a day by ten yoke of oxen (which
would probably be considerably more than ten acres) would
yield a mere nine gallons of wine. This is not simply a reversal
of fortune for these men; it is God's judgment upon them. (In
v. 9, RSV gives, much more clearly than AV, what was probably the meaning of the original text.)

11-13. Drunkenness and indulgence
The vice of drunkenness is mentioned not infrequently by

the prophets (cf. v. 22; Hos. 7.5; Amos 6.6; Joel 3.3). The fact
that it is placed immediately after the section on the land-
grabbers probably means that drunkenness was a vice particularly of those who had money in plenty. On the one hand,
the rich took advantage of some men's financial embarrass-
ment in order to increase their holding of heritable property,
while, on the other hand, they indulged to an excessive degree
their own physical appetites (v. 11). It might be thought that
the fact that these persistent tipplers had music at their feasts
indicates that they wanted to make at least some show of
elegance; but it is more likely that the music also served their
physical pleasures. The result was that their senses became
utterly dulled and they became quite incapable of thinking at
all of anything but the satisfaction of their own appetites and
desires. No thought of God ever entered their minds; his works
they never saw in the world around them.

The connection of v. 13 with the verses immediately preceding it is very doubtful; but the link is probably to be found
in the words FOR WANT OF KNOWLEDGE. These words do not
mean simply ' because they are ignorant ' in the general sense,
but because they have no understanding of God and his works
—like the drunkards described in v. 12. If this link was intended, then it must be assumed that the drunkenness which
was rampant became widespread and very corrupting in its
effect, so that the penalty is said to fall upon ' the people '.
The fact that exile is mentioned means that the Assyrian
danger had by this time become serious and the possibility of
the land being invaded and some of its inhabitants taken into
captivity had become real. The honourable or honoured men
spoken of in v. 13 may mean those who had suffered loss
already; they would continue to suffer in a devastated, uncultivated land.

14-17. Men abased, God exalted

Verses 14-16 have sometimes been thought to be out of
place here and to have their proper association with 2.6-22;

compare, for example, v. 15 with 2.9 and v. 16 with 2.11, 17.
That is plausible, both because haughtiness has no place here
in the catalogue of vices, v. 21 being rather concerned with
self-esteem and self-complacency, and because there is no woe
in this section to suggest that it constituted one in the series of
vices libelled. In the judgment which befalls the land the
deaths, of noblemen and commoners alike, are so many that
Isaiah uses the strong figure of saying that ' Sheol has enlarged
its appetite and opened its mouth beyond measure ' (cf. Num.
16.30 ff.). Sheol was the place of the departed, of good and
bad alike, where they maintained a shadowy, passionless existence and where there was no remembrance of Yahweh; there
at least the slave had some consolation in being free from his
master (cf. Job 3.17 ff.; Ps. 6.5). Verses 15-16 express the contrast which is expressed more than once in 2.6-22 of the abase-
ment and humiliation of man and the exaltation of God in
righteousness and his self-revelation in that awesome, subduing
quality of holiness in the presence of which man is forced to
recognize his own creatureliness and unworthiness (cf. 6.5).

17 is clearly a fitting sequel to v. 13, so that once again the
isolation of vv. 14-16 in their context is made clear. The translation THEN LAMBS SHALL GRAZE AS IN THEIR PASTURE, FATLINGS
AND KIDS SHALL FEED AMONG THE RUINS (RSV) should be followed; otherwise, on some evidence from LXX, AND KIDS SHALL
FEED IN FAT PASTURES NOW WASTE. In each case the line means
that what had been well-cultivated, richly-productive land has
become pastoral again, and a simpler economy has supervened
upon the former wealth and ostentation which Isaiah criticizes
(cf. 7.23-25).

18-19. Defiant unbelief
The figure used in v. 18, not current among us today, must
have had meaning for people who knew the ways of an agricultural economy. The second is the clearer of the two parts of
the verse. Sin must often have been a burdensome, weary

business for many in Judah; it must have absorbed so much of their energy (cf. Isa. 57.9-10; Jer. 9.5). But they drove on unrelentingly, like oxen pulling after them the laden cart to which they are yoked. The first part, which is largely parallel in expression to the second, raises one query: what is meant by CORDS (or ropes) OF VANITY? The figure again is of a yoked animal pulling some vehicle or implement after it; RSV uses the phrase CORDS OF FALSEHOOD; but it is not the cords which are false, it is the sinners themselves and their sins which may be so described. There is much, then, to be said for the proposal that the original phrase may have been ' bullock ropes ' (the words for ' vanity ' and ' bullock ' being very similar in Hebrew), so that the two parts of the verse are then wholly parallel.

19 expresses defiant unbelief. Those who show this attitude say that they have seen no signs of God's activity upon the earth and are not prepared to believe what the prophets have to say about God's judgment and correction of his sinful people. If God proposes to do anything, let him do it at once that it may be seen. This is the same unbelieving attitude as is expressed in other passages in the Old Testament in which men describe God as silent or asleep, or as having forsaken the earth (cf. Isa. 42.14; Jer. 1.12; 14.8 f.; Ezek. 8.12; 9.9). It is an attitude which quietens its fears by the protestation that there is nothing to fear, and which attempts with easy mind to defy the moral law by saying that there is no God who can judge, and earth's judges can be suitably controlled and made amenable.

20. Moral perversion

This, the first of three briefly expressed woes, indicts, and calls for judgment upon, those who pervert the moral law, who say, ' Evil, be thou my good '. These are the people whose only good is that which is advantageous to themselves; they are un-compromisingly utilitarian in all that they do; they deride altruism as a principle of human conduct. We may, indeed, properly describe them as morally unprincipled, as perverts.

21. Self-conceit

The class designated here are not the haughty in the strict sense of that term; they are not the people who think they are a cut above their neighbours and show it in snobbishness and exclusiveness. Rather they are thoroughly pleased with themselves, have a very pronounced self-conceit, believe that they are thoroughly able to look after themselves and, being thus self-sufficient, have no need for the aids and the comforts which weaker people seek in religion. They conceive religion to be fundamentally an attitude of subservience, and they have no intention of being subservient to any person, in heaven or in earth. Before their fellow-men they are self-assured; before God they are presumptuous.

22-23. Heroes in their cups

The men who do great deeds only when they are intoxicated to the point of unwonted geniality and cheerfulness and who talk like heroes only when drink has withdrawn them from the hard realities of life—these are known and are found in every age. Their conduct may be harmless enough, it may be easily dismissed as empty boasting; but the retreat from reality which wine and strong drink can provide may be sought for its own sake, so that men are in this way made morally flabby and shirk any difficult situation. Verse 23 shows how the corruption can be carried one degree further; the drink-addict not only becomes morally flabby and lax but he more and more transgresses moral standards in his dealings with others. Such standards introduce a rigour into life; they demand moral discipline. But the life of the drink-addict becomes progressively more and more undisciplined; he can be induced to acquit the guilty at the price of a bribe, and, for mercenary advantage, to withhold from the innocent the acquittal to which he is entitled.

The connection of vv. 24 f. with the preceding verses is very much open to question; they certainly do not seem to have any particular applicability to the drunkards described in vv. 22 f., but may be thought to refer to all the types condemned in the woes. In this case the statement in v. 24, that their root will become rotten and THEIR BLOSSOM GO UP LIKE DUST, must mean that these wicked types who are condemned in the woes are like a tree which, having lost all vigour and vitality, becomes dry and withered, so that the root disintegrates and the parched blossoms are blown into the air like dust before the wind. It is an excellent figure and is made more effective if the tongue of fire mentioned at the beginning of v. 24 is taken to refer to the burning hot wind of the desert.

But the most notable feature of vv. 24 f. is the final sentence in v. 25, which is found as a recurring refrain at the end of the stanzas which constitute the long poem found in 9.8–10.4. The idea at once presents itself that these two verses might be another, displaced stanza belonging to this poem which might have had its place originally following 9.21. But there are two features of vv. 24 f. which argue against such a simple transference of these verses in the way indicated: the first is that the word THEREFORE at the beginning of v. 24 is not suitable at the beginning of a new stanza, but assumes a close connection with a verse or verses immediately preceding; and, secondly, the subject of reference in THEIR ROOT, THEIR BLOSSOM, etc., now becomes undefined. That the two verses should be transferred to follow 9.21 is a suitable proposal, but it seems necessary to assume that something preceding, and defining, the subject of v. 24 has been lost. One detail: it should be noted that the second clause of v. 24 should be rendered as in RSV: AND AS DRY GRASS SINKS DOWN IN A FLAME.

26-30 describe the invader from the north. In subject they are closely associated with the poem in 9.8–10.4. They do not, however, describe existent evils, like the other stanzas, but

invasion; for that reason they may fittingly be read following
10.4, at the end of the poem. The invaders are the Assyrians.
In brief phrases, which give a fine impression of speed of movement and urgency of intention, the passage describes their
unflagging energy and disciplined progress (v. 27), their
weapons at the ready and their mounts swift as the wind, and
their whole clamorous, ravenous, onsweeping attack like the
fearsome assault of a pride of lions. Verse 30 seems somewhat
unconnected with the verses which precede it, the figure being
suddenly changed from the roaring of lions to the raging of a
troubled sea. Over all the land there is darkness, both the
darkness of anguish and distress and the physical darkness of
a day in which the natural light is obscured by clouds, as if
the heavens themselves had put on mourning garb. For SEEM
LIKE FLINT in v. 28 we may read ARE THOUGHT OF AS A FIERCE
WIND (Arabic ṣarṣar).

ISAIAH'S INAUGURAL VISION

6.1-13

The fact that this inaugural vision has its place here in the
book, and not at the beginning, may indicate that it once stood
at the head of a small collection of utterances and biographical
passages (such as 6.1–9.7) which was later incorporated into
the book as we now have it. But we have to remember that
the record of the call of Amos is in 7.14-16 of his book, so
that the need may not have been felt in every case to record
the inaugural vision, or the experience which brought the
sense of vocation, at the beginning of the record of a prophet's
life and work.

To understand all that this visionary experience meant in
the life of Isaiah and in the thought of his contemporaries, it
is necessary to remember that in much of the Near Eastern
area, particularly in Babylonia, there was celebrated annually

a great New Year Festival when the divine king was enthroned, the narrative of the Creation and of the victory of the supreme god over the great deep (or chaos) was celebrated, and the king, as representative of the people, made confession of their sins and pleaded for the continuance of the divine blessing for the coming year, especially for the rains in their season and for victory over their enemies. In Israel there was no such belief in a divine king, although there was the practice of anointing the king as for a holy office; but—although the matter is disputed—there may have been kept at Jerusalem a form of the New Year Festival in which the enthronement of Yahweh was celebrated. That the prophet's vision took place during a celebration of this festival in which he shared is a very plausible idea but one which cannot be proved.

The chapter can be considered appropriately in three parts, vv. 1-4, 5-8, and 9-12, with v. 13 as a postlude.

1-4. IN THE YEAR THAT KING UZZIAH DIED (742 BC) may simply indicate the date when Isaiah had the experience here related; but it does not seem wholly fanciful to suggest that a long and prosperous reign of fifty-two years (cf. II Kings 15.1 f.) must have given a sense of stability and security to the people of Judah so that the end of it must have been a reminder of man's mortality and of the transience of human institutions, of kings' reigns and of kingdoms. In contrast, the Lord is HIGH AND LIFTED UP, exalted in power and glory above the earth, untouched by the limitations of finite man, not subject to man's mortality—the exalted, transcendent God, the Maker and Ruler of all. In terms of being, therefore, God and man stand apart; but God has established a relationship across that divide, he has made a bridge. The words HIS TRAIN FILLED THE TEMPLE mean that the skirt of his robe was seen in vision to do so; thus he is God of heaven and earth, he is present among his people, in his own house which Israel had built for him; therefore, man dare not think he can disregard God, and he ought not to think that he is forsaken by God. But God's presence among his people necessarily involves his activity among them, to judge or to comfort, to build up or to destroy, as the need may be. This activity of God among his people is indicated in the text in a way which is strange to us. The Israelites believed that the power of a prophet is active in the words he speaks (cf. Balaam, Num. 22.1-6), especially in blessing and cursing, in the clothes he wears and in the staff he carries (II Kings 4.29-31; Matt. 9.20-21). Therefore, the fact that the skirt of the Lord's robe filled the Temple doubtless meant for them that his power was present and active there, for they analogically used of God the same ways of thought which they used of his servants the prophets (cf. Isa. 55.11).

The seraphim are mentioned only here in the Old Testament; the guardians of the ark in the Jerusalem Temple are named cherubim. The word seraph (of which seraphim is the plural) comes from a verb meaning ' to burn ' and originally signified a serpent-like figure (cf. Num. 21.6 ff. for the use of it in connection with the brazen serpent). The word may, therefore, have been used in this connection because of the burning sensation consequent upon snake-bite. Here, however, the upper part of the figure is human; what the lower part was must remain doubtful and is not significant because it was covered in the prophet's vision. The seraphim were at once the guardians and the attendants of the heavenly throne; in God's presence they covered their faces, being unworthy or unable to look upon God; and, in reverence, they covered their own bodies. They praised the holy God who is apart from all his creatures in majesty and in glory, but of whose majesty and glory man may find ample evidence in heaven and earth, his own creation. Verse 4 speaks of the physical, visible effect upon the Temple of the song of the seraphim. The guardians of a Temple normally had their place at the threshold, so that we can easily appreciate the meaning of the statement that the foundations of the threshold shook. All that the Temple represented became alive for Isaiah that day; the whole shrine vibrated with spiritual power and it was filled with smoke, not simply with the smoke from the altar but the smoke or cloud which veiled from man the divine presence.

5-8. The prophet's response

One aspect of the prophet's response was immediate. Before God the seraphim covered their faces; but he, with his own eyes, had seen the King. How could any man have such an experience and survive? (cf. Ex. 33.20). As he stood there in Jerusalem, the prophet was acutely aware, not only of his own creatureliness and unworthiness, but of the fact that all his people were as he was. The next step could not be with the prophet; from his predicament he could not find a way of escape.

It is important, therefore, to note that the way out was provided from God's side. The prophet was cleansed from his sin as by fire, by means of a glowing ember carried by a seraph from the altar. That a prophet should have had a sense of cleansing in this way is very notable, because the prophets (not least Isaiah; cf. 1.12-15) had often hard things to say about the Temple and all its works. But this day he found the spiritual realities which lay behind the Temple forms and rituals. To say, as some scholars do, that it was a hot stone and not a glowing ember which touched the prophet's lips is surely to miss the point; the glowing ember and the cleansing by fire must have been recognized as fitting symbols, if not authentic instruments, of the God who had revealed himself to Israel in the wilderness among the fires of Sinai and to Elijah by fire on Mount Carmel.

Isaiah at once learned that he had been cleansed by God, not simply that he himself might have the assurance of sins forgiven and live in the joy of that experience. It was now his responsibility to go and tell others of the experience he had had, that they might seek to enter into a similar experience. But Isaiah was not directly commanded to fulfil that responsibility; the existence of the responsibility was made known to him in the question which was addressed to him: WHOM SHALL I SEND

AND WHO WILL GO FOR US? And the prophet made willing
response, not pointing to someone else who was, as we would
say, 'eminently suited to the task', but offering himself. He
responded as, in any age, men will respond who have had
experiences to which they owe much. They know themselves
debtors and this is the only way in which they can try to pay
the debt.

9-12. The prophet's commission

If Isaiah had resolved that he must now go and call upon
people to find the cleansing and spiritual renewal which he had
found, the words which constituted his commissioning for this
work must have sounded peculiarly discouraging. It is not
easy to conceive that any preacher, in addressing his audience,
ever used such words as HEAR YE INDEED, BUT UNDERSTAND
NOT; he could not possibly have forbidden them either to hear
or to understand. Even if we moderate the words somewhat
and say: 'Go on hearing but you will never understand', they
are still very hard. They so emphasize the people's hardness
of heart and obduracy that we wonder if Isaiah ever could have
begun in this way; but the bitter irony of 29.9, for example,
shows that it is possible. Many scholars, however, find the
words so hard that they are persuaded that this section was
written down some years after the event, possibly at the time
when Isaiah had to interrupt his prophetic activity for a period
(cf. 8.16 f.). By that time he was aware of the stiffness of the
opposition he had to face, he had learned that preaching to the
resolutely antagonistic may merely increase their antagonism
and make their ignorance and prejudices more impenetrable;
and so he wrote down words which sharply say: 'Go on hearing but don't understand lest some day you should turn and
be healed, as I was.'

The inevitable question was asked by Isaiah: 'How long
am I to continue such a profitless and exasperating ministry?
Could not I find something better to do than waste my time
on such people?' But the answer came to him that he must

continue the work so long as any people were left in the land. Punishment would come upon the sinful land, ruin and dereliction; its inhabitants would be removed; but so long as he had any congregation at all, the charge remained his. Isaiah, therefore, was called to an unremitting and apparently unrewarding task. Jeremiah recoiled at the beginning from his prophetic commission when he thought of his inexperience, but the promise was given to him that he would receive strength for his task (Jer. 1.6, 17-19). No such comfortable assurance seems to have been given to Isaiah.

13 sounds at once like an addition and a qualification; the former because the chapter seems complete without it, the latter because v. 11 speaks of utter desolation and gives no hint that a tenth may remain. But that Isaiah did speak of a remnant which would survive the great day of judgment is not in doubt (cf. 1.9, 25; 4.2-4, 5 f.; 10.20-23; 11.11-16; etc.). This verse about the tenth, which at least temporarily survives, may have been introduced in order to strike this essential note of the prophet's teaching in this chapter. But the final sentence of the verse, THE HOLY SEED IS ITS STUMP, is not found in the Greek version and should be regarded as an addition introduced into the chapter. It is a comment on the word STUMP (not SUBSTANCE as in AV) which is used earlier in the verse. The devastation of the land and the clearing out of its inhabitants is likened to the felling of a tree; the tenth which remains is likened to the tree-stump. But whereas the main part of the verse states that even this stump will in turn be destroyed, the additional words speak of the stump as that from which the new shoot will come, because holy seed remains in it (Isa. 4.2; 11.1; etc.).

THE RAVAGES OF WAR AND
THE WAY OF PEACE

7.1–12.6

A NATIONAL CRISIS

7.1–9.7

IMMANUEL

7.1-17

Following upon the intimately personal record of Isaiah's in-augural vision in ch. 6, this passage 7.1-17 appears at first sight to be a piece of historical recording; but its primary importance lies in the account it gives of the part played by the prophet during the political crisis to which it refers. The nature and circumstances of the crisis can be understood more fully with the aid of the evidence from II Kings 16, II Chron. 28, and the relevant Assyrian records.[1] The reigning king in Judah at the time was Ahaz, so that the event took place some years after the prophet's call (7.1; cf. 1.1). According to a commonly accepted chronology, Jotham reigned 742-735 BC (eight years, following upon a regency of eight years at the end of Uzziah's reign; so the sixteen years of II Kings 15.32 f.); II Kings 16.1 states that Pekah of Israel was already seven-

---

[1] Cf. D. Winton Thomas, *Documents from Old Testament Times*, pp. 53-58.

teen years on his throne when Ahaz of Judah, Jotham's
successor, became king, but a chronological problem is involved here, for whose solution reference must be made to II
Kings.

Tiglath Pileser of Assyria was in the west on several occasions to quell revolts during the years immediately following
743 BC. II Kings 15.37 implies that the alliance of Ephraim and
Syria against Judah began before the death of Jotham; but the
full danger to Jerusalem and Judah developed in 735-4 BC,
when the two confederate kings, Pekah of Ephraim and Rezin
of Syria, attempted to force Judah to join them in revolt against
Assyria, and brought their armies against Jerusalem to force
the issue.

2-3. The result was a state of emergency in Jerusalem and fear
for the safety of the city. Isaiah was moved to go out and meet
King Ahaz when he was engaged in taking practical measures
for the city's water supply; this was an essential precaution if
the inhabitants were to be given a chance to survive a siege.
The so-called upper conduit was a channel by which water
from the spring of Gihon in the Kidron valley was led into
the upper city (cf. II Kings 18.17). It is to be noted that the
prophet was accompanied by his son Shear-jashub (' A remnant shall return ', i.e. shall return (as from exile) to their
native land, or shall return in penitence to God); the significance of this fact will be considered later.

4-9 record the prophet's words to the king. Verse 8b surely
cannot be part of the original text, for two reasons: first, it
breaks the close connection and obvious parallelism between
8a and 9a; and, secondly, it could not possibly have been a
comfort to Ahaz to be told that within sixty-five years Ephraim would be annihilated. When 8b may have been added
is not certain; sixty-five years later would mean 669 BC, in the
reign of Esarhaddon of Assyria, who is reported as having
settled Assyrians in Ephraim (cf. Ezra 4.2). Such a mixing of

the population might conceivably have been interpreted as the end of Ephraim as a distinct people.

Isaiah's words to the king draw a sharp contrast. On the one hand, there are two human beings, ruling petty kingdoms, fuming in their wrath and trying to work out their plans to subdue Judah for their own ends and set a puppet, the son of Tabeel, on the throne, a docile creature willing to do their bidding. On the other there is God, the supreme ruler, whose kingdom has no end, whose word to Ahaz is: 'It (the counsel of the two confederate kings) will not stand, nor will it be translated into accomplished facts' (v. 7). Verses 8 and 9 say, either that the two kingdoms have their own appointed place and their own limited sphere, or that their heads are mere men whose threats should not be treated with undue fear or respect; they are tails of smoking firebrands almost burnt out.

But how could the king with equanimity accept and act on such a message? To do so might be interpreted by some of his people as an act of implicit faith in God; by the majority it would be regarded as manifest dereliction of duty and a failure to take the appropriate defensive measures dictated by a proper sense of responsibility and by common sense. The acuteness of the king's problem at its fundamental level Isaiah makes plain in the memorable words recorded in the final part of v. 9: 'If you do not have faith, you can have no assurance' or 'Without faith [in God] you can have no confidence.' In other words, if a man does not have steadfast trust (the basic meaning of the verb used) in God, he can have no steadfast purpose in life and no confidence in meeting the emergencies of the human situation. That is a test which confronts the believer and the would-be believer in every age. If, of course, such trust in God guaranteed to a man the object or result towards which his own practical endeavours would otherwise have been directed, the test would not be so acute; but it guarantees no such thing; God's way is often through loss to gain, and through humiliation to renewal of life.

Again, such trust in God's care need not dispense with

human effort. A righteous man will not normally believe that, if his house goes on fire, his righteousness will save it; rather will he try fire-buckets and every available fire-fighting appliance, and maintain his trust in God, even if the worst should befall. But Isaiah's call to Ahaz to have no fear because the purpose of the confederate kings would not be realized seemed to imply that all his practical measures for the safety of the city were needless, because God had decreed that the danger was merely temporary and would pass.

10-17. Presumably to ease the king's predicament, Isaiah offered him a sign. Amos 3.7 and Jer. 23.16-22 affirm that the true prophet stands in God's counsel and is entrusted with a true word to speak; but a false prophet who uttered only his own imaginings might claim to be a genuine prophet. How could their hearers distinguish the true prophet from the false? A prophet, it is said, might predict a future event, and the fulfilment of that prophecy would be a vindication of him as a true prophet; but that was not an easy test to apply (Deut. 18.21 f.; 13.1-3). Isaiah offered to give such a vindicating sign, that the king might be assured of the fact that he was confronted by a true prophet; let the sign, he was told, be DEEP AS SHEOL OR HIGH AS HEAVEN (so RSV in v. 11, rightly). The range of choice given to the king was made as wide as it could be.

12-13. The king refused, as he said, to tempt the Lord (Ex. 17.2, 7; Deut. 6.16). The question remains: Was that the genuine answer of a humble man who believed that faith in God ought to be without such extraneous assurances, or was it a respectable cloak for an unwillingness to be driven into a position in which to refuse to take the prophet's advice, when this was confirmed by a sign, would appear as open apostasy and unbelief? Isaiah's reply in v. 13 seems to support the latter interpretation. The prophet is now plainly impatient.

G

14. The nature of the sign has caused much discussion. Several
points should be noted before any attempt is made to arrive
at an interpretation. RSV is right in reading A YOUNG WOMAN
(lit. the young woman) instead of A VIRGIN (which comes from
the LXX); there is a distinctive word in Hebrew for 'virgin'
but it is not the word used here. Secondly, IS WITH CHILD (RSV
footnote) is probably to be preferred to SHALL CONCEIVE; if
this is accepted, the interval of time between the prophet's
interview with the king and the birth of the child is shortened.

Now for interpretation. That we should read 'the young
woman', and make it refer to a woman in the crowd listening
to the prophet and designated by him, is most unlikely and
would serve no particular purpose. But two other meanings for
'the young woman' have been proposed. The one is that it
means the prophet's own wife (8.3 f., can be claimed to give
support for this), but the fact that she is named the prophetess
in 8.3 is against such a use. The other is that it means the
queen, so that the child to be born would be the successor to
the throne of Judah; that is possible, but the use of such a
designation for the queen is unparalleled in the Old Testament
and must remain doubtful, even if examples of its use can be
quoted from peoples who were neighbour to Judah. The in-
definite subject 'a woman' seems the most likely of the renderings of this type. Within a few months, therefore, this
woman, when she gives birth to her child, will name him
Immanuel, 'God with us'. If that name had the meaning 'May
God be with us', it might signify that the child was born at a
time of national calamity, so that the name was a prayer for
God's help. But v. 10 implies that the sign will confirm the
prophet's message which is that Ahaz should be rid of all his
fears about the safety of Jerusalem in the present crisis; and
the birth of a child named, in effect, 'God help us' would have
increased rather than allayed the king's fears. Therefore, we
take the name to be a profession of faith 'God (is) with us',
a name given to the child in joyful thanksgiving because the
danger and threat to the city and land had completely passed

away. But the fact that Shear-jashub was with the prophet on this occasion is presumably a token that punishment is about to come upon the sinful nation, at the hands not of these petty, upstart kings, but of the king who is chosen as the rod of Yahweh's anger (10.5). On this interpretation, the child Immanuel is not himself a deliverer, but his name is a token of the deliverance which will have taken place by the time he is born.

One other line of interpretation has been suggested; it is that 'the woman' means the community. Now it is true that 'daughter Jerusalem' and 'virgin daughter Jerusalem' are used as designations of that city (e.g. Jer. 8.21; 14.17; 18.13; Amos 5.2 etc.), but there is no parallel to the use of 'the woman' alone with such a reference, although the meaning would be excellent and the person named Immanuel would in this case be a deliverer.

15-17 also have a problem of interpretation. In Babylonian cultic texts BUTTER AND HONEY are mentioned as food of Paradise. If this line is followed, it would mean that the child Immanuel, feeding upon this food, will thus learn how to refuse the evil and choose the good, in contrast to the sons of men since Adam who have fallen into the sin of refusing the good and choosing the evil. And it would mean that this Immanuel will be a deliverer blessed by God.

But the fact that the next verses (16-17) tell of disaster very soon to come upon the land of the two kings of whom Ahaz had been so much afraid, and of such days of calamity for Judah as had not been since the disruption of the kingdom upon the death of Solomon, and give no hint of deliverance, induces us to seek another interpretation. Butter and honey are the best that the nomad can hope for by way of nourishment; and the fact that the first word is properly rendered 'curd' and is not the ordinary word for 'butter', supports this. But no one can be said to eat these in order to know how to refuse the evil and to choose the good (which is the meaning of v. 15 in AV); such fare can bring neither moral discernment nor

the ability to distinguish the harmful from the beneficial. But
the LXX reads 'before' in place of 'in order that'; this
reading should be accepted. A child begins early to reject
what is harmful or disagreeable and to choose what is beneficial and pleasant; but before Immanuel has reached this
stage, Judah will have been reduced to nomad fare. That
means that, although the prophet Isaiah had promised deliverance from Pekah and Rezin, the present verses confirm that
within a few years disaster will come upon Judah, as the
presence of Shear-jashub certainly implies (cf. vv. 1-3).

18-25. In that day

The concluding verses of the chapter now follow in easy
and intelligible sequence, describing in various ways the condition of Judah (or of Judah and Israel) in the day when,
stripped of all her glory, she is reduced to a very simple
pastoral economy again; the reference may be to the years
between 734 and 721 BC.

18. Yahweh summons Egypt and Assyria to invade the land.
The figures of FLY for Egypt and BEE for Assyria may be used
to indicate the swarming, pestilential and devastating effect
of their armies when they take possession of the land, occupying not only the bushes and the pastures and stripping them of
all greenery, but occupying even the ravines and the clefts of the
rocks so that the inhabitants are left without a place of refuge
or escape; or they may have been well-known symbols for these
countries, like the rose for England, the thistle for Scotland,
etc.

20. It is notable that here Egypt (cf. Hos. 9.3) is no more
mentioned, but the onsweeping invasion of the Assyrians in
the land is likened to the action of a razor; not only is the land
laid bare but it is treated with, and laid open to, ignominy (cf.
II Sam. 10.4). THE HAIR OF THE FEET is a euphemism, the feet
meaning the private parts, as in 'to cover the feet' (cf. Judg.
3.24; I Sam. 24.3).

21-22 do not speak of abundance; a man with a young cow and two sheep was ill provided; but even the few cattle which remained afforded adequate food for the small population which now survived. Valuable land which formerly had carried a thousand vines had now gone wild again, overgrown with briars and thorns; all the cultivated land likewise had become untended and had reverted to waste, becoming again a hunting-ground for men with bows and arrows. In these lands the cattle and sheep which remained found their range and roamed at will.

A word of retrospect. It will have been noticed that according to the line of interpretation of ch. 7 which is presented above, it is the name of the child Immanuel which is significant, not the office he is to fulfil; but for the support of this view the LXX text has to be followed in v. 15. The Hebrew text as it stands, meaning 'curd and honey shall he eat, in order that he may know etc.' means surely that this must be regarded as food of Paradise which makes men wise. Taken in this way, the passage has messianic significance, and Micah 5.2-4 shows that this was the interpretation of it which developed.

MEN CONSPIRE, GOD RULES

8.1–9.1

This section consists of various portions which are closely related to, and refer to much the same circumstances as, ch. 7. They speak of the peoples' plans for political security and national safety and of God's rule which is not mocked, of the refusal of the people of Judah to trust in Yahweh for their welfare, and of the hostility shown to Isaiah and his associates on the one hand and of the nature of the judgment decreed by Yahweh on the other.

8.1-4 The fear of man and the fear of God

These verses are closely parallel in meaning to 7.16; they proclaim the imminent destruction of Damascus and Samaria, involving the whole of Syria and Ephraim. As tablets of stone were used to publicize laws which had to be obeyed, so in this case a polished tablet (of metal, stone, or wood; we do not know which) had inscribed on it a message expressed in brief, memorable words. THE PEN OF A MAN probably refers to the style of writing (viz. writing in the common script or style) and not to a type of pen.

MAHER-SHALAL-HASH-BAZ, i.e. ' Speeds (the) booty, hastens on (the) spoil' signifies that the day of devastation is now near at hand. The fact that v. 4 speaks specifically of the spoliation of Damascus and Samaria suggests that judgment upon Judah is not referred to here at all, so that the message must have brought comfort to the faithful section of Judah's population and may, therefore, have been delivered when the danger from Rezin and Pekah still threatened the land (7.1 ff.). The preposition ' For ' prefixed to the message as quoted has the meaning ' belonging to ', ' the property of ' (as is illustrated in the use of ' For the king ' on Israelite royal jar handles which have been discovered in Palestine), so that it has the effect of making the words of the message into a personal name (cf. v. 4). The tablet with its significant name is given the value of an official instrument by being duly attested (v. 2, in which RSV should be followed). The priest Uriah, who is named as one of the witnesses, is mentioned in II Kings 16.11 as consenting to foreign innovations in religious practice in Judah in the reign of Ahaz.

3-4 accentuate the message given in vv. 1 f. (cf. 7.3 for the name of the prophet's first child); and the fact that the coming spoliation of Damascus and Samaria will take place before the child Maher-shalal-hash-baz can utter the words 'Father' and ' Mother' confirms the view taken of 7.16 that ' good ' and ' evil', as used in it, mean ' beneficial' and ' harmful', and that the verse indicates an event in the near future. The king of

Assyria, referred to here as in 7.20, must be Tiglath Pileser III (745-27 BC). II Kings 16.17-18 gives a record of negotiations between Ahaz and the Assyrian king, and the inference must be drawn that, possibly before Isaiah's encounter with him (cf. 7.1-16), Ahaz had already sent a request to that king for help against his adversaries, II Kings 16.8 speaking of the gift of silver and gold which had to be sent to ensure that help.

5-8. The quietly flowing waters of Shiloah or the Assyrian flood-waters

These verses have the same subject as vv. 1-4, but the mode of presentation is different; in the latter the coming judgment is proclaimed, here the reason for it and the full effect of it are expressed. In their distress and perturbation (cf. 7.2) the people should have trusted in Yahweh for deliverance. THE WATERS OF SHILOAH THAT GO SOFTLY (AV) cannot refer to a stream flowing through the valley of Siloam, since such a stream, which would have been both seasonal and open, could neither have brought nor even symbolized security to a be-leaguered city. The reference should be taken as being to the conduit bringing the waters of the Virgin's Fountain to the pool of Siloam which was inside the city. This conduit was probably the precursor of the rock-hewn tunnel, built in the time of Hezekiah or later, which was made for the same pur-pose and has been discovered, and in the middle reach of which there was found the famous Siloam inscription.[1] To trust in such slowly flowing waters meant to trust in Yahweh for safety.

The contrast between such an attitude and *rejoicing* in the two confederate kings seems wholly inapposite; there was never any question of rejoicing in them. But the word ren-dered ' rejoice ' in AV is closely similar to a root meaning ' to melt ' or ' dissolve '; thus RSV reads suitably AND MELT IN FEAR BEFORE REZIN etc. Otherwise, to speak of the waters of Shiloah which go ' softly and meltingly ' (i.e. intermittently) may be a

[1] D. Winton Thomas, *Documents from Old Testament Times*, pp. 209-11.

reference to the intermittent flow of the waters of the Virgin's
Fountain (cf. John 5.7); in this case the words REZIN AND THE
SON OF REMALIAH are regarded as an addition in the text. The
gentle flow of the waters of Shiloah is contrasted with the
flood-waters of Assyria which will not only destroy Ephraim
and Syria (cf. v. 4), but will sweep devastatingly into Judah,
overflowing the whole land. Thus the appeal by Ahaz to
Assyria, which it was hoped would bring relief to Jerusalem
and Judah, would simply involve them together with Ephraim
and Syria in a common fate.

In the first half of v. 8 the Greek version has a text which
reads: 'And it shall remove from Judah anyone who can raise
his head and can do anything', meaning it will reduce the land
to a state of utter helplessness. This Greek text may be a
variant to the first half of v. 8 as we have it in AV and RSV,
or additional to it.

In the second part of the verse the figure used ceases to be
that of a devastating flood, and becomes that of a bird with
outstretched wings. It may be taken as a bird of prey, signifying
destruction, as does the flood. But, in that case, why should the
address be to Immanuel? Surely, it should rather be to the
people of Judah who had refused to trust in Yahweh. The
alternative is to separate the second half of v. 8 from the first
half, to note that vv. 9 f., form a stanza with the ending 'for
God is with us' (i.e. Immanuel) and, hence, to take the second
half of v. 8 as the final part—all that remains—of another
stanza with the same ending, thus:

' ....

And the stretching forth of his wings will fill the land,
   for God is with us.'

In this case, the figure is not of destruction, but of protection.

9-10, in either case, follow in close association, but probably
support the second interpretation which has just been given

of v. 8b. In v. 9 the PEOPLES addressed are not the Gentiles
alone; they are exemplified in Ephraim and Syria because of
what they have done (cf. 7.1 ff.), and in Ahaz and those
in Judah who followed his counsel of seeking Assyria's help
(II Kings 16.7 ff.). Verses 9-10 describe the futility of all such
plannings and actions; peoples may make alliances and try
to work out their purposes in the field of practical politics, but
their plans miscarry and their works are frustrated (cf. Ps. 2);
for 'God is with us'. Here GOD IS WITH US (Immanuel) is
obviously a protestation of faith, as was the use of the name
in 7.14. There is inherent in these verses the belief that the
land would not utterly be destroyed, the belief which is likewise expressed in the name of Isaiah's first child, Shear-jashub.
Amos (9.7) seems to speak as if another people might take the
place of a faithless Israel; but that idea never had a real place
in Israelite thought. Their hope was of a chastened and purified
remnant.

11-15. The only true sanctuary

These verses record a vision of the prophet's, in which the
figure of the strong hand laid upon him is paralleled by certain
usages in the Book of Ezekiel (cf. 1.3; 3.14, etc.). The instruction given in the vision is that Isaiah and his followers should
not be carried away by popular fears or emotional excesses,
nor be frightened when words like plot and conspiracy are
tossed from mouth to mouth. They ought to have grounds of
assurance and confidence beyond those available to faithless,
unbelieving men (cf. 7.9). There is only one true way of personal assurance and of social stability, that men should fear
God and obey him.

There are several uncertainties of text in this passage; one
in particular should be mentioned.

12-13. A measure of parallelism can be discerned in the final
phrases of these two verses, which has raised the question of
whether the parallelism was originally fuller than it is in the

present text. Now the Hebrew words for 'holy' and 'make holy' or 'sanctify' (v. 13) have a certain similarity to the word for 'conspiracy', so that the suggestion has been made that one or other of these was used in the two verses, not both. The alternative interpretations then would be:

- (a) 12. Call not holy whatever this people calls holy. . . .
       13. Honour as holy [only] the Lord of hosts. . . .
- (b) 12. Call not a conspiracy all that this people calls a conspiracy. . . .
       13. Make your conspiracy [i.e. alliance] with the Lord of hosts. . . .

Verse 12, as interpreted in (a), would require to be taken as a reference to popular idolatries, a subject not dealt with in this section; on the other hand, while the interpretation of v. 12 in (b) suits the context very well indeed (cf. 7.1 ff.), the phrase 'make your conspiracy with the Lord of hosts' is unparalleled.

Probably, therefore, the text as it stands may be accepted as more likely to be the original than any reconstruction of it. The words 'fear' and 'dread' are, in this case, used in different senses in the two verses. In v. 12 Isaiah and his followers are told not to be disturbed by popular cries of conspiracy nor to share popular fears and apprehensions about political events. They must regard as holy only Yahweh of hosts and seek a refuge in him (cf. v. 14); there is nothing sacrosanct about the plannings and devisings of the kings of the earth.

14. The first phrase of this verse follows closely. The Lord of hosts will be a refuge and, as it were, a place of security to those who trust him (cf. Ex. 21.14; I Kings 1.50; Ezek. 11.16; etc.). The second part of the verse is then seen to be in sharp contrast; the Lord of hosts is a stone against which unbelievers stumble and a rock over which they fall (cf. Matt. 18.6; Mark 9.42; Luke 17.2). In other words, those who disregard God do not escape with impunity; God cannot be by-passed. We are reminded of the words in Luke 20.17 f.: 'The very stone which

the builders rejected has become the head of the corner. Every-
one who falls on that stone will be broken to pieces; but when
it falls on anyone, it will crush him.' It is interesting to note
that the Targum read 'snare' for 'sanctuary' at the beginning
of v. 14 and thus made the whole verse uniform in meaning
and integral with v. 15.

16-18. Seal up the testimony

Isaiah's advice to Ahaz remained unheeded, the king per-
sisting in his reliance upon Assyria for help (cf. II Kings 16.
7 ff.). The signs are that in view of the opposition he had en-
countered, Isaiah withdrew from active prophecy for a period.
The testimony (v. 16) which is to be bound up means a record
of his prophetic utterances, while the law which is to be sealed
away in the safe keeping of his disciples is not the Sinai law
or the Ten Commandments but the teaching or instruction
which he as a prophet had given. This reference to his disciples emphasizes their existence as a community of faith within the general community of Judah; but since the primary
qualification for membership of such a community was faith
rather than kinship, there was involved the as yet unrecognized
correlate that such a community must be open to the faithful
among all peoples. Thus, it has been said, we have here the
germ of the conception of the Church as the community of the
faithful. Verse 18 contains the reminder that the names of
Isaiah and his children will remain during this time as signs
and wonders to the people (cf. Deut. 4.34; 7.19; etc.); and the
final phrase may mean that Yahweh will still dwell in Mount
Zion. The people may have forsaken him but he has not
forsaken them.

This is then a time of waiting for Isaiah (cf. Isa. 30.18;
40.31; etc.; Pss. 25.5; 27.14; 31.24; 37.7-9, 34; 42.11; etc.). The
next bit of instruction or warning must come to the people
from their own experience, probably their own suffering; they
may respond to that more willingly than they had done to the
prophet's words.

8.19–9.1. Superstitions revive when faith fails

19. When people forsake the fountain of living waters, they hew for themselves new cisterns or return to old ones, even if these can hold no water (cf. Jer. 2.13); so now they turn back to old superstitious practices (cf. 19.3). The two technical terms used in v. 19 may be rendered as 'ghosts' and 'FAMILIAR SPIRITS' or as 'WIZARDS' and 'MEDIUMS'; the verbs related to them, 'CHIRP' and 'MUTTER', make the former rendering the more likely (cf. 29.4). 'Mediums' or 'soothsayers' had once been common in Israel (cf. 3.2 f.) and had never died out; wizardry and necromancy stand forbidden in the law (cf. Deut. 18.11; Lev. 19.31; 20.6 f.). Saul is said to have forbidden such practices, although he himself resorted to a witch in his extremity (I Sam. 28, espec. v. 9).

There are two ways in which v. 19 may be interpreted:

(a) 'When they say to you: "Consult ghosts and familiar spirits which chirp and mutter. Should not a people seek unto their gods? Should not they seek unto the dead on behalf of the living?"' That is the way in which the people justify their conduct; they see nothing reprehensible in it. In opposition to that attitude Isaiah calls upon his disciples (v. 20) to turn to his own testimony and instruction for Yahweh's guidance.

(b) Take the first part of v. 19 as expressing the popular attitude: 'When they say . . . mutter.' Then take the second part of the verse as a rejoinder: 'Should not a people seek unto their *God*? Ought they to consult the dead on behalf of the living?' That is possible, although the transition to the positive question from the preceding negative form is a doubtful one, so that the first way is preferable.

20. The first part of the verse reminds us at once of 8.16. The second part is very doubtful; the original will not bear the meaning given to it in the AV. While the translation in RSV meets one of the main difficulties linguistically, to speak about a word as having no dawn is a strange expression. Two possible lines of interpretation lie open to us.

(a) Assume that something has been lost from the text, and that we have two distinct fragments left:

'If they do not speak according to this word (i.e. the prophet's instruction) . . . which shall have no dawn.'

(b) Follow the Syriac version, which read a word for 're-ward' instead of 'dawn', and take the phrase closely with v. 21:

'Assuredly they (the people whose words are quoted in v. 19) speak according to this word which is without reward (i.e. this is the unrewarding way in which they talk) when they pass through the land, greatly distressed and hungry.' This certainly gives suitable sense.

21-22 describe the privations and sufferings of the faithless, superstitious people in the land; in their frustration they curse (or curse by) their equally faithless king and their God whom they have forsaken. They look upwards and around them, only to find a scene of unrelieved misery, suffering and gloom. In the last phrase of v. 22, 'THEY SHALL BE DRIVEN (RSV, WILL BE THRUST) INTO DARKNESS', is very doubtful indeed; follow the Greek version and get the rendering, 'and darkness impene-trable' (or unillumined) which follows smoothly upon the DIMNESS OF ANGUISH of the preceding part of the verse.

9.1 is numbered in the original as 8.23. The content of the first part of it suggests that it should be taken with 8.21 f. But the rendering in AV and RSV seems utterly contradictory of v. 22, if the fem. (HER VEXATION, AV) is given its normal reference to Jerusalem or the land of Judah, and it cannot be made to refer to Isaiah and his faithful followers; the tense varia-tion in 'BUT THERE SHALL BE NO GLOOM TO HER WHO WAS IN ANGUISH' (so RSV) has no warrant in the original. The words should rather be read as a comment, possibly a later comment, on the preceding verses, thus: 'Does not he have darkness who is in distress?' The believers are the children of light; but the unbelievers, when they suffer, are in impenetrable darkness, because they have no answer to their perplexity and do not know which way to turn.

The rest of the verse is difficult; the rendering in AV cannot be supported; that in RSV is more reliable. Here we have what serves as a transition from the judgment and distress recorded in ch. 8 to the prophecy of salvation in 9.2-7. A contrast is drawn between the shame which rested on Zebulun and Naphtali (i.e. Galilee, part of Ephraim) IN THE FORMER TIME and the return of God's glory to THE WAY OF THE SEA, THE LAND BEYOND (i.e. east of) THE JORDAN, GALILEE OF THE NATIONS in the latter time. A note on the geography first; Zebulun and Naphtali are in that part of Ephraim which the Assyrians must have invaded first, and so may be used to designate Ephraim as a whole; in this way the shame spoken of refers to the circumstances described e.g. in 7.23-25; 8.21 f. In the future the shame is to cease and the glory of God is to return to a defined area. The way of the sea is often used to designate the route along the coastal plain of Palestine. The land beyond the Jordan may mean Syria and Gilead which, in the time between the death of Solomon and the days of Isaiah, had been so often disputed territory. GALILEE OF THE NATIONS or, more likely, ' circle (or area) of the nations ' cannot be defined geographically with certainty. It has sometimes been defined as an area in Galilee in the neighbourhood of Kadesh, or the area around Megiddo on the Carmel ridge. Neither of these propositions seems plausible. May the reference not be to the circle of nations (Moab, Ammon, Edom, Philistia, etc.), against which Amos, for instance, delivered words of judgment (chs. 1-2), and with which Israel and Judah had had more or less close relations since the time of King David (cf. Zeph. 2.4-11)?

Two possible explanations may be offered for the specific mention of these areas. They may designate the areas in the neighbourhood of Judah which the Assyrians had devastated; to them the glory of God will return. Or, much more likely, the meaning may be that the glory of God will return to the land

of Judah as it was in the days of King David (cf. 9.7; 11.14-16);
the land east of the Jordan will again be within the kingdom as
a possession of Yahweh's people, as will the land of Galilee,
and the Philistine country through which ran the way of the
sea (cf. Obad. 19 f.). This line of interpretation makes THE
FORMER TIME refer to the events recorded in most of chs. 7 and
8, so that, if 9.1 is from Isaiah, it is from a later period in his
career when he could look back to the events of 735 BC and
the immediately following years and speak of them as belonging to a former day.

THE PRINCE OF PEACE

9.2-7

These verses are in notable contrast with the contents of the
preceding chapter and take us back in thought to 7.14. Here
is not only the promise of a new day of light, joy and peace
and of a kingdom established in justice and in righteousness,
but a statement that all this has taken place.

2, speaking of a time of darkness now past, immediately recalls
8.22 and 9.1, and makes us think also of Isa. 60.1 and John
1.4-9; the darkness was that of a people who were perplexed
and involved in tragic suffering and who had forsaken their
faith in God to follow idolatrous ways and superstitious practices. The statement that they had been living in a land of
gloom (not 'shadow of death', as AV) implies that their predicament had been very serious and complete ruin had been
very near; while the words HAVE SEEN A GREAT LIGHT readily
suggest the interpretation that the new day had come suddenly
and unexpectedly.

3 makes it plain that it was neither the people nor their leaders
who had brought about the change, but God himself. An increase of population is a token of God's blessing and, also,

evidence of days of peace and security when the casualties of
war are no more. The text of the first part of the verse is not
certain; AV, with its two contradictory phrases, cannot be
accepted; the RSV rendering is possible and has a long tradition behind it; but 'thou hast made them greatly happy, thou
hast given them much cause for gladness' is another rendering
very close to the existing text. The joy and gladness are un-
restrained, as in the day of a harvest home or vintage festival,
or as in the day when, with victory won and all danger past,
men divide the spoils of war.

4 describes the oppressive régime which the people had experienced (cf. 10.24, 27; 14.25). The first two phrases should
be taken together: THE YOKE OF HIS BURDEN means his heavy,
burdensome yoke. The yoke of an animal was a heavy beam of
wood which was laid across its shoulders; through holes in it
there were set, at right angles to the yoke, wooden rods, one on
each side of the animal's neck, below which the two rods were
tied, so that the neck was enclosed in this harness.[1] It is these
rods which are probably referred to in the following phrase
THE STAFF OF (or 'for') HIS SHOULDER; we might describe them
as 'the collar on his shoulder'. 'The rod of his oppressor', the
taskmaster's rod or club, a weighty and potentially devastating
weapon[2] (so 10.26 and Ex. 21.20; Ps. 23.4), clearly implies that
the people had undergone a period of hard service, presumably
as subjects of a foreign power to which their land was a
tributary province.

What is the reference of THE DAY OF MIDIAN (cf. 10.26)?
Num. 31 has been suggested, which tells how the Israelites were
delivered from the baneful influence of the Midianites who had
seduced them to worship Baal; but that was not a deliverance
from an oppression such as this verse describes. It must have
been the deliverance from the Midianites by Gideon (Judg.
6-8), which gave rise to the comparison; they devastated the

[1] See E. W. Heaton, *Everyday Life in Old Testament Times*, pp. 99-101.
[2] Cf. E. W. Heaton, *op. cit.*, p. 50.

country and must have been an unbearable scourge (Judg. 6.1-6). But the fitness in the comparison consists not only of the oppressive effect of the Midianite depredations, but of the fact that deliverance from it was achieved by a notably small army of devoted soldiers who went to the attack with the battle-cry, 'For Yahweh and for Gideon' (Judg. 7.18). The Midianites were a nomadic or semi-nomadic people whose range was the wilderness south-east of Judah, but they spread to the territory east of the Dead Sea and the river Jordan as occasion offered or their needs demanded, and they made predatory incursions into the land west of the Jordan, especially at harvest-time.

5. The meaning of this verse is not in doubt; it describes the end of war, for Judah at least. The word rendered 'armour' in AV means 'shoe' or 'boot', so that the first phrase of the verse may be taken as in RSV or, more simply, 'for every boot of warrior tramping noisily'. (EVERY) GARMENT ROLLED IN BLOOD i.e. every blood-soaked garment, is both intelligible and fitting; there seems no need to read a closely similar text to get the rendering 'every blood-polluted garment'. Boots and blood-soaked garments represent all war's accoutrements; they are to be burned to ashes; the day for them is done (cf. 11.6-9).

6, with its announcement of the birth of a son to the community, comes in very suddenly. 7.14 speaks of the coming birth of a child who will be named Immanuel, because, by the time he is born, the danger prevalent at that time (735-4 BC) will have passed away. Here it is said that the child has been born, and he is born to fulfil an office. Not now, as in 7.14, is it said that the child is born to a specific woman, but 'to us'. to the community (cf. Immanuel, God with us). In other words, it is a God-given deliverer who is spoken of.

This son is not to have a name which will be for a sign, like the names of Isaiah's sons (cf. 7.3; 8.1), but one which will be descriptive of his office. Clearly the name is in four com-

H

posite parts (so RSV); WONDERFUL COUNSELLOR, a ruler of un-
failing wisdom who will, unlike Ahaz for instance (cf. Isa.
7.12; II Kings 16.7-9), never make false choices or foolish
decisions but will guide his people in the right way.

MIGHTY GOD is a possible rendering of the original, but the
word for 'God' as used here can mean, for example, hero.
'God of a hero' (the literal rendering) may mean divine hero
or warrior. That means that as a hero or warrior he will not
use the ways of violence and force and the weapons of war, but
he will rule in justice and righteousness, a divine warrior, who
reminds us of Elijah and Elisha and their unseen auxiliaries
(cf. II Kings 2.11 f.; 6.17). EVERLASTING FATHER, which could be
a title of God, can also be used to describe the constant,
paternal rule of this son; he will never cease to care for his
people and be a father to them. The alternative rendering sometimes proposed, 'father of booty', has nothing to commend it.
PRINCE OF PEACE means prince ruling in peace and securing the
peace or welfare of the community. The king, anointed to rule,
had the responsibility of guarding the welfare of the community; but many kings had failed in their office. This one
will not fail.

Upon his shoulder will rest the rule, the office of government; he will be prince, not king, maybe as a reminder that
there is only one King, namely God, or because the people had
suffered so much at the hands of their kings that the name is
no more to be used (cf. Ezek. 34.24; 37.25; 44.3; 45.7; etc.).
That the rule is to be UPON HIS SHOULDER, as his burden, may
be in contrast to the burdensome yoke which, in former days,
had been on the people's shoulders. Indeed, the phrase might
be rendered: 'The symbol of rule (e.g. the key, cf. Isa. 22.22)
shall be on his shoulder.'

7. 'Great shall be the dominion, and unending peace shall
rest upon the throne of David and his kingdom that it may be
established and upheld in justice and in righteousness. . . .'
So the verse should run. Before the fall of Samaria in 721 BC,

the kingdom of Israel had suffered from many dynastic changes and Judah had experienced lesser vicissitudes. But now there would be stability within the realm, based upon that foundation of justice and righteousness which the prophets had demanded. Justice means essentially that rule of law and order which is set forth in the commandments, statutes and ordinances contained within the Pentateuch; righteousness is that obedience to the law and fulfilment of it, in virtue of which a man may be blameless before the law. In such a kingdom of justice and righteousness God's rule will have full scope, his spiritual gifts will be fully enjoyed and his community will be established.

The final phrase of v. 7 may appear to be additional; it is found in Ezekiel (36.5 ff.; 38.19) and elsewhere in the Old Testament. But its use here is an affirmation that all that is described in the preceding verses is brought about by the zeal of Yahweh, who in love cares for and disciplines his people and, as a jealous God, will not overlook their unfaithfulness and apostasy.

A brief comment upon the interpretation of 9.2-7 must be given:

(a) It has been suggested that the passage must be understood in terms of the ritual of the Enthronement Festival which was celebrated annually at least in Judah's cultural environment and *may* have been celebrated in Jerusalem, and, particularly, in terms of the actual enthronement of a new king (Ahaz or Hezekiah). That might seem to explain some of the terms used, e.g. light, joy, victory, and the birth of a son as indicating the adoption of the king as God's son and his assumption of a regnal name; but it is not adequate. It does not explain the expectation that all wars will cease and an unending kingdom be established, nor the reference to a great deliverance which appears as the prelude to it.

(b) The passage has been interpreted wholly eschatologically, as representing the last great struggle with the forces of darkness, their complete destruction and the establishment of

the unending kingdom of righteousness. Such an interpretation
can be sustained, but the whole passage seems to make clear
in its references that there was a great historical occasion of
deliverance and emergence from mortal danger which evoked
this great hope.

(c) It seems essential, therefore, to seek such an occasion.
Many have found the beginning of the second half of the sixth
century BC as the most likely period—a time much later than
the life-time of Isaiah. There were signs that the dark night
of the Jewish exile in Babylon was coming to an end, there
was a growing expectation of release and joyful return to
Judah to rebuild the Temple and restore the kingdom under
a scion of David's house, and the hope that, the people having
paid the penalty for their sins, they would now enjoy the
blessings of peace and prosperity (cf. e.g. Isa. 40.1-11; 42.1-16;
43.1-13; 45.1-8; 60; Zech. 6.9-15; etc.). But it is doubtful if this
period could be described as one of such grim bond-service
as v. 4 implies; and Cyrus the deliverer mentioned in Isa.
44.28 and 45.1 would not be described by a Jewish prophet as
'a son born to us', so that, on this interpretation, the phrase
quoted would require to be referred to a son or grandson of
the exiled King Jehoachin, who, even when in exile, continued
to be regarded as the rightful king of Judah.

But the presence of the reference in 7.14 to the child Immanuel about to be born makes it imperative that the suit-
ability of the passage to some phase of Isaiah's ministry must
be examined, and the contrast of the emergent light of the
new day with the preceding darkness, as described in v. 2,
seems to have immediate reference to 8.22 and 9.1. That the
deliverance of the country from the invaders Pekah and Rezin
(7.1 ff.) could have provided the occasion seems unlikely; there
is no hint that they exercised oppressive rule (they were but a
temporary, if acute, danger) and deliverance from them could
not have given nourishment to great hopes for the future. Besides, the deliverance was brought about by the response of
Assyria to Ahaz' call for help (II Kings 16.7 ff.), it was not a

deliverance 'as in the day of Midian'. But some years later (in 701 BC) Jerusalem and Judah were in deadly danger (cf. 10.24, 27; 14.25) and did experience a wonderful deliverance which was not achieved in any sense by force of arms; the armies of Sennacherib gave up the siege of Jerusalem without having captured it, because they were smitten by a devastating plague (II Kings 19.20-36). It was an act of God, an act of deliverance more wonderful than that of the day of Midian, for there was not even a Gideon with his three hundred assaulting the enemy. With a God who could so deliver, what had Judah to fear from any world power which would vaingloriously rule and oppress? There was only one enduring, unending King (cf. 6.1); and if Judah were established as God's kingdom in justice and righteousness, it too would be an unending kingdom, by God's power, not its own. So, we can believe, there arose the expectation expressed in these verses; in this case the reference to 'the son born to us' may be to the Immanuel of 7.14, or to a son born to the reigning Hezekiah after 701 BC.

THE DOWNFALL OF EPHRAIM AND OF ASSYRIA AND THE RISE OF THE SHOOT OF THE STEM OF JESSE

9.8–11.9

EPHRAIM'S ARROGANCE AND INIQUITY

9.8–10.4

It is at once to be noted that a sentence which has the effect of a recurring refrain occurs four times in this section of the Book of Isaiah: 9.12, 17, 21 and 10.4. In addition, the refrain is to be found at 5.25 also, and the view is presented in the Commentary at that point that 5.24 f. formed part of the poem whose greater portion is in 9.8–10.4, and that 5.26–30 formed a sequel to it.

9.8–12. The first stanza of the poem tells of a revelation which had come to the prophet from God and which will fall like a thunderbolt among the people, AND ALL THE PEOPLE WILL KNOW (v. 9). The phrase quoted must mean that the people too will come to know God's word, not with the swift insight of the prophet but, possibly, only after bitter and humiliating experience. Another rendering of the verb is possible, viz. 'will be humbled' (cf. Isa. 53.3, 'humbled by grief', and Hos. 9.7; Ezek. 25.14); that also gives very good sense. Ephraim had suffered greatly; houses had come down in ruins, trees had been cut down (v. 10); but they had shown courage and spiritual resilience, which the prophet regarded as self-assurance and vain presumption. They had resolved to build more securely (stone in place of brick) and more magnificently (costly cedar for common sycamore). It was Assyria which had devastated and impoverished Ephraim after Ahaz of Judah had appealed to them for help in 735-4 (cf. II Kings 16.7 ff.). The mood of confidence in Ephraim now presumably means that Tiglath Pileser of Assyria had recently died (he died in 727), so that hopes of freedom revived among his subject peoples.

'The adversaries of Rezin' (v. 11, AV) who are to be raised against Ephraim can hardly be correct, because the Syrians (of whom Rezin was king) are named as one of them. Read 'ADVERSARIES' (RSV) or 'their adversaries' or follow the Greek version which had 'the adversaries of Zion', i.e. the Syrians and the Philistines (cf. II Chron. 28.18) who had formerly been their allies.

13–17. Anarchy and violence

The second stanza describes how sheer anarchy and confusion developed among a people who would not read the signs of the times. The judgment of God which came upon the people cut off headman and commoner, dignitary and poor

man together (for the terms used, cf. 19.15). The punishment of
the worthy and unworthy alike, as v. 15 explicitly says, seems
contradictory of v. 16, which says plainly that the leaders of
the people had failed them. It may be that, instead of 'the
honoured elder' in v. 15, we should read 'the proud (or
toadied) old men'. The full effect of v. 16 is:

> 'Those who should have guided this people have led them
> astray, and those who should have been guided have been
> engulfed.'

The only reason one can suggest for the specific mention of
the young men in v. 17 is that they were the future leaders and
might have been spared to have their opportunity. The use of
the verb 'have joy in' (AV, v. 17; 'rejoice over', RSV) with
regard to these young men is probably an improper rendering;
read 'have mercy upon' or 'be gentle to'. Even the widows
and orphans, who are so often commended to mercy in the Old
Testament, receive no mercy now. The stanza describes a
situation of corruption and disregard of every social obligation,
in which all classes of the population are equally involved.
The common people are not merely confused; they are actively
presumptuous and vain (v. 16).

18-21. The fire of God's wrath
It has to be carefully noted that this stanza speaks of two
devastating fires. It speaks predominantly of the consuming
passion of the people's wickedness which burns men up so
that nothing is left in them that can be salvaged, just as a
prairie fire, feeding on briars and thorns, sets fire to thickets
as the smoke clouds roll upward (v. 18); and it speaks incidentally of the fire of God's wrath, for which the people are as
fuel (v. 19, except the last phrase). The fact that the last phrase
of v. 19 and vv. 20 and 21a return to describe man's consuming
wickedness has induced some scholars to read 'like a consuming fire' or 'like devourers of men' in v. 19 instead of

LIKE FUEL FOR THE FIRE; but no such modification, minimal
though it is in each case, is necessary. We must believe, of
course, that in their wickedness, which rent asunder and
devastated the land, the men of Ephraim were paying the
penalty for their sinfulness and so were under the punishment
of God's wrath. They knew sin as a consuming fire which
would not let them go even as it consumed them. That men in
this condition should rampage insatiably and in their awful
hunger eat the flesh of their own arm (so AV v. 20) is not in-
conceivable, but in the context most unlikely. One ancient
version reads 'his neighbour's flesh', a very suitable sense;
'the flesh of his children' (lit. his seed) is also possible but not
so probable. The point of v. 21 is that Manasseh and Ephraim
were neighbours and close of kin; they are at daggers drawn;
yet both can unite in the old hostility against Judah.

10.1-4. The accents of Amos
1-2. 'Writers that write perverseness' (RV) does not convey
the meaning of the original, nor is the translation given in RSV
at all clear. The writings referred to are official documents or
decrees, so that v. 1 condemns not common criminals, but the
leaders of the community who make iniquitous laws and heavy
(i.e. oppressive) or mischievous decrees, whose purpose is to
obstruct the course of justice, and to rob and defraud, beyond
any chance of remedy or appeal for restitution, the poor, the
orphans and the widows who are so often easy, unchampioned
victims.

3-4. But when their day of punishment comes, to whom will the
oppressors turn for help? Where will they commit their pelf for
safe keeping? There is a problem of interpretation in v. 4. AV
and, more clearly, RSV take it as it stands; these people will
have to accept the situation which confronts them; all they can
do is to crouch among the captives and fall among the slain
and hope that they will escape notice and survive. That strains
the original somewhat but is just possible. But the text will

bear another rendering: 'Beltis bows down, Osiris is broken;
they fall beneath the slain.' But there is no evidence that the
Israelites worshipped Beltis (or Baalath), the consort of Bel (or
Baal) although the Phoenicians commonly did; the worship of
Osiris, an Egyptian god, is found in Palestine as the worship
of Tammuz (cf. Ezek. 8.14) but it was probably practised
seasonally only and not widely. There is no evidence to support the view that the worship practised by the people of
Ephraim who had forsaken Yahweh was at this time predominantly the worship of Beltis and Osiris; and even if it had been,
it is impossible to understand how, when punishment came
upon Ephraim, it could be said that 'Osiris is broken'. The
fate of Osiris was not bound up with that of Ephraim.

After the close of this stanza 5.26-30 fits in, with its description of the enemy who is to invade the land, the instrument
of the punishment which Yahweh has decreed against it; and,
in turn, 5.26-30 serves as a suitable introduction to 10.5 ff. But
whereas 5.26-30 is related to the Assyrian campaign in response to the call of Ahaz for help (cf. II Kings 16.7-9) when
Damascus was captured and towns on the border of Ephraim
were incorporated in the Assyrian empire, or describes that
invasion of Ephraim which resulted finally in the fall of
Samaria and the end of Ephraim as an independent kingdom,
10.5 ff. (cf. vv. 9-12) seems to refer to the later Assyrian invasion at the end of the eighth century when the army of
Sennacherib devastated Judah and besieged Jerusalem.

THE PRIDE OF ASSYRIA HUMBLED

10.5-34

5-11. The rod of Yahweh's anger

These verses begin with words of great significance and
startling assurance. That Yahweh should bless or rebuke, use
or forsake his own people or any individual member of his

people, was the common conception; but other peoples had their own gods who cared for their interests. Amos had indeed already broken through the confined range of such national-istic religious ideas; he had spoken of Yahweh as having brought the Israelites from the land of Egypt, the Philistines from Caphtor and the Syrians from Kir (Amos 9.7). Here Isaiah, in similar vein, speaks of Yahweh as using the Assy-rians as a punitive instrument against his own people; thus he interprets a devastation of Judah by the Assyrians, not as a failure by Yahweh to save his people from disaster at the hands of a mighty foe aided by mighty gods, but as a punish-ment by Yahweh inflicted on his unfaithful people by means of one who was not a professing servant of his. Here is faith in a rule more powerful than that of the Assyrian king and in a kingdom greater far than his (cf. Jer. 27.6). The second half of v. 5, as in AV, cannot stand; the Assyrians are not wielding Yahweh's fury, but he is wielding the Assyrians as the staff of his fury. RSV gets that meaning by abbreviating the phrase; but since ' hand ' often means ' power ', we might render the whole phrase as ' the staff empowered to convey my fury '. The zeal (cf. 9.7) which expresses itself in the care and salvation of a penitent or faithful people, and in love for them, expresses itself as wrath against a faithless, presumptuous people. The Assyrians are commissioned to plunder them and tread them underfoot.

But vv. 7-11 are an amazing contrast to the two preceding verses and no less significant. Assyria is no less presumptuous than Israel. For the Assyrian king has no thought of a divine overlord directing his step or of the possibility that the cam-paign in which he is engaged is for any other purpose than that of imperial aggrandizement. The limited commission to punish Israel or Judah he knows nothing of; the subjection of many peoples is his objective (v. 7) and, he believes, that should not present any serious obstacle. He is a king of kings (v. 8) not a petty prince of a puny people. What are Jerusalem and Samaria when compared with the cities which already have opened their gates to him, and what are their images compared with images of greater shrines? The Assyrian knew nothing of the second commandment given to Moses; the God of the Jerusalem Temple was like the god of any other shrine, represented by an image which had no power against him (cf. 45.4 f.; Ps. 76.10).

For NOT SO, i.e. 'not in this manner' in v. 7 we might read 'not rightly' to give the rendering: 'Not in the right way does he think of it, nor in the right way does he plan it.' But the other rendering should probably be preferred.

Carchemish, on the upper reaches of the Euphrates, lay on the route of an Assyrian army marching westward; here they would cross the river and turn south-west, to find Calno and Arpad about fifty miles on from the river crossing. Hamath lay on the Orontes another hundred miles south. Verse 8 implies that Samaria was already destroyed, like Damascus; therefore the date of this section must be after 721 BC, and probably belongs to the end of the century (cf. 5.26-30).

12-19. Assyria's vain boasting and the end of it

When Judah's pride and arrogance (cf. 9.9 f.; 10.6) have been rebuked, the pride and arrogance of Assyria will suffer punishment (v. 12). In v. 12 read HE WILL PUNISH; and, instead of the very stilted AV rendering, read: 'he will punish the king of Assyria for his arrogant vauntings (or deeds—lit. fruit) and for his proud disdain.' In v. 13 the king speaks as if he were almighty, claiming for himself not only strength but wisdom (cf. 11.2); that is accentuated in the final part of the verse, which not only describes him as plundering national wealth and removing boundaries in order to destroy all sense of national cohesion, but as trampling down their inhabitants like a bull. This last phrase is difficult; the verb is not 'trample down' but 'bring down', and a bull does not characteristically bring down anything. But the phrase rendered 'as a bull' can be rendered 'as a god' (cf. Gen. 49.24; Isa. 1.24; 49.26; 60.16; etc.) or 'as a mighty hero'; either of these renderings would fit well: 'and I brought down (to the ground) their inhabitants like a god' (or 'like a mighty hero').

14 uses a homely metaphor. The boy who rifles a bird's nest meets no effective opposition but only an ineffective clamour. The Assyrians captured the treasures of cities with even less ado; none of the inhabitants fled away, none chirped in protest —a very effective figure. But it seems more fitting in the context to read 'laid there' for LEFT (AV) or FORSAKEN (RSV) in respect of the eggs.

15 very effectively describes the presumption of the Assyrians (cf. Isa. 45.9 ff.; 64.8; Jer. 18.6; Rom. 9.20 f.); it is like the rebellion of an uncomprehending instrument against the agent who purposefully uses it for a salutary end. The last phrase should be understood as: 'As if a staff should lift up that which is not wood.'

16-19. The punishment of 'leanness (*or* wasting disease) in his well-fed limbs' must have touched his pride and brought humiliation; and a devastating fire will undermine and bring down his splendour (not 'he shall kindle' AV, but WILL BE KINDLED). This is like the punishment meted out to sinful Israel (cf. 9.18 f.); it is Yahweh's doing, who is the Light of Israel and their Holy One (v. 17). It is a great destruction; trees might sometimes be spared in war (cf. II Kings 3.19) and the law has a regulation concerning the sparing of fruit-trees (Deut. 20.19 f.), but here only a handful survive. The last clause of v. 18 seems to be out of place and may originally have belonged to the end of v. 16. It is very notable that, as a remnant of Israel will survive (cf. 1.9, 25; 4.2-6; 7.3; 10.20-27), so it will be with Assyria (v. 19).

20-27. The remnant of Israel which will survive

These verses are divisible into two portions, of which the second, vv. 24-27, seems more closely related to the foregoing

vv. 12-19 than the first. But the connection of vv. 20-23 with what precedes is probably to be found in the reference to the remnant (of Assyria) in v. 19.

20-23. Time after time Israel and Judah had relied on a neighbouring power for help and deliverance from danger. Isa. 30.1-5; 31.1-3 give evidence of a pro-Egyptian party in Jerusalem, while Ahaz had himself appealed to Assyria in 735 (II Kings 16.7-9). Such tactics brought national disaster, but now the lesson has been learned (v. 20); the people are now ready to trust in the waters of Shiloah which go softly (8.6), to rely with steadfast faith (cf. 7.9) on the Holy One of Israel. It is a repentant remnant which survives (v. 21). Verses 22 f. do not follow on easily; they speak only of utter destruction, with a short phrase about the survival of a remnant sitting like an inconvenient stranger in the midst of the message of 'a full end'. Probably these two verses belong to an early stage of Isaiah's ministry, before the doctrine of the remnant became prominent.

24-27 are closely united in thought with vv. 12-19. The terror of the Assyrians will soon be over; they will pass away (cf. vv. 12-19). The ROD AND . . . STAFF of v. 24 remind us at once of 10.5, and of 9.4, and in the latter of these also there is a reference to the deliverance of the day of Midian (v. 26; cf. Judg. 6-8) and to the burdensome yoke that is to be removed from the neck. This deliverance from the Assyrians is not only like that in a former day from the Midianites, but like that greater deliverance from Egypt at the Red Sea (cf. Ex. 14.16, 21 f.). The final phrase of v. 27 has no meaning in AV. Follow RSV, taking the words AND HIS YOKE WILL BE DES-TROYED FROM YOUR NECK as the end of v. 27, and the remainder as the beginning of v. 28 in the form: HE HAS GONE UP FROM RIMMON.

28-34. The Assyrian invasion

This is not a sequel to the preceding passage at all, but

might suitably follow vv. 5-11, and is parallel with 5.26-30.
Its period is almost certainly 701 BC. The passage is a literary
masterpiece, the brief phrases graphically conveying the impression of a swift, relentless advance. The places mentioned[1]
are all close to Jerusalem on the northern side, so that the
danger to the capital is now very real. Rimmon (*or* possibly
Pene Rimmon; cf. Gen. 32.30; Judg. 8.8 etc.) is some five miles
east of Bethel (cf. Judg. 20.45 ff.), Aiath is a little south of
it; Migron and Geba are still closer to Jerusalem; after Mich-
mash a narrow passage, beset with cliffy slopes, made the
troops leave their baggage there (v. 29) and pass through un-
encumbered. The other places mentioned were all within half-
a-dozen miles of the capital. In v. 30 DAUGHTER OF GALLIM
means the township, as DAUGHTER OF ZION means Zion, Jerusalem (v. 32).

11.1-9. The shoot of the stem of Jesse

7.14 spoke of the coming birth of the child Immanuel; 9.6 f.,
spoke of the child who had been born and upon whose
shoulders the responsibility of government is to rest and who
is to be given a wonderful name descriptive of his attributes.
The passage now before us must be considered in close connection with these.

1 raises a question at once. Is the new SHOOT or BRANCH which
is spoken of to be regarded simply as a new growth from the
tree of Jesse (i.e. David's house), or should we assume that the
word STUMP (lit. what is cut down) must refer to a tree which
has been stripped, so that we must find the occasion of the
utterance in the sequel to a national disaster when Judah suffered greatly and was reduced to a naked, impoverished condition? The parallel phrase A BRANCH . . . OUT OF HIS ROOTS
would seem to support the latter interpretation. The word
SHOOT (AV, ROD) is not in the original the same as that used

---

[1] Consult L. H. Grollenberg, *Shorter Atlas of the Bible*, map on p. 118.

for 'shoot' or 'branch' in Isa. 4.2; Jer. 23.5; 33.15; Zech. 3.8;
6.12. Nor is the second one which is translated in both AV and
RSV as BRANCH. SHALL GROW (or bear fruit) is the proper rendering of the verb in the second half of v. 1 but a very similar
text would give 'shall sprout', which is a closer parallel to the
verb of the first part.

2. The Spirit of God (or of Yahweh) signifies his life-force,
energy, vitality; it can be communicated to men. The effect of
it in men is unusual power which may express itself in skill
(Ex. 31.3; 35.31), courage (Judg. 6.34; 11.29; 13.25; etc.), wisdom (Gen. 41.38), prophetic insight (Num. 11.25 f.; Isa. 61.1),
etc. Here the Spirit of Yahweh bestows might (cf. 9.6, divine
hero) and wisdom, knowledge, insight and understanding (cf.
9.6, wonderful counsellor). Certain Old Testament passages
express the belief that in the messianic age there will be a
great outpouring of God's spirit upon men (cf. Isa. 32.15; Joel
2.28 f.).

3a. The word translated in RSV as DELIGHT means literally
'smell'; as 'sweet smell' (cf. Lev. 2.12; 3.16; 4.31; and frequently) it could easily mean satisfaction and delight. To have
delight in the fear of Yahweh i.e. in religion (cf. Ps. 1.2; Isa.
9. 3;35.10; 52.9; 61.3; Luke 2.10; John 15.11; Rom. 14.17; etc.)
is to have found the true way of life in which the law is not a
burden and duty is not an irksome yoke, but obedience brings
goodly fruit and the blessing of God makes rich.

3b-5. This prince of David's house will judge the poor right-
eously, i.e. they will not be oppressed but will get their rights
in the community; and he will decide fairly the cause of the
humble in the land, so that those who, by their nature, will not
fight aggressively for their rights will not be forsaken. In the
later part of v. 4 read 'he will punish the proud tyrant (not
the earth) with his sentences of judgment'; that, we presume,
is the meaning of the figure THE ROD OF HIS MOUTH. The GIRDLE

or loin cloth was obviously in close association with a man
(cf. Jer. 13.1-11); this figure, therefore, means that moral integrity and steadfast loyalty will be the prince's constant garment. It reminds us of the NT use of the armour of righteousness (as in Rom. 13.12; II Cor. 6.7; Eph. 6.11, 13 ff.) which the
Christian is to wear.

6-9 tell of the cessation of the hostilities which exist among
God's creatures; they are all reconciled and live in concord
and willing association and co-operation. It is a picture of
Paradise regained, with all the penalties of man's sin (cf. Gen.
3.14-19) wiped out. In v. 6 we should follow the Greek version
and read the third clause as 'and the calf and the lion shall
pasture together' and in v. 7 we should translate the first
clause as 'The cow and the bear shall associate together'.
Verse 8 means 'An infant shall play with glee by the hole of
a cobra and a young child lay his hand on the nest of an asp.'
Verse 9 sums up the non-combativeness of nature reconciled;
doubtless, IN ALL MY HOLY MOUNTAIN does not mean in Jerusalem alone in this context, but throughout Yahweh's land
(cf. Isa. 14.25; 65.25). It is essential to note that such non-
combativeness cannot be secured by human compact, however
sincerely that may be attempted; such an instrument may have,
for a time, the respect due to the pledged word, but in the
end it may be 'a scrap of paper' to the man who chooses, for
his own ends, to disregard it. Only the knowledge of God and
fidelity to his will can bind men together in willing fetters and
in true community.

As with 9.2-7, this passage has sometimes been regarded as
part of the ritual for a celebration of the Enthronement Festival (cf. note on 9.2-7). Verses 2-5 could be used readily to fit
such an interpretation, and on such an occasion prayer was
offered for victory over the people's enemies in the coming
year. But vv. 6-9a and, separately, 9b, seem to go beyond anything in the accustomed ritual of this festival; indeed, it seems
necessary to find some great occasion for such a vision of

universal pacification. According to the suggested interpretation of v. 1 above, it would appear that some occasion of great
national suffering must be looked for. That has sometimes
been found in the devastation of Jerusalem and Judah in 586
and the subsequent exile of the Jews in Babylon, with the
return to Jerusalem permitted by royal decree of the victorious
Cyrus and the rule of the branch Zerubbabel in Judah as the
ground of the new hope. That interpretation can be supported
and the title given to Zerubbabel seems particularly important;
but that title is not the same as either of the terms for 'shoot'
or 'branch' used here in v. 1. There remains the other possible
interpretation, that the occasion of 11.1-6 was the same as that
of 9.2-7, viz., the wonderful deliverance of Jerusalem and
Judah in 701 from the Assyrian army encamped against the
city. 9.2-7 saw that as harbinger of the end of wars (9.5); 11.6-9
has the vision of a wider peace, embracing the whole animate
creation.

THE INGATHERING OF THE DISPERSED

11.10–12.6

TWO ENSIGNS

11.10-16

This section follows suitably after vv. 1-9, even if it is
possible that it contains several originally separate fragments.
The general subject is the shape of things in the new day and,
in particular, the restored fortunes of the remnant of Israel and
Judah and the gathering home of their dispersed sons and
daughters. Whether IN THAT DAY (v. 10) indicates a day in the
near or the distant future cannot be answered.

I

10 is probably to be taken separately. In thought it is close to 2.2-4. In terms of Isa. 53.2 the phrase ROOT OF JESSE might refer to the 'shoot' or 'branch' mentioned in 11.1; but the fact that the word used is different from both of these words makes it more likely that the reference is to the stump of a tree which has been cut down to the root, and thence to the remnant of Israel and Judah. The fact of its survival after such suffering evokes wonder and curiosity concerning the source of its endurance. It is like an ENSIGN, to which the peoples assemble; they are drawn towards this people whose God has so wonderfully blessed them and seek association with it in faith and loyalty, so that its dwellings become now honoured and glorious. In AV HIS REST (or resting-place) is an accurate rendering; but the word can mean 'dwelling-place' (I Kings 8.56; Ruth 1.9).

11 speaks of the gathering home of Israel and Judah from Egypt (Pathros is Upper Egypt, with Ethiopia or Cush further south) and from Assyria (to which Shinar or Babylon, Elam to the east of it and Hamath in Syria on the Orontes were tributary) and from the coastlands and islands of the Aegean. Even in the days of David and Solomon Egypt had provided asylum for hard-pressed men of Judah and for political adversaries (cf. I Kings 11.14-25, 26-40). And Isa. 30.1-7; 31.1-3 show that there was a pro-Egyptian faction in Jerusalem in Isaiah's time, so that we may presume that there was even then a considerable number of Israelite and Jewish settlers in that land. Of people removed from Palestine by Assyrian conquerors and placed throughout her empire we have ample evidence;[1] and the troubled times which the Assyrians invasions brought may have induced many others to seek a refuge in the coastlands and islands of the Aegean.

12-14 describe the conditions of life of the returning men and

[1] Cf. D. Winton Thomas, *Documents from Old Testament Times*, pp. 58-63, 67.

women of Israel and Judah. The significance of the term EN-
SIGN in v. 12 may be the same as in v. 10, or it may designate
the banner of the returning companies. Hostilities against the
two lands will cease, and they themselves will make an end of
their own bickerings and strife (v. 13; cf. 9.20 f.). Into such a
picture of restitution and peace v. 14 seems to introduce a
discordant note by speaking of pillaging and occupation (if
not of revenge; cf. I Sam. 11; 14.47; II Sam. 8.3 ff.; 11.1; II
Kings 8.20-22; etc.). But its point may be that the empire of
Israel is to be restored as it was in the time of the son of Jesse
(cf. 9.1). A passage will be made for the dispersed of Israel
from Egypt, and from Assyria over the Euphrates, as was done
from Egypt in ancient times (cf. Ex. 14.16, 29; 14.21 f.); and
once more there will be a highway in the desert for the journey
of Yahweh's people.

A few minor notes should be added: 'the shoulders of the
Philistines' were the hill-sides sloping down westward to the
coastal plain (v. 14; cf. Gen. 48.22). The first verb in v. 15 is
DESTROY or 'devote', but several ancient versions read 'dry
up' which should probably be preferred; while, in the same
verse, whether we should say 'violent wind' or SCORCHING
WIND is not certain, the versions giving support to the former.

As for the occasion of the utterances contained in these
verses 10-16, it has been held by many scholars that they are
much later than the period of Isaiah and that they belong to
the final part of the sixth century BC (reflecting the return of
the Jewish exiles from Babylon to Jerusalem), or later still. It
cannot be denied that the final part of the sixth century was a
time of great expectations of the return of the people of Israel
and of Judah from many lands and of the tribute of the Gentiles (cf. e.g. Isa. 60). Yet the language used in vv. 10-16 is, on
the whole, characteristic of Isaiah. The fact that he does not
elsewhere use, for instance, THE CORNERS OF THE EARTH or THE
COASTLANDS OF THE SEA cannot be made a convincing argument against Isaianic authorship. By the end of the seventh
century many people, both of Israel and Judah, had been

carried off to many lands; it is, therefore, arguable, to say the
very least, that the survival of Jerusalem inviolate from Sennacherib's assault in 701 BC must have been interpreted as a
divine deliverance and as a token of God's blessing which gave
hope for the future. Surely now the hope of a termination of
the bickerings between Israel and Judah (cf. 7.1 ff.), and of
attacks on these lands (v. 13), was particularly apposite, and
the hope that from humiliated Assyria and from Egypt the
dispersed of Israel and Judah would now be gathered home.
Surely the deliverance from Assyria now would be as great
and memorable as it had been from Egypt of old (vv. 15 f.).
The fact that in v. 11 Babylon is not specifically mentioned is
surely in favour of this date rather than a date in the sixth
century when its name could not have been omitted.

THANKSGIVING AND PRAISE

12.1-6

This chapter appears to be in two portions; vv. 1-3 express
an individual thanksgiving, whether or not it was used in the
congregation of Israel at worship; vv. 4-6 is in the plural and
is a call to the congregation to rejoice before the Lord. Notice
how both portions begin with YOU WILL SAY IN THAT DAY, in
v. 1 the 'you' being singular, and in v. 4 plural.

1-3. This first portion gives thanks after a time of God's anger
(cf. 10.5); that means after a time of suffering. But that time
is now finished; the God who punished has himself brought
comfort and relief (cf. Hos. 6.1; Job 5.18). Since it was God
who thus saved his people, they now rejoice in him and sing
his praise.

4-6. The second portion is in less personal tones. It calls for
thanksgiving, but also for the proclamation of God's mighty

deeds in all the earth, that he may be duly celebrated and known for the great God he is (vv. 4-5). God is now in the midst of his people (i.e., he no more withdraws in displeasure or hides himself so that he cannot be found); therefore, let Zion SHOUT AND SING FOR JOY.

These two portions (two separate psalms, perhaps) are not in the customary, prophetic language, but their phrases can readily be paralleled from the Book of Psalms. That such psalms should be found in a prophetical book is not without parallel (cf. Jonah 2; Hab. 3). It is possible that ch. 12 did not come from Isaiah but was added as a fitting conclusion to a collection (chs. 1-12, or, more likely, a section of it) of the prophet's utterances and biographical narratives about him. The chapter itself bears no clear evidence of the date at which it was added.

UTTERANCES AGAINST FOREIGN NATIONS

13.1–23.18

This section contains principally a group of utterances against foreign nations, although a few sections of different type are included within it. The title which is used in 13.1, with its specific use of the name of the prophet, suggests that it stood at the head of a collection of Isaianic material composed of the whole or part of this section of the book. By no means all this section is regarded by most modern scholars as authentic, quite a few parts of it being adjudged to belong to a date much later than the second half of the eighth century; but that question is considered in the course of the Commentary.

ISRAEL'S ADVERSARIES

13.1–20.6

Within these chapters are contained utterances against peoples who were at various times adversaries of Israel: Babylon, Philistia, Moab, Damascus (i.e. Syria), Ethiopia, Egypt.

THE DOOM OF BABYLON AND PHILISTIA

13.1–14.32

These two chapters do not contain one connected literary

unit, and may, for the purpose of comment, be considered
in several parts, viz. 13.1-22; 14.1-4a; 14.4b-21; 14.22-23;
14.24-27; 14.28-32.

13.1-22. Babylon

The word BURDEN (AV) or, rather, UTTERANCE (RSV) occurs
frequently in this section of the book. 13.1-22 is a poem of
great power and literary skill, divided into a number of more
or less clearly defined stanzas, with a distinct break between
vv. 16 and 17.

1-3. A threefold summons—a signal (cf. 11.10, 12; 18.3) made
from a bare height (hence clearly visible), a gathering call, and
a beckoning with the hand—calls peoples unnamed to gather
for the conflict; Yahweh himself has summoned his own hosts,
his proudly exulting ones who are zealous for his honour (vv.
2-3). In v. 2 read WAVE THE HAND FOR THEM TO ENTER THE
GATES OF THE NOBLES (or grandees), or, possibly, 'wave the
hand for them, draw (your swords), ye nobles.' Since every
war against God's enemies was a holy war in his name, those
taking part are described as CONSECRATED to the task (v. 3).

4-5. The second stanza pictures graphically the people gathering for battle, the mustering, the din, the hosts FROM THE END
OF THE HEAVENS, all the instruments of God's indignation. It
is THE DAY OF THE LORD (cf. Amos 5.18-20).

6-8. The third stanza speaks of the dismay and anguish of it,
the pain and the terror, the speechlessness, the words of comfort which no one can find to offer, the FACES . . . AFLAME.
The last detail is unexpected; faces aflame normally betoken
anger; in this case we should have expected them to be pallid.
We must presume that they were red for very shame rather
than white with fear and apprehension.

9-12. The fourth stanza speaks not only of the desolation of
the earth, and the punishment of wickedness and pride until

men are rarer than gold, but of the convulsions of nature which, by its very disorder, shows that it is involved in the upheavals; for all creation is a co-ordinate unity, and all nature is affected by the great work of God upon the earth. Ophir (cf. I Kings 9.26-28) was reached by ship from Ezion-geber at the northern end of the Red Sea; its location is not certain, probably in south-west Arabia (Yemen), or on the African continent opposite, or much further down the African east coast, opposite Madagascar.

13-16. The doom is inescapable. From this great city and people, now humbled and under judgment, foreigners who had shared in its wealth and magnificence, run off, like A HUNTED GAZELLE, to their own homes; no loyalty induces them to share the sufferings; they are passengers who accept no responsibility for the ruin (cf. Nahum 2.8). All who remain perish, children and all; the end is utter violence.

Up to this point no city or people has been mentioned; vv. 2-16 do not refer specifically to Babylon; indeed, vv. 5 and 11 make the reference to all the earth. It has, on that account, been argued that this passage represents a point of view later than that of Isaiah as expressed in the comparable passage 2.10-22; and the mention of the convulsions of nature, which reminds us of Joel 2.1-11, 30-32; Zeph. 1.14-18 and other passages, is thought to support this view. But Amos himself did not think of the Day of Yahweh as having reference only to Israel and Judah, and Isa. 18.3, in an authentic passage, has reference to all the earth. As for the convulsions of nature, these figure more prominently in later descriptions of the great Day of Judgment, but the form of Amos 8.9 shows that this idea was active in Isaiah's day. Therefore, in spite of v. 1, the evidence is clear that vv. 2-16 are not concerned exclusively, or even particularly, with Babylon; and there is no definitive argument for denying them to the prophet Isaiah.

17-22. Verses 17-19 speak specifically of the destruction of

Babylon by the Medes, a people who could neither be bought off nor bribed, and were merciless in their warring. Babylon will be utterly destroyed and the final stanza, vv. 20-22, makes it a place of utter desolation, regarded as a place accursed. Neither shepherds seeking shelter nor nomads passing by enter its ruins (v. 20), wild beasts of the desert and shrieking creatures of the waste occupy it; owls (or, less likely, ostriches) are there, and hyenas and jackals, the scavengers of deserted places (v. 22). In v. 21 satyrs or goat-demons seem, in the context, much more likely than goats, for Babylon now is no place for domestic animals. Also in v. 22 the word rendered 'desolate houses' in AV means literally 'widows', but it is probably a by-form of a common word meaning 'towers' or 'palaces'.

Is it possible to attribute vv. 17-22 to Isaiah? Babylon in his time was certainly active and for a period was a thorn in the flesh of Assyria (cf. ch. 39; II Kings 20.12-19). Might, then, these verses refer to Sennacherib's capture of Babylon in his campaign against Merodach Baladan at the beginning of his reign? 22.6 speaks of Elamites in the Assyrian army, so that the presence of Medes need not present difficulty; and we must remember that Merodach Baladan may have appeared a bigger menace to the people of Judah then than he does to us who read the historical record now. But two difficulties stand firmly against this view: (a) the mention of Medes alone in v. 17 (and not at all the Assyrians), and (b) the description of Babylon as THE GLORY OF KINGDOMS, THE SPLENDOUR AND PRIDE OF THE CHALDEANS (v. 19), surely too grandiose for the Babylon of Merodach Baladan. And the specific mention of the Medes alone in v. 17 is an obstacle in the way of those who suggest that 'Assyrians' stood in place of 'Babylon' in v. 19 in the original form of the utterance, and that it was later revised in view of the subsequent course of the history of Judah and the name Babylon was introduced. It seems impossible, therefore, to maintain the authenticity of this section. The Medes became a significant force in the Near East only after they united with the Babylonians to destroy the power of Assyria (Nineveh fell in 612 BC); and in the sixth century, after the death of Nebuchadnezzar in 561 BC, they rose to power under Cyrus (cf. Isa. 44.28; 45.1) and brought about the downfall of Babylon in 539 BC. It is, therefore, to this period between 561 and 539 that it seems necessary to ascribe 13.17–22.

14.1–4a. The doctrine of the return of the dispersed people of Israel and Judah is found several times in chs. 1–12 (cf. e.g. 10.20–23; 11.10–12) and the statement that foreigners will seek to learn of Yahweh and serve him because of his wonderful works is found in 11.10. This portion, 14.1–4a, which is concerned with these subjects and is in prose, serves as a link between 13.2–22 and 14.4b–21. 14.1–2, like 13.2–16, has no specific reference to Babylon and might well come from Isaiah, but vv. 3–4a, like 13.17–22, mention Babylon in particular, so that the whole passage may be dated as is 13.17–22, if not later. Verse 2 speaks of a complete reversal in the fortunes of the returned people in that those who were formerly their captors and masters are now their servants (cf. Isa. 61.5, etc.). Israel, now disciplined for her sin and restored by God and reconciled to him, is once against his chosen servant; the old covenant relationship established in the wilderness is fully restored.

14.4b–21. This is a magnificent taunt-song, describing the reception in Sheol of a dead tyrant who is not named. Once we have commented on some details of it, it will be necessary to consider whether some of the ideas concerning life after death which are expressed in it are to be taken as matters of belief on the author's part, or simply as part of a notable imaginative conception or myth whose purpose is to present certain truths but which must not be pressed in all its details.

4b–11 constitute the first movement of the poem, in two stanzas (4b–8, 9–11). A great oppressor's rule is ended. THE GOLDEN CITY CEASED! (AV) has no meaning; to apply the term 'golden city ' to the oppressor's capital city is forced. But the Dead Sea Scroll 1 Q Isaᵃ has, not the word meaning ' golden city ', but a similar one which has the suitable meaning of INSOLENT FURY, ' arrogance ' (cf. RSV).

5, speaking of THE SCEPTRE OF RULERS, seems to extend the reference, against the rest of the passage, to more than one oppressor; possibly, therefore, SCEPTRE should be taken as symbolic of royal power and the phrase read as ' the sceptre which ruled rulers ', or else the plural should be regarded as used for emphasis (the preceding plural for ' WICKED ' supporting this), meaning ' the sceptre of the ruler '.

6. AV is not easy; with the aid of an ancient version we may read the verse as :

Who smote peoples down in wrath, with blows unrelenting, and ruled nations in anger, with oppression unsparing.

Now he has gone; the whole earth has found relief and is at peace again (v. 7); the trees of Lebanon which had been mercilessly felled by him are now unmolested (for such felling of trees, commonly practised by Assyrian and Babylonian conquerors, cf. note on 10.18 f.).

9-11 describe the reception of the dead tyrant in that subterranean region which is the abode of the departed, those limp, weak SHADES, who there have a living death rather than a sentient life. There is excitement in Sheol for the tyrant's arrival; the shades are stirred to interest, kings rise from their thrones to receive him, surprised that one so mighty has now become as weak as they, that all his grandeur and magnificence have become rotten, that he who lived luxuriously (cf. Amos 6.3-6) has now maggots for his bed, and worms for his coverlet (v. 11).

12-21 constitutes the second movement of this poem.

12. It is important to catch the significance of this verse. Lucifer is not to be understood as meaning Satan (cf. Luke 10.18); the term, from a verbal root meaning ' to shine brightly ', means the morning star, which is particularly bright throughout the Near East; it fades out before the rising sun. But the morning star *fades out*, it does not fall from heaven (v. 12). It is clear, therefore, that the tyrant, of whom this poem speaks, is compared with the morning star because of his brilliant splendour; but account must be taken of the Canaanite myth that Helal, the morning star, rebelled against the most High God and was frustrated and cast down to Sheol. The value of using that ancient myth in illustration becomes clear in vv. 13-15.

The last phrase of v. 12 is very doubtful. YOU WHO LAID NATIONS LOW is very questionable. It is the figure of a felled tree encumbering the ground which is used now. The tyrant has been laid prostrate before the nations which he had ruled and which had for long lived under his burdensome and life-destroying shadow.

13-14 reveal the tyrant's unbridled ambition and gross presumption. It is the spirit of those who built the Tower of Babel illustrated again, and the spirit of Helal, son of the morning. The tyrant presumes to set his throne in the heavens, to preside in the assembly of the gods (cf. Job 1.6 ff.; Ps. 82; etc.) in the far north, or, as it may be rendered, on the top of Zaphon (the mountain of the assembly of the gods located in the far north). Man's mad ambition and passion for power can go no further.

15-17 record the tyrant's downfall; he dies and descends to Sheol, to be a spectacle which makes others gape in wonder and meditate how the mighty are fallen and how the proud rulers of the earth are brought down among the weak shades.

18-20a. But his lot in Sheol is as bitter as his place on earth was resplendent. All the kings he conquered, whether they remained as captives or were used as lieutenants in his armies (cf. 10.8), lay honoured, in their own burial places (v. 18). This need not be taken to mean, in the former case, that they must have been permitted to return home, in contradiction to the last words of v. 17; it simply means that they were decently and honourably buried in their long homes, their graves. But the tyrant lies unburied (v. 19; *not* ' away from your sepulchre ', RSV, nor ' out of your grave ', AV), like a loathed carcase (lit. rottenness, putrefaction), wrapped around with the slain. The final part of v. 19 should possibly have a slight change of order, thus: ' wrapped around with the slain, those pierced by the sword, like a dead body trodden underfoot (v. 20). Those who go down to the stones of the pit (from 19)—you will not be associated with them in burial. . . .' The phrase THE STONES OF THE PIT has been variously interpreted; but in this context the reference probably is to the mode of burial of bodies found lying uncovered, by casting stones over them. Even this mode of burial is denied to the tyrant.

20b-21. The final clause of v. 20 may be rendered as in RSV, or with the Greek version, as having reference specifically to the tyrant: ' The descendants (lit. seed) of an evil-doer shall never have honoured names.' That would mean that the punishment of the father falls also upon his children after him. They, too, are destined for destruction, lest the spirit of their father should live in them and they in turn should build their great cities and possess the earth (v. 21).

Now a brief retrospect on the whole section 13.1–14.21. We have already noted that, while the introductory verse 13.1 and the prose fragment 14.3-4a as well as the long, rhythmic passage 13.17-22 make specific mention of Babylon as the subject of reference, there is no mention at all of any specific people in 13.2-16, 14.1 f. and 14.4b-21. It has already been argued that the passages which speak of Babylon must be attributed to the sixth century BC at the earliest, but 13.2-16 may well be authentic. It now remains to consider ch. 14. 14.1 f. has little evidence upon which to base any conclusion; but by the end of the eighth century Israel and Judah had had sufficient experience of the oppressive methods of Assyria to hope, after the deliverance of Jerusalem in 701 BC, for a situation in which their captors would be captives, and their oppressive rulers would be ruled.

14.4b-21 is a much more complicated problem. For example, take what is said about Sheol in it. Whereas, before the time of Isaiah, the doctrine of Sheol, as far as our evidence expresses it, remains undeveloped, and, even at a much later period (cf. Job 3.18 f.), it is held that the social distinctions of the earth have no place there, the departed being together in an amorphous, listless society, in the passage before us kings still sit on their thrones and, apparently, have knowledge of what is happening on the earth, and v. 20 even hints at rewards and punishments in the hereafter. Now these ideas concerning life after death arose much later than the time of Isaiah; yet it must be admitted that a person of Isaiah's time might have composed this passage as an imaginative conception of the fit fate of such a tyrant as he describes. But granted this possibility, did Isaiah write it? Is it in his style and spirit at all? The contents of ch. 10 might warrant the conclusion that it is in his spirit, on the assumption that the reference is to Assyria; it is not in his style. Therefore, the authorship of the passage must remain uncertain in terms of its style and content.

But another question remains. Do the characteristics of the tyrant, as detailed, indicate that one, notorious tyrant was in mind? Let us see. He is described as unrelenting in persecution (14.6), greatly presumptuous and ambitious (14.13 f.), as slain in battle and left unburied (14.19) and as incurring a punishment whose deadly effect continued upon his children after him (14.21). Does any one emperor, of Assyria or Babylon, fit the picture? Sargon of Assyria (who captured Samaria in 721 BC) would fit the bill as warrior and tyrant, and he died

a violent death and was not buried in his own house; but peace
did not ensue upon his death. Sennacherib of Assyria was a
presumptuous tyrant; the losses sustained by his army in 701
might be thought to give warrant to a statement that he had
ruined his own country and to the expectation that a period
of peace and quiet would now ensue. Even the statement in
14.20 that the tyrant would be left unburied might be thought
to apply to Sennacherib in terms of 18.6. Of the emperors of
Babylonia, Nebuchadnezzar might be reckoned a likely candi-
date; he was a mighty campaigner, a great builder, so that the
cypresses and cedars of Lebanon might well have heaved a sigh
of relief at his death. But, whereas Dan. 4.25 contains the
prophecy that he will be driven out of human society and eat
grass like oxen, there is no extant record to the effect that he
was not given ordinary burial and after his death there certainly
was not peace and quiet. None of these rulers wholly fits the
picture drawn in our passage, even if Sennacherib and Nebuchadnezzar may be deemed to come near to it. But another
passage of the Book of Isaiah has relevant evidence, viz.
30.27-33. In particular, it speaks of the Assyrian being broken
in pieces, every stroke of the rod being accompanied with
tabrets and harps; ' and for the king Topheth will be prepared.'
For such an utterance against Assyria the reigns of Hezekiah
and Josiah seem the fitting occasions. Ahaz, who had sought
Assyria's help, had caused his son to pass through the fire (II
Kings 16.3); so now the king of Assyria would perish. If, therefore, 30.27-33 (q.v.) can be regarded as authentic, it seems
defensible to regard Sennacherib as supplying many of the
details of the picture of the fallen tyrant and to consider it an
open possibility that Isaiah was the author of the figure of the
tyrant.

The conclusion of the argument seems to be that, while part
of the passage may have come from Isaiah, as a whole and in
its present form it belongs to a later date.

14.22-23. A prose fragment, not the continuation of vv. 4b-21,

but like 13.1 and 14.3-4a, which also have specific reference
to Babylon, and, in content, similar to 13.19-22. Babylon is to
be deserted and desolated, not even a remnant will remain.
In v. 23 the rendering HEDGEHOG (RSV) is very doubtful;
BITTERN (AV) seems more suitable, but the word so translated is of uncertain meaning.

14.24-27. A passage very important for the appreciation of the
grandeur of Isaiah's conception of God's judgment. Verse 25
reminds us of 9.4 and 10.27 and, in content, of 10.12-19. It
may have been Assyria's pretensions to be a world power
which evoked in Isaiah's thought a world judgment, which
would concern not only Assyria but all the nations. The fact
that Assyria is to be judged in Yahweh's land does not necessarily mean that all the nations, over whom his hand is
stretched out, will necessarily be judged there, although it is
doubtful if Isaiah could have conceived judgment executed
upon them in any other place. This world judgment is planned;
it is inevitable and it cannot be frustrated (v. 27; cf. 43.13).
This is the regnant God of human history, whose is the kingdom, the power and the glory, to whom the nations are as a
drop from a bucket and as the fine dust on the pans of a
balance (Isa. 40.15).

14.28-32. Utterance on Philistia
The problems of interpretation in this utterance are considerable. Verse 28 dates it in the year King Ahaz died, which
was probably 715 BC. Philistia then experienced relief from a
time of oppression (v. 29) but is warned not to rejoice because
FROM THE SERPENT'S ROOT WILL COME FORTH AN ADDER;
another of the same brood will arise to take the place of the
one who is gone. The idea that the rejoicing was at the death
of Ahaz and that the warning of renewed oppression was intended to refer to his successor Hezekiah is ruled out for three
reasons: (a) Ahaz, as far as we know, never treated Philistia
oppressively; (b) the new scourge is to come from the north

(v. 31); (c) the messengers (v. 32), if they came to Zion, would
not have resorted to their people's oppressors for guidance or
help. The reference, therefore, in the case of oppressor suc-
ceeding oppressor must be to two Assyrian kings. The likeliest
event must have been the death of Sargon in 705 (he had certainly subdued Philistia six years before); the years following
705, when Sennacherib had trouble consolidating his seat on
the throne, may well have inspired hope. But such an interpretation at once raises the question of the authenticity of v.
28.

As for the content of the verses, the reference of v. 30 cannot be to the poor and the needy of Philistia (FIRST-BORN OF THE
POOR meaning 'the poorest of the poor', cf. Job 18.13); that
would not make sense. By a slight vowel change in a word in
the original, the first phrase of v. 30 would read: 'The poor
shall feed in my meadow', which would make the reference at
once to Jerusalem and would mean that, while Philistia is completely destroyed, Judah is secure under Yahweh's protection.
Read with RSV at the end of v. 30 I WILL SLAY; in v. 31 'melt
with fear, Philistia, all of you', and in the final clause of it:
'and no straggler in his battalions'. In v. 32 the messengers
are presumably from Philistia to Jerusalem, seeking help. They
are not given the help which we can imagine they expected;
they hear a confession of faith (cf. 7.9).

UTTERANCE ON MOAB

15.1–16.14

These chapters describe a grim disaster which has befallen
Moab, making the country a desolate ruin and her people
fugitives. It has often been maintained that 15.1-9, together
with 16.8-11, constitute an elegy upon the fate of Moab composed by a sympathetic author (cf. 15.5; 16.9, 11), while 16.
1-7, 12 are an independent poem describing an embassy from

K

Moab to Judah, and 16.13 f. is a postlude to the whole, stating
that within three years the oracle will be fulfilled.

Relative to that literary analysis of the chapters, certain
arguments have been adduced. For example, the notable parallels between the elegy and Jer. 48.29-38 have been quoted,
and the conclusion reached that it is the elegy which is the
primary source; but since there are parallels also between
16.6 f. and the Jeremiah passage, there is no reason here for
separating the elegy from its context in chs. 15-16. Again, it
has been maintained that the language of the elegy is quite
unlike that of Isaiah; but that is an argument very difficult to
handle and very easily overweighted. On the other hand,
Isaiah's ability to make a graphic and effective recital of place-
names, such as is exemplified in 10. 27b-32, might be used to
support the view that he might have been responsible for the
similar effect in 15.1-9. But, these lines of argument apart, it
is the sympathy expressed with Moab in the elegy which makes
it most difficult to attribute it to Isaiah or to any man in Israel
or Judah.

15.1-9. Ar-Moab and Kir-Moab were two very important
towns in Moab, the former on the left bank of the river
Arnon and the latter about 25 miles further south. The towns
named in vv. 2 and 4 lay between the Arnon and a line due
east of Jericho, all being thus north of the river. The sudden
disaster which came upon the land sent the people of Dibon
(not as in AV) TO THE HIGH PLACES (i.e. the hill-shrines) to
make lamentation and to plead for divine mercy (cf. Judg.
11.37). The whole country was involved in mourning (vv. 2 f.).
The rhythmic form is broken in v. 3, and there is some evidence that the second clause of the verse should be read as
'on the housetops there is lamentation'. The second part of
v. 4 may mean that the distress is so great that even the men
of war cry out; but a minor vocalic modification would give
the much better rendering: 'therefore the strength (lit. loins)
of Moab trembles, her whole being trembles.' Verses 5 f., in

which the places named are of unknown site except Zoar
which was at the south-eastern end of the Dead Sea, tell of
the flight of the people of Moab southward to Edom, away
from the inhabited area north of the Arnon where the enemy
must have concentrated their forces; the fugitives take with
them what they can carry. THE BROOK OF THE WILLOWS (v. 7)
is probably the Wadi Arabah, that deep depression which
stretches from the Jordan valley to the Gulf of Akaba on the
Red Sea. Verse 9, it is to be noted, strikes a typically prophetic rather than an elegiac note; it proclaims further disaster
for Moab. The lion may signify the Assyrians or simply a
fiercely destructive foe.

16.1-5. The interpretation of some of these verses is very uncertain; RSV is a better guide to the meaning than AV, especially in vv. 4 f. Verse 1 clearly speaks of an embassy from the
people of Moab, now fled to Edom, to the city of Zion. Read
the first part of v. 1 as in RSV or as: THE RULERS OF THE LAND
HAVE SENT A MESSENGER (as in Hebrew?). Lambs as a gift from
a pastoral country like Moab are what might be expected (cf.
II Kings 3.4 f.). Sela (later, Petra) was a famous centre in
Edom. Verse 2 breaks the connection between vv. 1 and 3,
and probably had a place originally in the passage 15.5-9. Note
that vv. 3-5 are direct speech, without any introductory for-
mula. 'Give (us) advice; grant (our) request', such is the
opening. The request is for a hide-out and a refuge for the
fugitives of Moab (v. 3); that being so, the AV rendering in
v. 4 is inconsistent. By means of a slight modification we may
read it consistently as 'let the outcasts of Moab receive hospitality with you', and read 'destroyer' rather than 'spoiler'
in the next clause. But the main interpretative difficulty is in
4b-5: 'for the extortioner . . .' etc. The words of 4b AV
could never have been used by the Moabite messengers; follow
the RSV rendering: WHEN THE OPPRESSOR IS NO MORE, AND
DESTRUCTION HAS CEASED, and the oppressor HAS VANISHED
FROM THE LAND, (v. 5) THEN A THRONE WILL BE ESTABLISHED IN

. . . LOVE, etc. That means when Moab has been delivered from her present predicament. There are then two possible ways of understanding v. 5 and each can be supported: (*a*) we may recognize that the phrase IN THE TENT OF DAVID is rhythmically superfluous according to the literary form of the passage and take the verse to mean that an honourable and just régime will then be established in Moab which will have peaceful relations with Judah in contrast with the hostilities of the past; or (*b*) we may retain the phrase mentioned and regard the verse as a gracious (and, it may have been hoped, ingratiating) compliment to Judah to the effect that such a deliverance for Moab with their aid would be to the glory of the house of David and to its establishment in justice and righteousness on the throne of Judah.

6-7. That v. 6 is to be understood as the response to the cry of the Moabites for help is clear; v. 7 may be taken in association with it, a course which seems preferable to conjoining it with the following verses. We must conclude that the graciousness expressed in the final part of the cry was not accepted as genuine. Moab is condemned for its pride and arrogance (cf. 25.11). 'Therefore Moab shall wail for Moab' sounds as if it must be part of the response; they must face their own troubles, for they lack sympathizers.

The final part of v. 6 is somewhat uncertain of meaning; his boastings are nought or are false, is the probable meaning. The so-called RAISIN-CAKES OF KIR-HARESETH (v .7, RSV), a town of Moab, were made from pressed grapes and seem to have been a delicacy used particularly on festival occasions, especially at the Festival of Ingathering (cf. II Sam. 6.19; Hos. 3.1; cf. Jer. 7.18).

8-12. Of these verses, 8-11 are elegiac like 15.1-9; these two passages may be parts of a whole which is broken by 16.1-7, or we may take 16.8-11 to be a resumed elegy after the rebuff given to the Moabite messengers which is narrated in the intervening passage. The speaker in vv. 8-11 is obviously greatly stirred by the sufferings of Moab (cf. vv. 9 and 11). For fruitful Moab and the loss of her vintage joys he feels great sorrow. THE VINE OF SIBMAH (like the grapes of Eshcol) must have been celebrated and so it exemplifies the greatness of the loss. By the use of hyperbole he makes its roots stretch to Jazer in Ammon to the north, to the wilderness east and south, and westward to the Dead Sea (v. 8). In v. 8, THE LORDS OF THE NATIONS HAVE STRUCK DOWN ITS BRANCHES is possible but causes an awkward change of subject in the verse: Isa. 28.1 shows that it is possible to render it as 'its fruitful branches struck down the lords of the nations', so potent was its wine. In v. 11, after the statement in v. 10 that all JOY AND GLADNESS ARE TAKEN AWAY, the speaker expresses his own feeling, saying in our own idiom: I tremble like a leaf for Moab, my heart quakes for Kir-heres.

Verse 12, which seems to be responsive to 15.2, is prophetic, not elegiac (cf. 15.9); Moab may pray on the high places but she shall not prevail.

13-14 is a postlude in prose which proclaims heavy judgment within three years for Moab. It is quite generally attributed to Isaiah.

A few words must be said about the authorship and date of chs. 15 and 16. We have already noted in 15.5; 16.9, 11 strong expressions of sympathy for Moab in her suffering and, in 16.9, 11 particularly, very strong language is used to express these feelings. Now it might be suggested that 15.5 could be interpreted as an example of interjected direct speech, so that the verse expresses the feelings, not of the author, but of Moab; but 16.9, 11 are not amenable to such treatment. It seems necessary, therefore, to conclude that the elegy at least (and probably the intervening narrative in 16.1-7) was written neither by Isaiah nor by any other man of Israel or Judah. 16.9, 11 would lead to the conclusion that it was composed by a Moabite and Isaiah took it over, introducing in 15.9 and

16.12 his own contributions and supplying the postlude
(16.13 f.).

The occasion of the poem is more difficult to determine. The
conquest of Moab by Omri has been suggested as the occasion
(cf. II Kings 3.4 ff. and the Moabite Stone[1]), but Judah was at
that time weak and a Moabite appeal to Judah for help would
not have been made. Jehoram has been regarded by some
scholars as the oppressor (cf. II Kings 3) but that does not
suit the needs of the passage either, because he and Jehosha-
phat of Judah were allies in the campaign against Moab. More
likely than either of these is the view that Jeroboam of Israel
was the oppressor (cf. II Kings 14.25; Amos 6.14) and that the
Moabites made their appeal to Uzziah of Judah. But it is
doubtful if the relations between Judah and Israel at that time
were such than an appeal to Judah would have seemed to
Moab likely to be successful. Another suggestion may be made;
it has the support of at least some scholars. The Annals of
Sargon of Assyria speak of a campaign he conducted in 715
BC against certain tribes in north-west Arabia. His route most
probably passed through Moab. His oppression and devastation of Moab *en route* could explain the absence of any mention of a battle in chs. 15-16; and this view would make the
embassy to Judah take place at a time when the fear of Assyria lay heavily upon all the peoples of the west land. It would
also make the chapters belong to Isaiah's own time and the
form of words used in 16.5 would give support to that. The
epilogue (16.13 f.) would then refer to Sargon's later campaign
of 711 BC, or to Sennacherib's, which caused great havoc in the
whole area.

[1] Cf. D. Winton Thomas, *Documents from Old Testament Times*, pp.
195-98.

UTTERANCE ON DAMASCUS AND EPHRAIM

17.1-14

The title mentions Damascus alone, but Damascus is the subject of vv. 1-3 only, unless v. 4 is regarded as an intrusion in its present position, in which case we may take under the title vv. 1-3, 5-6. There is, however, no warrant for extruding v. 4 in this way.

1-3. In AV the rendering of v. 1 is very stiff; read: 'Look at Damascus, no longer a city; she shall become a ruin heap.' 'The cities of Aroer' (AV, v. 2) must mean the two cities of that name in Moab, the better known of which lay a little to the north of the river Arnon; but these cities, being in Moab, have no relevance here in an utterance against Damascus. Therefore, follow the Greek version and read with RSV: HER CITIES WILL BE DESERTED FOR EVER; they will become a place where flocks will lie down unmolested. Verse 3 describes Syria and Israel as sharing the same fate. The fortress which will be taken away from the latter might mean the Syrian capital, Damascus. which served as a defence bastion and bulwark against Assyria; but parallelism suggests that it was intended as a reference to Samaria, the capital of Israel, both countries thus going down in ruin.

4-6. The harvest and the gleaning

Three figures are used here to describe the fate which will befall Jacob (i.e. Israel or Ephraim); (i) wasting disease (cf. 10.6): a loss of vitality and comeliness which cannot be counteracted; (ii) harvest: the people will be gathered away in the harvest of judgment, so that the land will be left bare and empty, like the harvested valley of Rephaim which Isaiah's audience, the people of Jerusalem, knew so well; (iii) gleaning: which suggests the little which remains, when a harvest field

is gathered or when an olive-tree is beaten with a stick (cf.
24.13; Deut. 24.20). In v. 6 read, not 'four or five in the out-
most fruitful branches thereof' (AV), but FOUR OR FIVE ON THE
BRANCHES OF A FRUIT TREE (RSV).

7-8. The return to Yahweh

These verses seem to have no particular relevance to the
preceding sections; they describe how suffering and calamity
make people search their hearts and amend their ways. The
return here is to the Holy One of Israel; they no longer pay
any respect to forms and images which they have made with
their own hands, which means they give heed to the Second
Commandment. There is a possibility that the reference to
ALTARS, GROVES and IMAGES (AV) is a later amplification of
the original text. It seems certain that the people did not forsake all altars, nor did Isaiah command them to do so, even
if he spoke strongly against formal sacrificial worship (cf. 1.11
ff.). The word rendered GROVES (Asherim) means the wooden
posts which were erected, together with stone pillars, beside
Canaanite altars in Palestine. The latter were sacred pillars,
representing the male god Baal. The former represented the
goddess Asherah, the wife of Baal; they represented also, in
residual form as it were, the tree of life. To destroy these meant
to forsake the fertility rites of Canaanite worship; the reference
to altars, if retained, should be taken to be to these Canaanite
altars. In v. 7 the word rendered as ALTAR OF INCENSE in RSV
is a special word *hamman*, which can also mean *Hamman*, the
Phoenician sun-god. For that reason *hamman* was one thought
to mean sun-image (so AV margin) or sun-pillar, but the
accepted meaning now is altar of incense (cf. 27.9; II Kings
23.5, 11; II Chron. 34.5; Ezek. 6.4; etc.).

9-11. Whether v. 9 should be associated with 7-8 or 10-11 is
not clear. The simile 'as a forsaken bough and an uppermost
branch' (AV) obviously does not fit the clause which immediately follows it; follow the Greek version and read 'like the

cities which the Hivites and the Amorites abandoned because
. . .' The term Amorites is commonly used in the Old Testament to designate the inhabitants of Palestine when the Israelites entered under the leadership of Joshua; at other times it is
the term Canaanites which is so used. When these two are
differentiated, the latter is used of the inhabitants of the coastal
plain and of the Jordan valley, the former of the inhabitants of
the hill-country. The Hivites and the Horites are now identified, being the Hurrians[1] whose home was in northern Meso-
potamia. The influence of the Hurrians culturally in ancient
Palestine is now generally recognized. The 'pleasant gardens'
which the people planted (v. 10) were probably gardens of
Adonis, which were pots or baskets of quickly withering
flowers used in the service of Adonis (or Tammuz; cf. Ezek.
8.14), the young god who dies with the onset of the desiccating
heat of summer when nature seems dead. The cult was widespread in the ancient Near East. 'Slips of a foreign god' (AV,
STRANGE SLIPS) is a phrase parallel in significance to 'the gardens of Tammuz'. The people may use these and other
methods to try to ensure to themselves the fruits of the fields,
but all in vain; the harvest will elude them (not 'the harvest
will be a heap' AV).

12-14. No problem of interpretation arises here. THE THUNDER
OF MANY PEOPLES amassing, reminding us of the opening of
Ps. 2, refers generally to the nations, like Syria and Ephraim
(7.1 ff.) or Assyria (10.5-11), which muster their war-hosts and
try, God disregarding, to carry out their plans and satisfy their
ambitions. But as God in the beginning gained supremacy over
the great deep (leviathan, rahab; cf. Job 41.1; Pss. 74.4; 87.4;
89.10; Isa. 51.9; etc.; cf. also Pss. 93.3 f.; 65.5-8; etc.), so will
he be victorious when the nations roar like the roaring of
many waters. Like an insubstantial thing, they will be whirled
away in a moment and leave nothing permanent behind them.
    Ch. 17 clearly belongs to a time when Israel was still a

[1] See W. F. Albright, *The Archaeology of Palestine*, Pelican, 1949, p. 182.

kingdom and when Israel and Syria were in alliance, and,
therefore, to the time before 734 BC (cf. 7.1 ff.), in the early
years of Isaiah's prophetic work. It thus is earlier than ch. 7.
The sections contained in vv. 7-14 bear no evidence which
binds them definitely to that time, but they fit it very well.
Verses 12-14 have sometimes been thought to refer to Assyria
(cf. 8.7 f.), but the mention of 'many peoples amassing' pre-
vents such a restriction of the reference.

UTTERANCE ON ETHIOPIA

18.1-7

1-3. This passage is compressed, has sudden transitions of
address and is sometimes cryptic in its references, but its
meaning can be discerned with reasonable assurance. The first
clause of v. 1 presents questions at the very start. 'Woe' (so
AV) is not suitable, because there is neither pity nor condemnation here; but exclamatory words are notoriously difficult to
translate suitably into current and acceptable English usage;
often only colloquialisms reproduce the true meaning and the
proper flavour. 'Ah', 'Ha', and others have been tried, un-
satisfyingly. 'Hail' might be nearer, but it is not in common
English usage today. The initial word of v. 1 is used in the
reception at Jerusalem of a group of Ethiopian ambassadors
who, fearful of the spread of Assyria's power, must be pre-
sumed to be appealing to Jerusalem for help and offering
co-operation.

LAND OF WHIRRING WINGS suggests a land infested by insects,
subject to depredation by mosquitoes, or tsetse flies, or such
plagues. The word rendered 'whirring' is rare and uncertain
of meaning, and at least two ancient versions and the evidence
of cognate languages support another meaning, 'ship' (or
ships), which would give, suitably in this verse, 'sailing ships'
(lit. ships with wings). Verse 1, then, describes their journey

from Ethiopia down the Nile (here named 'the sea') on
papyrus vessels, which were made of papyrus reeds or bul-
rushes bonded with pitch. Egypt had (and has) a serious lack
of timber, which she imported mainly from Syria. Verse 2,
from GO, is the instruction given to the ambassadors to return
home, without any practical result achieved but with the message contained in v. 3. In v. 2 read probably, in the first descriptive phrase, A NATION TALL (lit. drawn out, prolonged) AND
SMOOTH (smooth-skinned and anointed with oil) and, in the
second phrase, A NATION MIGHTY AND CONQUERING (i.e. treading
down, *not* trodden down, as in AV), and in the last clause,
'whose land is traversed by rivers'. The message of v. 3 is to
the effect that in due course, in God's own time, a signal will
be raised (cf. 11.10; 13.2) and nations will be summoned then
to action against the foe.

4-6 constitute the second stanza of the poem. God bides his
time, watching quietly in his dwelling-place (cf. RSV), neither
hastening nor delaying. The next clause may be a simile, LIKE
CLEAR HEAT IN SUNSHINE, and like the heavy dew IN THE HEAT
OF HARVEST. This suits the verse division. As the heat and the
dew are prelude to, and prepare for, the harvest, so God is now
preparing for the harvest of the nations and the time is near.
The other interpretation is to make a full stop at the end of
the first part of v. 4 and then take 4b and 5 together: 'When
the heat is clear in the (summer) sunshine, and the dew lies
heavy at harvest time, but before the harvest . . .'. This also
gives excellent sense. The rendering in AV 'a cloud of dew'
has no meaning; take as above. In v. 5a AV is a poor rendering; read: 'But before the harvest, when the blossom is
finished and the flower is turning into a fully-formed berry
. . .' Thus the devastation falls at the most unwelcome time
(cf. Amos 7.1-3); all is set for harvest, the fruit is formed, the
time for calamitous loss seems to be past, sunshine and dew
have done their vital work; but it is now that the blow falls.
All is cut down.

In v. 6 the reference is, presumably, not to the vines, but to the Assyrians. They have been enjoying their heyday of power and are about to gather in the full harvest. Now their bodies will be left to the carrion birds and to the beasts of the field, who will make an unremitting feast of them.

7. The postlude describes how the same Ethiopia, having seen the great deliverance wrought by Yahweh, will bring tribute to Mount Zion, to the King whose is the power, the glory and the victory.

Probably this chapter is to be attributed to the time between 705 and 701 when Sennacherib was making Assyria a power feared through the Near East, or earlier, to the years preceding Sargon's invasion of Philistia when various peoples including Philistia and Judah, incited by Egypt, revolted against Assyria.

UTTERANCE ON EGYPT

19.1-25

This chapter consists of two main parts; vv. 1-15 describe a time of severe economic and social distress in Egypt when all her wise men are baffled and her rulers are resourceless, the whole situation being interpreted as a judgment upon the land by Yahweh, while vv. 16-25 contain a series of announcements about days to come when the fear of Yahweh will be in Egypt. His worship will be established there, and the great powers, Assyria and Egypt, together with Israel, will be reconciled and an alliance of friendship and peace established among them. Whether all this comes to us from Isaiah or not has been much discussed; but let us first consider the contents of the chapter.

1-15. Anarchy and confusion in Egypt

1-4 describe the swift spread of panic and confusion. It is a judgment sent by Yahweh; Egypt's own religion can bring no comfort to the people, its barrenness and inefficacy are revealed in a moment; idols and people quake in fear. There is a resultant state of confusion, strife and anarchy; 'every man for himself' becomes the motive of conduct (v. 2). Any faith they had having failed them and the whole political situation being topsy-turvy, the people revert to superstitious practices, turning to idol and soothsayer, to ghost and familiar spirit, to find guidance wherever they may (v. 3; cf. 8.9). There follows the threat of a hard overlord, as if Yahweh were bringing on their heads the penalty of the hard service they once imposed on the Israelites (v. 4).

5-10 describe how the whole economic and social life of Egypt is shaken to its foundations. The waters of the Nile (lit. 'the sea'; cf. 18.2) fail, and a noxious stench fills the land (v. 6); the reeds and rushes by the river's banks languish (v. 7); the soil in which seeds are planted is dried up and blown away (v. 7). Fishermen spread their nets in vain; the flax-workers, and the women who card and the men who weave cotton (so the Dead Sea Scroll 1Q Isa[a]; AV, 'net works') grow pale (v. 9). The meaning of v. 10 is doubtful; AV gives no sense at all. The noun in the first half (lit. 'her foundations') should probably be parallel to that in the second half, which should be rendered 'all the wage-workers'. The Greek version in the first half gives suitably 'her (i.e. Egypt's) workers', and this should be accepted, thus: 'All her (i.e. Egypt's) workers will be crushed, her wage-earners will be vexed in spirit.' The evil of unemployment is in all the land and its woes are not difficult to imagine. Thus Egypt's main industries, corn-raising, fishing and the manufacture of cotton and linen are brought to a standstill.

What of the national leaders? Any plans which even the wisest can propose are utterly useless; all wisdom is made to appear as foolishness. The counsellors of Pharaoh are chal-

lenged to declare and make known (*not* know, as AV) what
Yahweh's counsel and purpose are. Verse 13 brings the rulers
under condemnation. THOSE WHO ARE THE CORNERSTONES (SO
RSV; AV, 'stay') OF HER TRIBES is a curious expression but,
since the word rendered 'tribe' can mean 'sceptre' or 'rod
of authority', the phrase may be taken to mean 'the chief
princes of the realm'.

Zoan, to be equated with Tanis and with the city of Raamses
which was built by Semitic slave-labour (Ex. 1.11), was one
of the most ancient cities in Egypt and was a capital city (cf.
Num. 13.22); it was situated in the delta area, near the eastern
border. Noph (v. 13 AV; cf. Jer. 2.16; Ezek. 30.13; Moph in
Hos. 9.6) was Memphis, a city on the left bank of the Nile,
celebrated from early times. The result of all that has happened
is that the Egyptians are infected with a distorted vision and
with an unbalanced judgment, so that they stagger and reel
like a drunken man, and have as little knowledge of where
they are going and as little ability to arrive there. Head and tail,
prince and commoner are alike baffled and impotent (cf. 9.14).

It is not difficult to believe that this remarkable passage came
from Isaiah. More than once he warned his countrymen against
seeking a way out of their political troubles by relying on
Egyptian help (cf. 30.1-5; 31.1-3). Egypt, in Isaiah's judgment,
was weak, irresolute and divided; and the final part of the
seventh century offers more than one possible occasion for the
utterance. Ch. 20 speaks of Sargon's campaign against Palestine (711 BC) and says that he will lead away captives from
Egypt and Ethiopia in shameful procession; and we know also
that, in the case of Sennacherib's campaign ten years later,
Egypt's help was late in coming and ineffective when it did
come. It has been said that the language of the section is unusual for Isaiah, but obviously, in describing economic, political and social life in Egypt in a time of chaos, he was dealing
with an unusual subject.

16-25. Here are five short passages, each beginning IN THAT

DAY; they form a fitting sequel and a progressive climax to vv. 1-15. First, their contents must be indicated.

16-17 speak of the fear of Yahweh in the land of Egypt, and it seems clear that physical fear is meant as well as moral fear. Yahweh apparently has revealed himself as the great God who carries out his purposes (cf. 19.12); therefore the Egyptians tremble before his judgments (cf. 19.1).

18 refers to five cities in Egypt which speak the Hebrew language and serve Yahweh of Hosts, one of them being named CITY OF DESTRUCTION (AV). The reference here, it must be assumed, is not to a few cities whose people become converts to Yahweh worship and represent the first stage in a larger, even a total, conversion of the Egyptians, but to five cities of Jews settled in Egypt. The fact that the RSV reads CITY OF THE SUN arrests attention at once; indeed, the Greek version gives a different reading still, ' City of Righteousness '. What the story of these variant readings was cannot be discussed here at any length and cannot in any case be handled with certainty. The first name mentioned above stands in the accepted Hebrew text, the second is supported by a group of Hebrew mss and by several ancient versions. The probable history of the reading is that one of the five cities was named ' City of Righteousness ' (cf. 1.26); it was the little Jerusalem among them. Later the reading was altered to the Egyptian name, CITY OF THE SUN, Heliopolis, a city situated in the delta area. The reading CITY OF DESTRUCTION, which in the original is very close in form to the second, came in later, either owing to orthodox zeal for Jerusalem as the only legitimate sanctuary of Yahweh worship (cf. Deut. 12.5; etc.), or owing to hostility to Egypt, or both.

19-22 speak of AN ALTAR IN THE MIDST OF . . . EGYPT; whether or not it was in the City of Righteousness is not said. There is also to be a PILLAR on the BORDER of Egypt. Presumably this pillar is not of the type which stood by a Canaanite altar and

certainly did not have its associations. It could be a memorial
pillar set on the border of the land, but commemorative of
what? The Exodus? That is not likely, especially in this context. Since it is described as a sign and a witness, it may be a
stone in the name of Yahweh, like a boundary stone, indicating
that the land of Egypt is his. This interpretation, it may be
believed, finds confirmation in vv. 21 f. Yahweh will make himself known to the Egyptians, as he has made himself known
to Israel, and the Egyptians in that day will know him, worship him and pay their vows to him. The fact that Yahweh will
smite Egypt and will heal it is a reminder of Hos. 6.1, and
signifies that he will punish the Egyptians for unfaithfulness
and evil, but with remedial and saving purpose.

23 tells how IN THAT DAY there will be a highway from Egypt
to Assyria, friendly relations will be established between the
two countries, and, as Egypt has come to know Yahweh, so
Assyria will come and will worship with Egypt.

24-25 describe how these two great powers, which had in their
great days ravaged countries and tormented peoples, will now
be a blessing and will be joined in a triple alliance, a wonderful
league of nations, with Israel.

Now it must be admitted that, in greater or less measure, this
section has been attributed to a time long after Isaiah's day,
v. 18 in particular to a time not earlier than the sixth century
and vv. 23-25, with their conception of Yahweh as God universal, to at least the same period. A few comments only can
be made here. When, we may ask, was Judah ever a terror to
Egypt (v. 17)? Certainly not in the sixth century and not at
any time thereafter before the close of the prophetic canon of
the Old Testament. But we have argued, in connection with
9.2-7, 11.1-9 and other passages, that the deliverance of Jerusalem from danger on the occasion of Sennacherib's invasion
must have seemed a divine deliverance. It was Yahweh trium-
phant over the mighty gods of Assyria. Egypt had sent an

army into Palestine on that occasion and it, according to the Assyrian record, had been defeated at Eltekeh; therefore, themselves humiliated, the Egyptians could claim no share in the humiliation of the Assyrians. Surely there we have circumstances, within Isaiah's lifetime, which are better fitted than any other of later date to evoke the fear of Yahweh and of Judah expressed in vv. 16 f. How soon this response will take place in Egypt is not said; it will be IN THAT DAY, an undefined future.

Such a respect for Yahweh and for Judah may well have been expected to have the results specified in vv. 18-22. Verse 18 really refers to hospitality given to Jewish colonists. It is true that, as far as we know, Jewish colonists were not numerous in Egypt until the time of Jeremiah at least (cf. Jer. 44.1; etc.), and their number was greatly increased in the sixth century; but no such extensive colonization by Jews in Egypt is required to give occasion to this utterance. The Jews after 701 BC will, Isaiah believes, be received into Egypt as people whom the great Yahweh has blessed, and they will name one of their cities ' City of Righteousness ', mindful of Yahweh and his prophet (cf. 1.26).

Verses 19-22 now follow without difficulty. The Egyptians, having seen the power of Yahweh in humiliating the Assyrians, now have an altar to Yahweh in their land and a stone pillar on the border. This worship and these symbols are witnesses for Yahweh, and the Egyptians will come to know him, worship him and serve him. They will be disciplined, as the Israelites have been, but the aim is that they may be healed.

So far we have contended that the passage 16-25, at least as far as v. 22, fits excellently into the circumstances of Isaiah's time. Is the theological outlook of vv. 23-25 too advanced for him? Those who refer these verses to a later, post-exilic date, have to make the name Assyria refer to one of the powers, Babylon, Persia or Greece, which succeeded Assyria in overlordship of the Near Eastern area; such a usage, of course, is not unparalleled. But when was Egypt of such importance in

these later days as to merit the mention it receives in these
verses? On the other hand, Assyria and Egypt were the dominant powers of Isaiah's days. Egypt, it was believed, would
come to know Yahweh; Assyria, humiliated before Jerusalem,
knew him. Surely the deliverance of that city, not by force of
arms, showed the futility of men's warring; surely, the use of
Sennacherib for purposes greater than he imagined (10.5)
showed how secondary and indeterminative are man's plannings. IN THAT DAY there will be an association of friendship,
instead of a state of war, between Egypt and Assyria, both
worshipping Yahweh (v. 23; cf. 11.16). And now, vv. 24 f.
follow as the climax of the prophet's vision of things to be; it
is a picture of reconciliation and peace. For such a vision to be
real, there was needed some great occasion; nothing in the
exilic or post-exilic age before the Maccabees provides the
requisite occasion. But can it not be maintained that 701 BC
was such an occasion and it was in Isaiah's time? The con-
tention presented here is that it can.

A SYMBOLIC ACT

20.1-6

Symbolic actions are not uncommon in the prophetic ministry of Jeremiah and Ezekiel; they have a small place (the
symbolic *names* of his sons apart) with Isaiah. But here is a
notable example. The expedition by Sargon which is mentioned
took place in 711 BC.[1] Ashdod was the centre of rebellion
against Assyria at that time and Egyptian help was sought.
Aziru, the king of Ashdod, was deposed by Sargon and his
brother was put in office in his place. He in turn was removed
by the people of Ashdod, who made a certain Yamani king,
but Sargon's commander-in-chief (his TARTAN, AV, v. 1) now
captured and plundered Ashdod and Yamani fled to Meluhha

[1] D. Winton Thomas, *Documents from Old Testament Times*, pp. 61 f.

(Ethiopia, Cush) but was extradited and delivered to Sargon. Such is the historical background to this chapter (cf. also 14.28-32).

Isaiah laid aside his prophetic garb (v. 2; cf. II Kings 1.8; Zech. 13.4; sackcloth was also mourning garb) and his shoes to go about naked (i.e. wearing his loin-cloth only), as a sign that the Egyptians and the Ethiopians would thus be led off as captives by the king of Assyria (cf. 19.4). There was a strong pro-Egyptian party in Jerusalem (cf. 30.1-5; 31.1-3), but Isaiah himself put no trust at all in alliance with Egypt for the safety of Jerusalem and the welfare of Judah. He believed, therefore, that Sargon would extend the power of Assyria into Egypt, so that the weakness of that country would be revealed and her pride would be humbled. When that happened, those who had expected much from Ethiopia and had boasted of the greatness of Egypt (v. 5) would lose face, and the coastland (which must mean here not only Philistia, but Judah also) would be at a loss to find another source of help. Clearly this chapter is closely related to 19.1-15; note especially 19.4.

A MIXED COLLECTION OF PASSAGES

21.1–23.18

UTTERANCE ON THE WILDERNESS OF THE SEA

21.1-10

Ch. 21 contains three sections, and of none of them is the interpretation easy. At the head of the first, 21.1-10, is the enigmatic title, WILDERNESS OF THE SEA. Southern Babylonia (cf. 'in the south', v. 1) cannot be named a wilderness, although there is some evidence in inscriptions that it was named 'the land of the sea', being situated at the head of the Persian

Gulf. But the Greek version omits any word for sea; that is probably correct. If so, the word 'wilderness', which is used very early in the utterance, was employed in the title simply for the purpose of designating it, and not to indicate a geographical area of reference for the utterance. That being accepted, the word in the original which is translated as 'sea' may be a fragment, or a corruption, of another word; very plausibly a word which means 'roar' or 'tumult' has been suggested, to give the translation:

A roar, like the onsweep of storms in the Negeb,
Comes from the wilderness, the terrible land.

That is difficult to understand; it seems to say that the prophet is apprehensive that a storm from the wilderness is about to break upon his country; yet the subsequent narrative seems to concentrate attention on the Euphrates-Tigris plain, mentioning Elam and Media in particular. We must assume that, in such a vision as this, danger from the area of that plain is described as coming from the wilderness which lay between it and Judah rather than from the north, the usual line of approach of invading armies coming against Judah from that area.

2-5 describe a vision which is told to the prophet (v. 2). First he sees traitor (not plunderer) and destroyer working havoc. There follows the summons to Elam and Media (both of which lie east of the Tigris) to attack it and to bring to an end all the sorrow and sighing this power has caused (read, at end of v. 2, 'bring to an end', imperative). The prophet is so filled with dismay and apprehension as he contemplates what he is told that he can neither listen quietly nor see clearly, but his mind reels (vv. 3, 4a). The final part of v. 4 can mean that the twilight hour of each day, in which he used to enjoy a period of quiet thought (the house-top, evening hour) is now filled with dark foreboding and fear; or the reference may be to the

evening of his life, when the prophet had hoped for peace and
quiet and now saw that hope shattered. If v. 5 is taken as in
AV and RSV, it seems necessary to take the first part as the
description of a comparatively carefree situation (except for
the posting of sentries) within the city so soon to be besieged,
and to make the second part: 'Arise' etc. as the introduction
to vv. 6-10. But there is a preferable way:

> Setting tables! Laying rugs [for diners]! Eating and
> drinking! To your feet, you princes! Oil your shields!

Thus vv. 2-5 would finish in a call to action, dispelling all
complacency; to oil the shields was to prepare them for use.
The polishing of shields may have served two purposes: to
preserve them, if of metal, from rusting, and if of leather, from
becoming dry and friable; and to make the enemy's weapons
glance off them more easily.

6-10 then give the word of Yahweh to his prophet, presumably
relevant to the situation just described. A watch is set, to be
on the look-out for riders bearing news. The watchman keeps
constant watch (v. 8) and in due course reports the appearance
of riders who bring the news that Babylon has fallen and that
her images have been SHATTERED TO THE GROUND. We must
now conclude that the unnamed power in vv. 2-5 is Babylon.
So the prophet announces the news to his own people,
THRESHED AND WINNOWED (v. 10).

Most scholars have no hesitation in referring this chapter
to the situation in Babylon in the period between the rise of
Cyrus (Isa. 44.28; 45.1) and the fall of Babylon in 539 BC.
Babylon had been a great oppressor; it was the Persians who
brought about her downfall and they might be described as
Media and Elam. By making a separation between vv. 2-5 and
6-10, it is possible to take the first part, which is a vision told
to the prophet to whom we owe the chapter as a whole (or a
piece of news translated into the form of a vision) as coming
from someone in Babylon, presumably a Jew resident there

and mindful of the storms from the Negeb which he once
knew in his homeland of Judah. He is greatly perturbed at the
course of events, fearing a new overlord or a time of utter confusion (or both) should Babylon fall, and he calls the people
to action. But the prophet to whom that vision (or that piece
of news) is told is in Judah; he receives the word from Yahweh
to set watchmen in Jerusalem to await the news of Babylon's
fate, and in due course he announces it to his people who have
been threshed and winnowed so often in their history. This is
a plausible interpretation; it avoids the difficulty that a prophet
in Judah should be seriously perturbed at the possibility of
the fall of Babylon; if it is followed, the date of the chapter as
a whole is determined viz. between 550 and 539 BC, long after
the days of the prophet Isaiah.

It has, however, sometimes been contended that a situation
in the time of Isaiah suits the contents of the chapter. Even
then Babylonia was a considerable force; Merodach Baladan
was a resourceful and intrepid Babylonian (Isa. 39.1-4). Sargon
of Assyria did battle against this antagonist in 710 and besieged
him in Babylon. The anguish felt by the visionary to whom we
owe vv. 2-5 may, in this case, be occasioned by the thought
that if the Babylonian is overthrown, the might of Assyria will
soon be turned against the west and Judah will suffer. So
Isaiah uses the situation as depicted and, according to the word
of Yahweh to him, sets watchmen to await news of Babylon.
This interpretation, which would, of course, trace the origin
of the chapter to Isaiah, has serious difficulties in it. That the
Persians, according to the first view, should be described as
Media and Elam, is notable but not impossible; that, on this
second view, only these two should be named (cf. 13.17) to the
exclusion of the Assyrians, is, to say the least, surprising.
Again, whereas in the sixth century there were many Jews
exiled in Babylon, it was not so in Isaiah's time, so that the
source of the vision recorded in vv. 2-5 becomes very difficult
and we are forced to attribute it to Isaiah himself in an ecstatic
experience. Finally, why, on this second view, should messen-

gers from Babylon be expected in Jerusalem to record its fall;
on the first view, the fall of Babylon was an event of first-class
significance for the Jews because of their exiles long resident
there.

On all counts it must be said that while the second view as
presented is not wholly ruled out. it is beset with difficulties
to a much greater extent than the first. The fact that the style
of the chapter is unlike Isaiah, while in itself by no means
determinative, also gives support to the first view. But the
issue is not absolutely clear; see below on vv. 11 f., 13-17.

UTTERANCE ON DUMAH

21.11-12

This utterance is so short that it is cryptic. Dumah, without
doubt, is Edom, which lay adjacently south and south-east of
the Dead Sea; the Greek text confirms that, and it may be that,
Dumah meaning ' silence ', there is a play on the name. The
watchman hears a call from Seir (i.e. Edom; cf. Judg. 5.4; Ezek.
35.2; etc.) asking how much of the night still remains, and he
gives an equivocal answer, which may mean that light and
darkness, peace and turmoil are both in store. The future
prospects, as we would say, are not yet settled. But the inquirer
is not fobbed off; he is invited to come again (so the last
phrase) and inquire.

Often this little passage is associated with the preceding
verses 6-10; the question is addressed to the watchman at
Jerusalem (v. 6) before the arrival of the messengers. But there
are certain difficulties in this when they are interpreted in the
way which is commended above (see note on vv. 6-10). The
time of the Jewish exile in Babylon, which finished with the fall
of that city in 539 BC, could not easily be described as a dark
night for Edom, since she used the opportunity to extend
her territory into Judah and, as a result, incurred fierce hostility
(cf. Ezek. 25.12-14; 35.14; 36.3; Isa. 63.1-6; Mal. 1.2-5; etc.).

But if we could take the other line of interpretation of vv.
6-10, which is outlined above, the relation of vv. 11 f. to them
might appear to be close. Sargon in 715 BC made a campaign
against some Arabian tribes. We have mentioned that this
campaign may have been the occasion of the elegy upon Moab
(see note on chs. 15-16). Edom as well as Moab may have
suffered during this campaign. Now Sargon was heavily engaged against Babylon which he besieged in 710; Edom was
naturally interested in this event and inquired if this might
mark the end of the night of suffering.

UTTERANCE ON THE STEPPE (ARABIA)

21.13-17

Kedar was a nomadic tribe of the Arabian desert; Tema and
Dedan were towns of the same area, about 250 and 300 miles
respectively south-east of the Dead Sea. The Dedanites have
been apparently driven away from their usual routes and water-
ing places by the stress of war and have sought refuge in the
rock-strewn wastes (*not* thickets) of the Arabian steppe, and
the people of Tema are summoned to bring food and water to
meet their need. The final two verses say that within a year
the power of Kedar will be blotted out and only a few will
remain. ACCORDING TO THE YEARS OF A HIRELING means, one
assumes, as the years which a hired labourer reckons up with
care (cf. 16.14); a hireling will not work longer than is required
of him.

There are no clues within these verses as to the occasion
which called them forth, and in the troubled days of the Assyrian empire, not to speak of later times, occasions were not
lacking. Yet it may be observed that the campaign of Sargon
against tribes of the Arabian desert would suit very well, and
such a view of their origin might unite them with vv. 11 f.
preceding.

UTTERANCE ON THE VALLEY OF VISION

22.1-14

The title is of uncertain meaning but it is obviously derived from v. 5. The Greek version has 'the valley of Zion' and that, taken with the evidence of the contents of the passage, has induced some scholars to think that the title originally may have been the 'valley of Hinnom' which lay immediately to the south of Jerusalem. Some valley in or near Jerusalem must be referred to, not as the one in which the prophet had this vision but one which was known as the valley of vision; we have no means of identifying it.

There are two contrasts between Isaiah and the people of Jerusalem thrown into sharp relief in the passage; the one is between his sense of impending judgment and sorrow over their continued, unrepentant sinfulness and their carefree revelry and irresponsibility (vv. 1-4, 12 f.); the other is between his call for trust in Yahweh for salvation and deliverance and their trust in material possessions and in weapons of war (vv. 8b-11).

1-8a form the first section of the passage. The first two verses describe an excited, jubilant city; the people are on the house-tops, not for evening rest and social intercourse, but to see all that is happening and to share in it. Verses 3 and 4 are unexpectedly different and certainly speak of circumstances and events which should have evoked anxiety and sorrow rather than joyfulness and levity. Verse 3 itself seems to be rather confused. It is not easy to understand how the RULERS FLED and WERE CAPTURED; if they were captured in flight from the city, that is not said clearly. On the other hand, the second half of the verse says that those WHO WERE FOUND (or better, following the Greek version, ' all the mighty men ') in the city

were captured and fled afar off—a comparable difficulty. Again,
CAPTURED WITHOUT THE BOW (AV, most unlikely, 'by the
archers') is an obscure phrase; if it means that they were captured without the enemy having to use their weapons of war
against them, it is a curious use of 'bow' for this purpose; it
is a no less curious usage if it means that the fugitives left the
city unarmed. If we may take the view that it is because the
Elamites (cf. v. 6) were famous bowmen that the bow is specified, there are two ways of interpreting the verse open to us:
(a) with a variation in the order of the component clauses:
'All your rulers scampered off together, they fled far away;
all your mighty men were taken captive together, taken captive
without a bow' (i.e. without a blow being struck)—excellent
sense, meaning, as it does, that the city's leaders abandoned
the people to their fate and its warriors were ignominiously
taken prisoner; or (b) on the basis of one ancient version
which, instead of 'were captured', read 'turned aside', i.e.
departed or fled, we may translate as follows, keeping the
clauses of the verse in the order in which they now stand: 'all
your rulers scampered off together, they fled from (the enemy's)
bows; all your mighty men fled together, they escaped far
away.' In the presence of such dereliction of duty on the part
of the leaders of the people and of such a national calamity,
the prophet refuses to be comforted (v. 4).

5-8a then record the vision in which the prophet looks away
from events which have taken place to see what is in store. He
sees greater distresses still to come upon the city, a day of
tumult and confusion when defence walls will be broken down
and the cry of the besieged people will rise to the hills. Elam-
its and Kir (the latter indicating Syrians; cf. Amos. 1.5; 9.7; II
Kings 16.9) are the named enemies but the intermediate phrase
of v. 6, which reads strangely WITH CHARIOTS OF MEN AND
HORSEMEN (so AV), should be rendered 'Syria rode on horses'.
The whole country is to be devastated and the defences (lit.
covering) will be laid bare.

8b-14 form the second section of the passage; of these verses, 8b-11 are in prose and their connection with the passage as a whole is open to doubt. Verses 1-2 had described the joyfulness in the city, undisturbed by anxiety, and v. 13 returns to the same theme, so that it is certainly possible at least that vv. 8b-11 break the sequence of thought in 1-8a and 12-14. But, as they stand, vv. 8b-11 imply that the people took heed of the prophet's warning and of the national danger, and we are reminded of 7.3 which speaks of practical measures which were taken in Jerusalem when Rezin of Syria and Pekah of Israel threatened it in 735 BC. To take a census of the houses of Jerusalem in order to requisition stone for the repair of the city walls is a realistic and urgent procedure, and to increase the storage of water within the city is another. The lower pool was probably a reservoir in the lower city, and the collection of waters into it may mean that various channels which conveyed waters from the spring of Gihon, outside the eastern wall in the Kedron valley, were diverted into the reservoir. The area between the two walls was at the south-eastern corner of the city (cf. II Kings 25.4; Jer. 39.4; 52.7); the old pool (v. 11) may have been the pool in the upper part of the city (cf. Isa. 7.3), situated north of the lower one but south of the Temple area.[1]

12-14 contrasts the prophet's call to mourning and the reckless attitude of the people. LET US EAT AND DRINK, FOR TOMORROW WE DIE need not be understood as meaning that the people had a sense of impending doom and intended to enjoy themselves as long as they could; the words may simply express their irrepressible levity and refusal to take any situation seriously.

The occasion of this section as a whole cannot be defined with assurance, but one crisis which occurred during Isaiah's career comes to mind as suitable. II Kings 18.13-16 records how Sennacherib made a great assault on the walled cities of

[1] See Map 4 in L. H. Grollenberg, *Shorter Atlas of the Bible*.

Judah, including Jerusalem, and Hezekiah offered the surrender of his capital city and paid heavy indemnity. That may
have been the occasion when the leaders and mighty men fled
from the city (v. 3) and, since battle was not engaged for it,
when the prophet could speak of the slain who were not
slain of the sword or killed in battle (v. 2). There may then
have followed a period of respite in Jerusalem before the
second great Assyrian threat to it (cf. II Kings 18.17 ff.); to
this period we may attribute the reckless, carefree attitude of
the people. Their city had escaped; why should they fear
further trouble? The reference to Elamites and Syrians is difficult on any interpretation of the occasion of the passage, but a
possible explanation of it can be given in terms of the occasion
to which we have referred it. The headquarters of Sennacherib
during the campaign were at Lachish; it was a detachment of
his army which he sent against Jerusalem. This detachment
may well have been composed of contingents of Elamites and
Syrians; the latter were subject to Assyria and parts of Elam
were. The fact that the Elamites were famous bowmen (cf. v.
3) is a confirmatory detail. Whether vv. 8b-11 refer to the first
or the second assault on Jerusalem is not clear.

DENUNCIATION OF SHEBNA

22.15-25

These verses contain a vehement condemnation of a certain
Shebna who was royal steward and master of the household.
Two marks of his pride and presumption are mentioned; he
had hewn out a rock tomb for himself as if he belonged to
the old aristocracy or, indeed, as if he had greater aspirations
still, whereas he had no title to such a place of honour and
no ancestral precedent for it (v. 16); and he had developed
the practice of riding in his chariot, like an Absalom or an
Adonijah (II Sam. 15.1; I Kings 1.5). Verses 17 f. are strong

and sarcastic, and the flavour of them is caught by RSV much
more effectively than by AV. The final clause of v. 18 which
in RSV is vocative (YOU SHAME OF YOUR MASTER'S HOUSE), is
probably better united with the preceding clause to bring out
the contrast between honour and shame: ' AND THERE SHALL BE
YOUR CHARIOTS (or chariot) of honour, now bringing shame on
your master's house '. The phrase A WIDE LAND (v. 18) was
probably made intentionally vague by the prophet; it may have
been used to signify a land in which Shebna would be reduced
to insignificance, a person of no account. Verses 19-23 speak
of Shebna's successor in office, Eliakim son of Hilkiah. It is
implied that the steward had an official dress (v. 21) and he is
given a key as a symbol of his office (v. 22); the fact that the
key was laid upon Eliakim's shoulder need not mean that it
was a large key, since to lay anything (robe, yoke, or what you
will) on a man's shoulder was the symbol of laying an obligation or responsibility on him; the key, indeed, made plain the
nature of the responsibility. Eliakim, as A FATHER TO THE IN-
HABITANTS OF JERUSALEM (v. 21), was to be their counsellor
and guardian (cf. Gen. 45.8).

Between v. 23 and vv. 24 f. we must, presumably, allow for
a lapse of time, great or small. Verse 23 speaks of Eliakim as
securely established in office, while v. 25 says that the PEG
fixed IN A SURE PLACE (a figure for Eliakim) will give way under
strain; it will then be cut down and all that was supported by
it will fall with it. Verse 24 tells us what put the strain on the
peg; all the members of Eliakim's family, all the ragtag and
bobtail (which is surely the meaning of the unusual phrase
THE OFFSPRING AND THE ISSUE) are given office in the royal
household through his patronage; they are the bowls and the
basins which by their weight loosen the grip of the peg on
which they depend and bring it down.

Shebna and Eliakim are mentioned later in the Book of
Isaiah (36.3, 22; 37.2) and in the parallel passages in II Kings
18.18, 37; 19.2. From these verses it is plain that by the time
of the second threat to Jerusalem by the armies of Sennacherib

in 701 Eliakim was already in office as steward, and Shebna is
named beside him as secretary. We must, therefore, conclude
that the presumption of Shebna had become manifest before
this and it may well be appropriate to associate it with the
wealth, ostentation and irresponsibility of the leaders in Jerusalem as described in the earlier part of the chapter (cf. espec.
vv. 1 f., 13). We are left with a problem we cannot solve. In
the verses quoted at the beginning of this paragraph, Shebna
appears as the secretary, whereas Isaiah had prophesied his
utter downfall and dismissal. Was it that a compromise was
arrived at, and Shebna, while he was demoted, was retained
on the palace staff as secretary, or do the prophet's words refer
to Shebna's ruin at a later date? In all the circumstances the
former seems much more likely. There may, of course, have
been other reasons for Shebna's downfall, as, for instance,
that he was a supporter of the pro-Egyptian party in the
capital (cf. 30.1-5; 31.1-3); that is a reasonable surmise. We
may, therefore, attribute vv. 15-23 to the period just before
701 BC and associate it with the earlier part of the chapter;
but it is necessary to attribute vv. 24 f., which tell of Eliakim's
downfall, to a later date.

UTTERANCE ON TYRE

23.1-18

The Israelites often had close ties of association with the
Phoenicians from the time of King David onwards. The
Phoenicians supplied the skilled craftsmen as well as much of
the materials for the building of the Jerusalem Temple (I Kings
5); and in the days of Ahab there was an attempt, chiefly under
the influence of his wife Jezebel, a daughter of a king of Sidon,
to impose Phoenician culture upon Israel (I Kings 16.31-33).
The Phoenicians, with their successful, far-ranging commercial
enterprise, their accumulated wealth and their blatant material-

ism, represented the very type of culture against whose vices Amos in particular warned the Israelites. But it had been a most prosperous culture, one which had apparently enjoyed, if not the blessing of God, at least a remarkable degree of impunity. Its fall now, therefore, caught the imagination of the neighbouring peoples and was a spectacular example of the transience of earthly greatness (cf. Ezek. 26-28).

Chapter 23 itself is in two main sections, vv. 1-14 and 15-18. The text, especially in the opening verses, is obscure in many of its details but, fortunately, the general sense is not seriously in doubt.

1-5. Tyre has fallen

So much did the sea mean in the life of Tyre that it is the ships of Tarshish (cf. note on 2.16) which are summoned to make lamentation and not the city's inhabitants. The next part of v. 1 may be rendered in various ways: (i) as in RSV (to which AV is largely similar), the final clause meaning that as the ships, voyaging home from Kittim (Cyprus), approach the Phoenician coast, they see the marks of Tyre's destruction; or (ii) a rendering probably closer to the rhythmic form of the passage:

> 'Make lamentation, you ships of Tarshish!
>   For their home-port is laid waste.
> Their entry-port from the land of Kittim
>   has been destroyed'

(or, alternatively to the third and fourth lines,

> 'As they come home from the land of Kittim
>   it becomes clear to them').

The AV of v. 2 is very obscure. RSV should be followed; it is right in joining the first clause of v. 3 to v. 2, and in reading YOUR MESSENGERS (or 'whose messengers') in place of the AV 'have replenished'. In this verse the call is to the inhabitants of the coastlands (AV ISLE, RSV COAST), a term which probably included in its reference not only the coastland of Phoenicia but also the offshore islands of the Aegean Sea. There is an element of doubt about the rendering of v. 3 in RSV which makes the revenue of Tyre the grain of Egypt (so Shihor; cf. Jer. 2.18); the revenue of the city did not come from that one source alone. It is possible that what the original meant was that the Phoenicians were so busily engaged in commercial enterprise that they had no time for agriculture; her harvest was the grain of Egypt, not that of her own fields. The word rendered in RSV as REVENUE means 'what comes in', and so can mean 'the increase of the fields', as well as 'produce', 'income', 'revenue'. We may take it, therefore, in the first of these senses, 'whose (only) ingathering from the fields WAS THE GRAIN OF SHIHOR, THE HARVEST OF THE NILE'. But she was THE MERCHANT (lit. merchandise) OF NATIONS.

In v. 4 it is not easy to have both THE SEA and THE STRONG-HOLD (or 'fortress'; AV, strength) OF THE SEA (i.e. Tyre) as the speaker; they cannot be equated. If we consider the word 'sea' as intrusive here and make 'the fortress of the sea' alone the speaker, there is made an unexpected separation between Sidon and Tyre, Sidon being called to shame when Tyre speaks. In view of the apostrophizing of the ships of Tarshish in v. 1 above (see note), it may well be that it is the phrase 'fortress of the sea' which is intrusive, and it is the sea which speaks; in this case, Sidon represents the Phoenicians. But a question remains: Could the Phoenicians be spoken of as the children of the sea, as is done in v. 4? The term 'motherland' is commonly used of the land which nurtures a people; it was the sea which nurtured the Phoenicians. For sea-girt Tyre the prospect was seawards, wealth came from her ships; 'mother-sea' is surely a possible conception. The destruction of Tyre meant the loss of her children; now it is as if they had never been. So we may understand the perfect tenses (I HAVE NEITHER

TRAVAILED, etc.); but it is also possible to give the translation: 'No longer shall I travail' etc. When the report of it
all reaches Egypt, there will be a deep sense of loss and
feeling of anguish, not only, we may assume, at the loss
of a market for her grain, but because she too had had her
times of greatness and can feel sympathy for Tyre in her
fall.

6-9. Who humbled the pride of Tyre?

In ancient days, as today, the destruction of a land scatters
refugees abroad. The summons to the citizens of Tyre and the
coastlands (cf. v. 2) to flee (lit. pass, cross) to Tarshish (cf. 2.16)
meant that they were to seek a refuge in a distant land, but
one in which they were known. Verse 7 has a note of biting
scorn in it. Is this (the ruin-heap of Tyre) your vaunted city,
whose foundations were so ancient that you imagined it would
never perish? The last phrase of v. 7 in AV would seem to
refer to the settlement abroad of the scattered refugees; RSV
gives a better translation, making it refer to the colonizing
enterprise of the Phoenicians in many parts of the Mediter-
ranean (the word 'feet' being an example of the literary usage
termed *synecdoche*, the use of a part to designate the whole,
like the 'hands' employed in a factory). So great was Tyre's
power and prestige that she could make and unmake kings
in her colonial dependencies and her traders were held in the
highest esteem (v. 8). Yet she fell in ruin. Who could have
contrived such a fate? A greater empire to which she had to
submit? A cruel chance? The prophet's answer is given in v.
9: Yahweh of Hosts planned it and brought it about. TO
DEFILE THE PRIDE OF ALL her GLORY is a strange phrase (v. 9);
its only possible meaning is 'to desecrate (or bring to dishonour; not stain, as AV) the pride of everything in which she
gloried'; but minor modifications of form or order may give
a simpler and more likely text: (*a*) 'to desecrate all her pride
and glory, to dishonour all the most honoured (or reput-
able) men in the earth'; or (*b*) 'to desecrate her pride, to

M

dishonour the glory of all the most honoured men in the earth'.

10-14. A ruin beyond repair

10. The meaning of this verse is difficult to determine. The word near the end which is rendered as STRENGTH in AV and RESTRAINT in RSV is uncommon and uncertain. The meaning 'strength' (lit. girdle) finds some support in Job 12.21. That might suggest the translation: 'Overflow your land as the Nile [overflows its banks], ye people of Tarshish, for strength there is no more (*sc.* in Tyre)', which might be interpreted as an invitation to them to take full possession of their land in freedom from dependence on Tyre. If we translate the final clause of the verse as FOR THERE IS NO MORE RESTRAINT (so RSV), it would, presumably, be necessary to make the reference to the restrictive rule of Tyre, which is more difficult. It should be noted, however, that the Greek translation shows some important differences: it omits 'like the Nile', and the initial verb is not that rendered by 'pass' (AV) and 'overflow' (RSV) but is one derived from a very similar Hebrew form, which yields the meaning: 'Till your land, you people of Tarshish.' That would mean that, with the fall of Tyre and the cessation of her commercial civilization, Tarshish must now return to an agricultural economy. This would fit in very well with the first rendering of the final clause of the verse as given above, but not with the second; the Greek text, however, gives support for a final clause of the form 'for ships come no more' and some scholars adopt this.

11. The order of the two parts of the verse should be reversed. Begin with: YAHWEH HAS GIVEN COMMANDMENT CONCERNING CANAAN TO DESTROY her harbours. 'Canaan' rather than 'the merchant city' (AV) should be adopted; the final word could be STRONGHOLDS (as AV and RSV), but 'places of refuge' hence 'harbours' or 'havens', is also possible, and suits the context much better. Now Yahweh has claimed and manifested his rule over the sea and the changed situation among the nations occasioned by the fall of Tyre has made many of them apprehensive about the future.

12 intimates that the days of the city's triumph and glory are finished; she is now the oppressed city; even in Cyprus her inhabitants will find no place of refuge. Dependencies may be friendly to a possessing power and get satisfaction from a derived and parasitic prosperity; but when the ruling power is overthrown, they make no attempt to heal the broken body or revive the corpse; they look towards the new day, even if it begins as a day of weakness and confusion. This modern age can offer many illustrations of that.

13. The attempts to make sense of this verse have been many, and there has been no lack of plausible proposals, but it is impossible to arrive at any assured result; the verse seems to break the connection between vv. 12 and 14. As it is translated in AV, it refers to an Assyrian conquest of the Chaldeans (see Isa. 39), which has no explicit relevance for Tyre at all. The translation in RSV has relevance to Tyre, saying that it was the Chaldeans, not the Assyrians, who conquered it and made of it a ruin; in this form it has all the appearance of a later insertion which was introduced here because the prophecy of the ruin of Tyre was not fulfilled until the sixth century (Ezek. 26 ff.), long after Isaiah's time. Two small points of interpretation may be added: FOUNDED IT FOR THEM THAT DWELL IN THE WILDERNESS (AV) gives a proper translation of the individual words of the text but does not give a clear sense. The verb rendered as 'founded' may also have the meaning 'ordained' or 'destined' (as RSV) and that should be adopted; 'them that dwell in the wilderness' means either the WILD BEASTS (which take possession of ruined places; so RSV) or 'the desert demons' (which likewise possess or haunt them). In v. 14 (as in v. 11) YOUR STRONGHOLD (so RSV) or 'your harbour' can be the rendering, each designating Tyre.

15-18. The restoration of Tyre

Jer. 25.11 ff.; 29.10 speak of a seventy years' captivity in
Babylon for the Jews; seventy years is spoken of in Ps. 90.10
as the full span of a man's life. Here it is said that Tyre in her
ruins is to lie forgotten for the same number of years ACCORD-
ING TO THE DAYS OF ONE KING, a doubtful phrase which probably means ' according to the span of a king's life ' (i.e. seventy
years) or ' for the period of one dynasty '. The final clause of
v. 15 should not be taken as in AV, and RSV should be modified to give the reading ' it will happen to Tyre as to the harlot
in the song ' (lit. ' as [in] the song of the harlot '). Verse 16,
therefore, contains a snatch from an old song, telling how a
forgotten harlot tried to resume her old trade and pick up her
old customers by singing songs they once knew as her own. So,
v. 17 says, at the end of the seventy years Tyre will resume
her old trade and hire out her services to her old customers.
Thus FORNICATION (AV) and harlotry (RSV) are not to be
understood literally; the prophets, particularly Hosea, speak
of foreign alliances and traffic among the nations as unfaithfulness to Yahweh who can supply all his people's needs; it is
in that sense that these terms are to be understood. In addition,
Tyre had, like a harlot, hired her services for mercenary gain;
in the day of her restoration, Yahweh will return to Tyre with
favour, and the profits of her trade will cease to be treasured
up for selfish gain and proud boasting but it will be dedicated to Yahweh. This will be part of that tribute of the
nations to Yahweh which is spoken of in Isa. 61.6 and
elsewhere.

To what extent this chapter is attributable to the prophet
Isaiah is very difficult to determine and has been much discussed. To say that all of it is centuries later than Isaiah and
had its occasion in the destruction of Sidon by the Persians in
the middle of the fourth century BC and the conquest of Tyre
by Alexander the Great in 332 BC (as some scholars have done)
leaves unanswered the question why any Jew of that period or
later should have prophesied that Tyre should lie in ruins for

seventy years (cf. vv. 15-18), as if that were a very belated re-
compense for the seventy years of Judah's desolation and servitude in the sixth century (cf. Jer. 25.11; 29.10). There is need
to look for a much earlier date.

Now vv. 1-4, 12-14 speak of Sidon, whose associations are
with Cyprus, which also is their chosen place of refuge when
disaster befalls them (vv. 1, 12); vv. 5-11, on the other hand,
speak of Tyre, which founded its colonies throughout the
world (v. 7) and had, in particular, trade associations with
Tarshish (v. 10), to which the refugees of ruined Tyre are told
to go (v. 6). But it does not seem possible, on the basis of
these distinctions, to separate vv. 1-4, 12-14, from vv. 5-11,
because the references to Egypt in vv. 3 and 5 appear to be
correlated, and vv. 11 f., which affirm that Yahweh has over-
ruled the course of events, are in close association. It seems
necessary to think of vv. 1-14 as a closely knit section, even if
the author may have brought into association two different
historical occasions, one on which Tyre was conquered and
one on which Sidon was the victim.

The possible historical occasions are these: (i) In the reign
of the Assyrian king Shalmaneser V (727-722 BC) Phoenicia
was conquered and Tyre was besieged for five years; we must
presume that it was eventually taken because tribute was paid
to Assyria thereafter. There is no word of its destruction but
it must have suffered material damage. (ii) The so-called Taylor
Prism[1] tells how, at the end of the eighth century, Sennacherib
of Assyria devastated Phoenicia and captured Sidon, whose
king sought refuge by taking to sea. These two events took
place during Isaiah's time and seem to supply a fitting background for vv. 1-14, with the possible exception of the difficult
v. 13 (see note on that verse).

Verses 15-18, which speak of a revival of Tyre after seventy
years, read like an addition of the sixth century, probably
added some time during the siege of Tyre by Nebuchadnezzar

[1] Cf. D. Winton Thomas, *Documents from Old Testament Times*, p. 66
and plate 4.

(585-573 BC) by a reviser or editor who was mindful of such
passages as Isa. 10.12-19; 17.3; 18.7; 19.21-25; 21.16 f. Such
a date seems to receive support from the fact that the dedi-
cation to Yahweh of the profits of Tyre's commercial enterprises is parallel in thought to Isa. 45.14; 60.11; 61.6.

YAHWEH'S WORLD JUDGMENT

24.1–27.13

This section comes in suitably here after the utterances concerning the nations contained in chs. 13-23. In 24.3 ff. there is found a word which may be rendered LAND (i.e. Palestine) or EARTH, but the use of WORLD as a parallel term in v. 4 makes it clear that the chapter is concerned with a world judgment and not with one confined to Palestine.

A curse is upon the earth, it is said (24.6); the whole of nature is affected; the earth is utterly broken and desolated. This is the Day of the Lord (cf. 2.12 ff.; 10.20-27; 13.1-16; 22.8b-14), not now in the sense of a national crisis and a specified punishment by sword, famine, captivity or the like, but in the eschatological sense. The style of writing of chs. 24-27 seems, in many respects, to be different from the rest of chs. 1-39, having some of the characteristics of apocalyptic literature. Nevertheless, it is possible to discern in the transition from chs. 1-23 to chs. 24-27 how prophecy, with its distinctive characteristics, could pass easily and by imperceptible degrees into apocalyptic. Condemnation of particular peoples for their sins passes into a comprehensive condemnation of all men for their depravity and transgression; a judgment announced for specified peoples in the immediate future and in specified historical circumstances becomes a general judgment related to an undefined future. It is still the Day of the Lord, but on a grander scale. The sun, moon and stars, the mountains and the streams, etc. are now mentioned as involved in the disorder which accompanies the day of judgment, but such a conception of co-ordinate nature, animate and inanimate, was known in Israel in Isaiah's day (cf. Amos. 8.9, Micah 3.6) and probably earlier. But whether these differences of style and thought-form between chs. 24-27 and the preceding chapters lead to the conclusion that they belong to a time later than that of Isaiah is a question which is considered most suitably when the contents of these chapters have been reviewed.

PREMONITIONS OF THE COMING JUDGMENT

24.1-23

1-13 of this chapter describe the existing situation in several ways: —

(*a*) Disorder and confusion reign. The Lord will empty all in the earth as a man might empty a bottle (cf. Jer. 19.1, 7). The whole texture of human society will be loosened, the social bonds will be broken (v. 2), and the original, divinely-ordained and divinely-established order (cf. Gen. 1) will be wholly cast into confusion. This is the word of the Lord (v. 3).

(*b*) The earth itself will become dry and withered (cf. 16.8; Amos. 1.2; Hos. 4.3; etc.) under the influence of the judgment. The reference to the haughty in v. 4 (AV) is clearly out of place; the meaning of the phrase, which is literally 'the height of the people of the earth', is doubtful; the rendering THE HEAVENS LANGUISH TOGETHER WITH THE EARTH (so RSV) is very questionable. The Greek version has no word for 'people' in its translation; we should probably follow this and translate as 'the heights of the earth wilt', which should be taken literally and not made to refer to heaven on the basis of v. 21 following. But the earth is not only arid and parched; it is polluted and defiled (cf. Num. 35.33; Jer. 3.9). In other words, man is the sinner, but the penalty for his sin does not fall on him alone (cf. Jer. 4.23-26).

(*c*) For the few survivors who remain no joy is in store (vv. 6-9). In v. 6 we may translate the second clause as 'those who live in it bear the punishment for their iniquity' (cf. RSV) or ' are desolate ' (AV). The statement in the third clause of the verse to the effect that they ' are burned ' (as by fire) is possible as a translation but unlikely in the context; another translation open to us is ' are pallid, sickly ' (i.e. because of their suffering) —a fitting sense; the Greek version has ' are brought to beggary '.

Not only are there no festivities now, there is no social intercourse (v. 10), only a sullen sorrow. That the reveller should turn away in disgust from his wine cup (v. 9), while people clamour for wine in the streets (as AV, v. 11), seems contradictory; but in v. 11 the rendering should be, not ' for wine ', but ' because of wine ', which would mean that the people clamour either because the wine has failed (so RSV; cf. v. 7) or because it no longer satisfies (v. 9).

(d) THE CITY OF CONFUSION (v. 10) has sometimes been taken to refer to a particular city, although there is no agreement as to which; it is probably better to see here a proleptic use, so that the meaning of the whole clause is ' the city is broken and confusion reigns '. The term CONFUSION means one of two things; idolatry, as exemplified in I Sam. 12.21, or, in terms of Gen. 1.2, it signifies the primæval state of chaos and disorder in the world before the God-given order came into being; v. 1 might seem to support the latter . In v. 11 ALL JOY HAS REACHED ITS EVENTIDE (so RSV) is a good rendering; it is the twilight before the darkness of night comes. In v. 13 the reference is not to the land (as AV); the rendering should be THUS IT SHALL BE throughout THE EARTH AMONG THE NATIONS. For the remnant, cf. v. 6, and for the figure used here, 17.6.

14-23 alternate sharply between the praises of the redeemed and descriptions of the ruin and devastation upon the earth. In vv. 14-16, which speak of people who proclaim and praise the glory of God, there is a certain doubt as to the subject; but it must surely be the surviving remnant mentioned in the preceding v. 13, and with this interpretation the Greek version agrees. It appears, therefore, that in distant parts of the earth, presumably among the Jews resident there, there was the belief that the judgment had now passed and they rejoiced in the fact. In v. 14 RSV specifies THE WEST; that is a doubtful rendering; it is better to render the last clause of the verse as 'their cry is heard above the sound of the sea '. On the other hand, in v. 15 the AV 'in the fires' has no meaning; a literal rendering would be 'in the lands of light (*or* shining)', i.e. in the lands of the east, to which, as complement, we may read in the second part of the verse 'in the coastlands of the west'. In v. 16 GLORY TO THE RIGHTEOUS (as AV) may be used, with reference to the people who have survived the suffering and disaster; but the rendering of RSV, GLORY TO THE RIGHTEOUS ONE, is also possible. The second part of v. 16 tells how the prophet cannot share in this joy and praise; he believes that the judgment is by no means past and that sorrow and suffering are still in store for the people. 'Leanness to me' (or 'my leanness', AV) is a literal rendering of the text; I PINE AWAY (RSV) is much better. Another possible rendering, 'the secret is mine', i.e. I know the secret of what is happening, I know the truth, would imply that the prophet was aware that God would return in mercy but believed that the time was not yet.

17-20 revert to the theme of vv. 1-13. The way in which an inescapable punishment is described in v. 18 reminds us very much of Amos 5.19. Judgment comes down from heaven through its windows like a devastating rainstorm (cf. Gen. 7.11); the very foundations of the earth are shaken (cf. Ps. 11.3) and it reels in helplessness and stupefaction. The word 'cottage' in v. 20 (AV) is not right; it does not suggest instability, as is required; read rather 'watchman's hut', 'frail shack' or something like that.

21-23 are very notable in that they express ideas which are not characteristic of the prophet Isaiah. The punishment is to fall,

not only on THE KINGS OF THE EARTH, but on the HOST OF
HEAVEN. Verses 21 f. make this term have reference to the
angelic powers, but v. 23 might be construed as giving it reference to the host of heaven in the sense of sun, moon and stars
also. The angelic powers are to be imprisoned and only after
a long interval are they to receive their punishment. It is as if
the defilement which man's sin has brought to the earth has
spread to heaven also. The angelic powers may, of course, be
thought of as the guardian deities of other peoples; all these
will be made subject to Yahweh, the only true God, so that he
will reign supreme and unchallenged. Verse 23 does not seem
to speak of the sun and moon paling into insignificance before
the presence of Yahweh, but of their being put to shame as if
they were guilty; this may mean that they are mentioned here
as objects of men's worship (cf. Isa. 60.19 f.; Rev. 21.23; 22.5;
and for wider reference, I Kings 22.19; Jer. 33.22; Pss. 58, 82).
Why the ELDERS are specified alone in v. 23, to the exclusion
of kings, princes, priests, etc., is a matter of conjecture; it may
be intended to indicate a restitution of the simple form of the
Israelite community which existed at the time of the Sinai
covenant.

PSALMS AND PROPHECIES OF THANKSGIVING
AND REDEMPTION

25.1-12

1-5 contain a psalm of thanksgiving, in which God is invoked
and praised, the address being to the deity in the second person.
The tone of the psalm matches vv. 14 f. of the preceding
chapter. The general sense of the first three verses of the psalm
is clear, but some phrases call for comment. For instance, it
will be noted that in v. 1 the last words are taken as a separate
clause in AV, THY COUNSELS OF OLD ARE FAITHFULNESS AND
TRUTH, whereas RSV has PLANS FORMED OF OLD, FAITHFUL AND

SURE in apposition to the WONDERFUL THINGS of the foregoing part of the verse. But according to normal Hebrew rhythmic form, the word 'counsels' itself should be construed with the words which precede it, so that the translation may be given as 'Thou has brought to fulfilment wonderful plans (or counsels), faithful and sure from of old.' Such a translation at once reminds us of the title Wonderful Counsellor in 9.6.

The saying in v. 2, THOU HAST MADE A (or THE) CITY A HEAP (cf. both AV and RSV), is a doubtful rendering of a questionable text; and it has set commentators a search for the city which was meant, Babylon being the most frequent choice. But the collective use of the word 'city' in v. 3 suggests a similar use here, so that in English translation we should use plurals, thus: 'Thou hast turned cities into ruin heaps.'

'A palace of strangers to be no city' (AV, v. 2) also is very doubtful, and the reading of 'impious men' (so Greek) for 'strangers' does not help; but without difficulty we can get the translation 'a palace of strangers' (i.e. 'enemies', almost 'infidels') 'to be a heap of rubble' (or 'to be laid bare', cf. 23.13).

4-5 are difficult and some of the similes used seem to be quite unsuitable; e.g. 'as the heat in a dry place' and 'even the heat with the shadow of a cloud', both in v. 5 (AV). RSV rightly incorporates the first of these into v. 4; probably both belong there, thus:

> Truly thou has been a refuge for the poor,
>   a refuge for the needy in his distress,
> a covert from the storm, a shelter from the heat,
>   from the heat with storm-clouds lowering;
> for the blast of ruthless men is like a winter-storm,
>   and like heat in a sun-scorched waste.

Thus the two similes make a notable contribution to the sense of the passage; to get 'winter-storm' in place of the unintelligible 'storm *against* a wall' requires only a simple change of vowel.

Verse 5 is now left as two parallel clauses, both of which require a comment. To BRING DOWN (or to SUBDUE THE NOISE (or DIN) OF STRANGERS is a curious saying; there is an overtone in the word NOISE which will be conveyed if we render it as 'noisy boasts' or 'braggart din'. As for the second clause, it is now generally agreed that not 'branch' (so AV) but 'song' (so RSV) should be read; THE SONG OF THE RUTHLESS is silenced.

6-8 contain a great prophecy of the new age. The verses follow closely in subject matter upon ch. 24. We may infer from 24.23 that THIS MOUNTAIN (v. 6) is Mount Zion. Here Yahweh is to be enthroned again in the hearts, not only of his own people, but of all peoples, and in celebration of this a feast is prepared of rich food and choice, well-matured wine (contrast the leanness mentioned in 24.16, the distasteful wine in 24.7, 9, 11 and the rebel angelic powers in 24.21 f.). Again, 24.7 f. had spoken of the time of mourning and sorrow which the people had endured; now the 'face of the veil' (the face-veil?), the sign of mourning, will be removed (cf. Isa. 61.3). The COVERING . . . SPREAD OVER ALL THE NATIONS may mean that which prevented them from seeing clearly and turning toward Yahweh, but it is more likely that the phrase should be made parallel to the one about the veil and have reference to mourning. Thus all the peoples are to join in Yahweh's feast and share the joy of the great, festival occasion. But v. 8 has promise greater still; the days of mourning are ended, sorrow is no more; God has even SWALLOWED UP DEATH FOR EVER (AV IN VICTORY; cf. I Cor. 15.54). This is surely the hope of immortality, not because men, by their nature, are children of immortality, but because God has destroyed death. Besides, as 24.1, 3, 10 speak of confusion and disorder and all their penalties, which befell sinful men, so in the new age (cf. 24.21-23) death, one of the penalties of man's disobedience, will be done

away (cf. Gen. 3.19). For THE REPROACH OF HIS PEOPLE cf.
Josh. 5.9; Jer. 6.10; Ezek. 5.14 f.; Luke 6.22; Heb. 11.26; I
Peter 4.14.

9-12 tell of the rejoicing of Yahweh's people and the humiliation of Moab. Presumably it is the righteous in Israel who
sing: THIS IS OUR GOD; WE HAVE WAITED FOR HIM TO SAVE US.
Now they rejoice in his salvation (or victory). The hand of
Yahweh peacefully resting upon Israel is contrasted with his
hand stretched out against Moab in judgment, a judgment
which is described in a coarse, loathsome figure. To say that
Moab is to be trodden down 'like straw in a midden' (v. 10)
is a figure which will not sustain the later figure (v. 11) of Moab
swimming about in it, trying to extricate himself. We should,
therefore, follow the well-established reading, 'AS STRAW IS
TRODDEN DOWN in the slime of a midden'.

In v. 11 it is a doubtful word in the original which is rendered as 'spoils' in AV and (tentatively) as 'skill' in RSV;
the word commonly means 'ambush' or 'treachery'. It does
not seem possible to make it refer to the *skilful* strokes of the
swimmer; rather the translation should be: 'He shall have
his pride laid low, and all his treacherous tricks with it.'

It is not possible to determine the historical occasion of this
utterance; it has some parallels with 16.6-8, 14, verses of the
utterance against Moab (chs. 15-16) which may be genuinely
Isaianic.

PRAYER FOR A FULLER SALVATION

26.1-19

These verses are so closely knit together in idea and there
is so clear a movement of thought that it seems necessary to
regard them as a unity. Yet, in spite of the words IN THAT DAY
which stand at the beginning of the passage, it contains more

than a declaration of what shall be in the future. Verses 1-6 tell of the triumph of the poor and needy over a mighty city which is laid in the dust and ascribe praise to the God who secures the welfare of his faithful and steadfast people. But vv. 7-10, showing a reflective mood, express aspiration after God, the hope that his laws will be held in honour in the earth, and the belief that the wicked, who disregard these laws, will be destroyed. Verses 11-15 continue the theme of the destruction of the wicked, and then reflect how once Israel served other lords; but they are dead and Israel now serves Yahweh alone and has been blessed by him. Verses 16-19 state how little Israel, as Yahweh's people, has been able to achieve and how few children it has brought into his family of faith. Suddenly at this point, v. 19 follows with its assured belief that the faithful dead shall live, an apparently clear expression of belief in the resurrection of righteous men.

But there are certain details of interpretation in particular verses which must be mentioned.

1-6. The words ' SALVATION WILL GOD APPOINT AS WALLS and rampart' mean that the welfare of Jerusalem will never be secured by material defences but depends on God who gives it on his own terms. These terms are stated in the following vv. 2 f.; it is the righteous nation and the man of steadfast trust (cf. 1.21, 26 f.; 7.9) who will be secure and at peace. Therefore, let the people so trust God; then he will be their salvation and their enemies will be vanquished (vv. 5 f.). In v. 4 the statement that God is AN EVERLASTING ROCK recalls many passages (e.g. Deut. 32.4, 18; I Sam. 2.2; II Sam. 22.2, 32; Isa. 30.29; Pss. 42.9; 61.2; Matt. 7.24 f.; I Cor. 10.4).

7-10. In v. 7 we may say that THE WAY OF THE JUST IS UP-RIGHTNESS (so AV) or LEVEL (so RSV), but the latter is supported by the second part of the verse in which the verb, which has to do with the use of a balance, must mean either ' measure out the path of the just', (i.e. appoint it, allot it) or make it level or smooth (cf. Isa. 40.4). In v. 8 THE WAY OF God's JUDGMENTS is probably to be understood, not as the way of his punishments of which the people must learn the lesson, but the way of his laws which they must obey (so in v. 9). The second part of v. 8 means that 'our earnest yearning is to name thy name (i.e. to call upon thy name in worship) and to remember thee (i.e. to remember thy works and ways).' But will the inhabitants of the world learn to do right? Verse 10 says that, by their very nature, they cannot recognize God's favour; they have no sense of reverence or awe.

11-15. The second and third clauses of v. 11 in AV do not make sense; they may be taken in one of two ways: (a) 'LET THEM SEE (THY) ZEAL FOR (THY) PEOPLE, AND BE ASHAMED; yea, let (thy) fire consume thine enemies'; or (following the Greek version) 'let them see it and be ashamed; let (thy) zeal take hold of the rebellious people and (thy) fire consume thine enemies'. The final part of v. 13 is curiously expressed in AV; we should read it as BUT THY NAME ALONE WE ACKNOWLEDGE. The DEAD MEN who do not live (v. 14) are presumably the LORDS who are mentioned in v. 13 so that we may be reminded of 14.9 ff.; for the first part of v. 15 cf. 9.3, the increase of a people being a sign of divine blessing. The final part of v. 15 should not, as in AV, be translated so as to express the expansion of the blessed people to the ends of the earth, but, as in RSV, the extension of their territory to the ends of it.

16 is difficult to handle. First of all, we should follow the Greek version and read the verbs in the first person plural, as they are in vv. 17-18. 'We visited thee' means called upon thee, sought thy help. The next part of the verse is of uncertain meaning, 'we poured out' being very doubtful and the word rendered 'prayer' meaning 'whisper' and usually referring to enchantments. Two possible renderings may be suggested, each of them uncertain: (a) 'We uttered a whispered prayer (i.e. a muttered, almost silent prayer; cf. II Sam. 12.19;

Ps. 41.7) because of thy correction upon us'; (b) 'We were distressed because of the whisper of thy correction upon us'—a very curious and unlikely rendering.

17-18. God's people should have produced children of faith but they had failed; all their work had been vain. That being the thought and mode of speech of these two verses, the last phrase of v. 18 must be given as 'but the children of the world do not come to birth' i.e. are not begotten unto a lively faith (cf. Acts 7.38; I Peter 1.3).

19 comes in suddenly and is contrasted with v. 14. Note that we should read with RSV: THY DEAD SHALL LIVE, THEIR BODIES SHALL RISE and, later, FOR THY DEW IS A DEW OF LIGHT. The final phrase, in view of the note just given on v. 18, should be read: 'And the earth shall give birth to the shades' (i.e. the dead). It does not seem possible to limit the meaning of this verse to a hope of national revival, when the people will have a renewed vitality; rather there is here an explicit belief expressed in the resurrection; God's dew will descend upon the earth, DEW OF LIGHT (not of herbs, as in AV, in spite of II Kings 4.39, which is quoted in support) and the dead shall be raised. The faithful in Israel must often have despaired of ever seeing the salvation of God in the land of the living; here, therefore, there is expressed the conviction that they shall rise again when God's triumph is complete.

RESTORATION AFTER JUDGMENT

26.20–27.13

This section contains a group of utterances, some of which have little if any connection with their context.

26.20-21 state again that the judgment is not yet finished; therefore the people must for a little longer seclude themselves.

N

The blood-guiltiness which still lies upon the inhabitants of
the earth is to be punished, the earth itself laying bare the
evidences of bloodshed and slaughter which lie buried within
her.

27.1 continues to speak of the judgment under somewhat
obscure figures. The term Leviathan, which is derived from a
verb meaning 'to twist', refers often to the primæval sea-
monster which, according to ancient mythology, was destroyed
by the great God; the great sea which stood in Solomon's
Temple in Jerusalem was a conventional symbol of this contest
(cf. I Kings 7.23 ff.). Likewise the term Rahab is used for the
same purpose (e.g. Isa. 51.9). But the references here are probably not to that primæval contest, but to the continuing contest of Yahweh with his enemies. Rahab, or THE DRAGON,
clearly means Egypt (cf. 30.7; 51.9; Ezek. 29.3; 32.2; etc), SEA
meaning the Nile as in 19.5; in which case the elusive (AV
swift) serpent and the wriggling (AV, crooked) serpent together
signify Assyria or Babylonia.

2-6 speak of Israel as Yahweh's vineyard and remind us at
once of 5.1-5; but whereas 5.5 ff. speaks of Yahweh's punishment of the vine because it produced evil fruit, here the first
words of v. 4, which properly belong to v. 3, say that Yahweh
bears no resentment towards it. In fact, v. 4 expresses the wish
that the vine should be beset by its enemies, BRIERS AND
THORNS, that Yahweh in his zeal might do battle with them
and exterminate them—an obvious reference to Israel's
enemies. Their only way of escape from such a fate would be
if they were to be reconciled to Yahweh and to serve him.
Verse 6 now promises to Israel success where formerly she had
failed (cf. 26.18).

7-11. The interpretation of these verses is very difficult; they
have no connection with what immediately precedes. The pro-
nouns in v. 7 are undefined; the meaning is this: 'Has Yahweh

punished Israel as Israel punished her enemies? Or has Israel
been destroyed in the way in which those destroyed by her
were?' 'No' is the answer implied; Israel has been treated
mercifully. The sequel is in v. 9 Israel's GUILT WILL BE EX-
PIATED, not by the punishment which she has to bear, but by
her forsaking the cultic practices in which she has so much
indulged and by returning in faithfulness to Yahweh (for a
note on the GROVES and IMAGES of AV see 17.8).

Verses 10 f. constitute another separate fragment. The subject appears to be the city of Jerusalem. It is now desolate and
in ruins; cattle have taken possession of it, stripping bare the
trees, and women gather the dead wood as fuel for their fires.
It is possible that, at this point, in the midst of v. 11, v. 8 may
be in place. There are some doubtful words in the original
language of this verse, particularly that rendered in AV by
IN MEASURE and in RSV by MEASURE BY MEASURE; but, by very
little vocalic adjustment, we may translate the verse as a twofold question thus: ' Wilt thou (i.e. God) strive with her (i.e.
Jerusalem) by driving her away or expelling her (as a man
might divorce his wife)? By removing her with the harsh blast
of the east wind when it blows?' That question of whether
God can bear any longer with his faithless people is followed
suitably by the remainder of v. 11: 'for it is a senseless
people.' Then the answer is given that God will no longer
have compassion or show favour.

12-13, each verse being a separate fragment, are in sharp contrast to v. 11. Verse 12 tells of the threshing of the grain from
the Euphrates to the Nile, in order that the good grain, the
faithful Israelites, may be separated from the chaff (cf. Ps. 1.4);
and not one will be lost. Verse 13 tells how the wandering (or
lost; cf. Deut. 26.5) Jews in Assyria and those who are scattered abroad in Egypt will be drawn to Jerusalem to worship
Yahweh there on his holy mountain.

It is difficult to determine, and it is impossible to discuss
adequately here, how much of the contents of chs. 24-27 may

belong to the prophet Isaiah. Those in the ends of the earth
who rejoice that the judgment is past (24.14 f.) are contradicted
by the prophet who sees further sufferings in store for his
people, when the noise of their feastings will cease and their
wine will taste bitter on their lips and few will be left (24.1-13).
This might be from Isaiah and fit the situation in Jerusalem
and Judah after the emergence of the city from the dangers of
the Syro-Ephraimitic war (cf. Isa. 7.1-2 and refs. given there)
or after the surrender of Jerusalem by Hezekiah in 701 BC
(cf. 22.1-14); but certainty is not possible.

Not a few of the passages which deal with coming judgment
refer to Yahweh's enemies who are to be destroyed (cf. 26.11;
26.21; 27.1); the earth will be shaken to its foundations; it
will fall to rise no more and man will suffer an inescapable
doom (24.16b-20). These may be genuine Isaianic material,
but 27.10-11, *describing* Jerusalem as a ruin, belongs to 586
BC at the earliest. Sometimes it is said that the whole of
nature will be involved in the judgment, and even the rebellious
angelic powers in the heavens (24.21-23; cf. 26.13 f.). The full
effects of the disorder brought to the earth by man's disobedience (Gen. 3) will be worked out, and the struggle of
Yahweh against the rebellious angelic powers will issue in the
re-establishment of Yahweh as supreme. This latter doctrine
is unparalleled in Isaiah and its authorship remains in doubt.

But hope remains. Yahweh's wrath against his people no
longer persists; he will be their protector against all their
enemies (26.12-15; 27.2-6). Those of their number who are
scattered abroad will be gathered home (27.12 f.); Yahweh
will be enthroned in Zion and his laws will be made known in
all the earth. But Israel will not succeed in turning other
peoples to the service of Yahweh; man's disobedience will still
remain (26.16-19; 26.7-10).

25.1-5, which speaks of proud conquerors and cruel peoples
being brought low and cities being reduced to ruin-heaps, does
not seem to suit the time of Isaiah; but 26.1-6, speaking of
the strong city of the righteous who trust in Yahweh and of the

downfall of a high and lofty city, could readily fit the situation
in Jerusalem and Judah after the deliverance of the city when
the troops of Sennacherib besieged it (II Kings 18). And that
may likewise have been the occasion of 25.6-8, which tells of
a great feast for all peoples and the end of mourning and sorrow. It might even have given rise to the hope of the end of
death (25.8). The sudden and specific reference to Moab in
25.10-12 presents no difficulty in view of 15.9 and 16.12-14
which are genuinely Isaianic verses and speak unrelentingly of
the suffering of Moab and of more trouble in store for it. But
whether the great hope of the resurrection expressed in 26.19
comes to us from Isaiah, who can say? It is an isolated verse in
its context, but that is by no means a definitive argument. It
must have required a great prophet and, almost certainly, a
great occasion, to call forth such a protestation of belief. It may
easily be described as too high doctrine for Isaiah's days; but
that is always a precarious basis for a judgment in the case of
a prophet who was, in spiritual stature, far above the common
levels of his day.

THE RULE OF GOD AND THE
PLANS OF MEN

28.1-32.20

These chapters, which deal with the situation in Ephraim and Judah in the final quarter of the eighth century, reveal the stresses and crises of that period, the behaviour of the Israelite leaders during it and the difficulty of inducing men to obey the call to faith in God which has so much the appearance of lazy inactivity when what is so much needed is positive and resolute action by men of political insight. They are, therefore, descriptive of a type of situation which is liable to recur in any age.

THE COVENANT WITH DEATH

28.1-29

1-4 are a vigorously expressed and easily understood condemnation of the drunkards of Ephraim. There are two phrases which have been interpreted as giving these verses reference to the capital city of Ephraim, Samaria. The first is THE CROWN OF PRIDE (vv. 1 and 3) when taken separate from the following phrase, THE DRUNKARDS OF EPHRAIM (as in AV). The other is ON THE HEAD OF THE FAT VALLEY(S) (vv. 1 and 4) which gives no sense at all in v. 1. The first phrase should be taken as part of the description of the drunkards' pride and vainglory, thus: WOE TO THE PROUD CROWN OF THE DRUNKARDS OF EPHRAIM (SO RSV), ' and to the fading bloom of its vaunted splendour '. The

first part of v. 3 in particular seems to give support to the view
that the reference is to the city of Samaria, but it may refer
to the dignity assumed and the pride felt by the besotted
leaders of Ephraim as a whole.

In the second phrase it seems necessary to assume that the
word for VALLEY has come into the original for a similar word
meaning 'pride', so that the phrase meant: 'on the proud
head of overfed men'.

Two other points require comment. The force of the last
clause of v. 2 is caught in such a translation as: 'he shall
forcibly lay low on his path'. The final part of v. 4 is curious.
If it means that the man who sees the first-ripe fruit swallows
it up speedily, what is the point of the words WHILE IT IS YET
IN HIS HAND (AV)? AS SOON AS IT IS IN HIS HAND (RSV) is an
incorrect rendering. It seems that we must interpret the verb
differently, thus: 'while it is still in his hand, he destroys it',
i.e. it is so tender and immature that to handle it is to ruin it.

5-6, in their use of the terms 'beautiful crown' and 'glorious
diadem', are clearly intended to be responsive to vv. 1-4, but
there is a notable difference. In the great day when Yahweh's
kingdom of righteousness is established (cf. vv. 17 ff.), Yahweh
will be the beautiful crown and glorious diadem to the remnant of his people, and A SPIRIT OF JUSTICE to those who dispense justice (cf. 11.2) and THE STRENGTH OF THOSE WHO TURN
BACK THE BATTLE AT THE GATE—which means that he will bring
to an end all injustice and corruption in the community and
defend the people from all the assaults of their enemies.

7-13 describe the besotted leaders of Judah in much the same
way as vv. 1-4 describe those of Ephraim. The subject of the
first part of v. 7 must be the judges and the defenders of the
city gates who are mentioned in the preceding verses. They, as
well as the priests and the prophets, have, through their
drunkenness, lost all power of insight and judicial discretion.
In vv. 9-10 these besotted leaders scoff at the prophet Isaiah.

' Are we babes but recently weaned,' they say, ' that he should presume to instruct us? What he has to offer as instruction is only the childish phrases of a kindergarten primer, toddlers' rhymes '. Isaiah's retort comes back to them at once in vv. 11-13. Yahweh, who had spoken in clear intelligible language to his people that they might find rest, will now speak in a barbarous language and in a strange tongue, and all they will make out will be a little here and there, some childish phrases; and that will be their downfall. So the scoffer, who, from afar off, tries to criticize the men of faith and the faith they hold, often fails to understand that all that he can learn of the faith is but a few childish ideas which he mistakes for the whole reality.

14-22. It is such scoffers and scorners in Jerusalem who are addressed in this section. They have made what is called A COVENANT WITH DEATH and a compact WITH SHEOL. The reference might be to their spiritual degeneracy and moral corruption (v. 15 might seem to support this interpretation); but, more likely, it is to their superstitious and idolatrous practices (cf. 8.19; 19.3; 29.4) which reveal their unfaithfulness to Yahweh. According to both interpretations the contrast is with faithfulness to Yahweh, who is the giver of life. But the FOUNDATION STONE which Yahweh lays in Zion represents not only his unchanging relation towards his people, but the truth that only upon that relation can the people build their personal lives and the life of the community upon a sure foundation. He who has trust to do so shall not make haste (v. 16). The Greek version has ' shall not be ashamed '; that gives good sense, but the other is in accordance with Isaiah's teaching (cf. 8.6) and reminds us of the oft-repeated call to wait on Yahweh (cf. 8.17; 25.9; 26.8; 30.18; 33.2; etc.).

17. THE LINE is the measurer's line and THE PLUMMET is the weight attached to the plumb-line of a builder or, more likely, to a levelling instrument; but when Yahweh is wroth, JUSTICE

will be his LINE and RIGHTEOUSNESS his PLUMMET, i.e. these are
the standards and tests which he will apply.

19. The first clause should be translated: 'whenever it passes,
it will take you'; and the final one, which is not intelligible in
AV, should be translated as: 'to understand the message will
bring only dismay' (or, as RSV, WILL BE SHEER TERROR).

20 is undoubtedly a proverb. The wicked have made their bed
and, perforce, will have to lie on it; but they will find no rest
on it (cf. v. 12) nor sufficient covering. For the significance of
Perazim (v. 21), cf. II Sam. 5.20 (I Chron. 14.11 f.), and for
Gibeon, II Sam 5.25 (I Chron. 14.16). The second part of v. 21
is expressed notably; Yahweh will rise up in his wrath, TO DO
HIS DEED—STRANGE (to him) is the deed! and to perform HIS
WORK—foreign (to him) is the work!—i.e. to punish his own
people (cf. Amos 3.2). In v. 22 'a consumption, even determined' . . . (AV) is ill expressed; A DECREE OF DESTRUCTION
(RSV) is clear; probably better is 'a decree of final destruction'.

23-29 contain a parable from the fields. Verses 24-26 are concerned with ploughing, harrowing and sowing. A farmer, it is
said, does not plough and harrow for the sake of ploughing
and harrowing; these are the ways in which he prepares the
soil to receive the seed. So Yahweh's judgments, which often
break and bruise men, should prepare the hearts and minds of
men to receive the seed of his Word (cf. Matt. 13.1-23; etc.).
Verses 27-29 speak of threshing the harvested grain. The
threshing is not uniformly done with the same instruments in
every case; dill (so RSV; or fennel) would be ruined with the
use of a threshing sledge on it, as would cummin if a wheel
were applied to it; these are annually sown herbs, tender and
soft; light instruments, such as a flail or a rod, must be used for
them. In v. 28 the first phrase is often taken interrogatively ('Is
bread-corn crushed?'), to avoid any contradiction with the
final part of the verse. That is possible. If we take the first

phrase as a categorical statement (as in AV), we must understand the grain is not *crushed* by repeated threshings nor by
rolling the wheel of a cart over it, but by an altogether separate
process. The last phrase in v. 28 is doubtful; horses, rather than
horsemen, should be the translation (so RSV); but there are
two objections even to the use of horses here. Firstly, they
were not used to draw a cart, but for riding or for drawing
chariots; secondly, WITH HIS HORSES belongs rhythmically to
the final clause (as AV has it). The suggestion has been made
that, by adopting a slightly modified reading, we may render
the second half of v. 28 as

> ' he rolls the wheels of his cart over it,
>   and spreads it out, but does not crush it.'

Thus these verses show, by the use of some of the processes
of husbandry, that Yahweh does not punish indiscriminately.
His punishment is intended to prepare men to work and to
serve, and to produce a harvest of good for the welfare of their
fellow-men.

YAHWEH'S PURPOSE FOR JERUSALEM
29.1-14

1-4. The name Ariel which is used in v. 1, 2 and 7 is clearly a
name for Jerusalem. The significance of the term has been
much discussed, but such verses as Gen. 46.16; Num. 26.17; II
Sam. 23.20, which are sometimes cited as providing helpful
evidence, have little to contribute. Two possible meanings may
be suggested: the form of the word yields most easily the
meaning ' lion of God ', but that seems completely unsuitable
in the final clause of v. 2. The second possible meaning is
' altar-hearth '. This finds support in the Moabite Stone[1] and

[1] Line 13; see D. Winton Thomas, *Documents from Old Testament
Times*, p. 197.

Ezek. 43.15 f., and it suits v. 2, in which the final clause would
mean that Jerusalem, in the day of its suffering and distress,
would be an altar hearth, not for the animal sacrifices of the
people, but for the sacrifice of the people themselves in the
great act of judgment.

The second sentence of v. 1 seems to mean: ' Let the years
come and go and let the festivals run their course.' That may be
intended in sarcasm, to the effect that, however religious the
people may appear in their attitude and however carefully they
may observe the forms of Yahweh's service, yet the distress
will come. Verses 3-4, which reflect the situation in Jerusalem
and Judah at the end of the eighth century, describe how the
city is besieged by the Assyrians, and the people are crushed
to the dust until their voices, as they lie prostrate, sound like
the eerie whisper of a ghost (cf. 8.19; etc.).

5-8. In these verses, which complete the first section of the
chapter, a question of interpretation presents itself. In the
original text there is no word having the force of MOREOVER
(AV; RSV BUT). The question, then, is this: Do vv. 5-8 continue the description of the devastation of Jerusalem or do they
speak of a deliverance of Jerusalem by Yahweh of hosts?
According to the former line of interpretation, the Assyrians
advance on Jerusalem as irresistible clouds of fine dust or
driven chaff, so that the city is suddenly visited (i.e. punished)
by the Lord of hosts as with wind and tempest. The whole
experience is like a bad nightmare to the people of the city.
According to the latter, the Assyrians will be like fine DUST
and driven CHAFF, i.e. will be driven away (the normal use of
this figure), and sudden deliverance will come for Jerusalem
when it is VISITED (for deliverance—not the usual meaning of
the verb) by Yahweh with his mighty weapons. Then the
enemy will awake as from a dream; they had expected plunder
in abundance (eating and drinking, v. 8) but they will be sent
empty away.

As has been noted incidentally, each line of interpretation

encounters difficulty, but the suggestion has been made that
the portion of v. 5 down to 'like driven chaff' (AV, AS CHAFF
THAT PASSETH AWAY) should be read after v. 6. If this is
done vv. 1-6 (minus the deferred portion of v. 5) refer to
the destruction of Jerusalem, and the deferred portion of
v. 5, together with vv. 7 f., refer to the deliverance of the
city.

9-14. A people blind and insensible

These verses speak bitingly of a people who have become
dull and lethargic, insensitive and insensible, and whose leaders
have lost both vision and wisdom. They seem to follow the
preceding verses in close sequence. The first words of v. 9 are
most strictly rendered as: 'linger on and be dumbfounded,
besmear your eyes and be blind'; but a very similar text would
give to the first of these clauses the meaning: 'be bewildered,
and dumbfounded', which is a better parallel to the second.
The words are, of course, spoken in bitter irony and prolepti-
cally, the full value of them would be: 'continue in your obtuse ways, and you will become more and more bewildered, be-
fuddled and blind' (cf. 6.9-10). The people are in a stupor
from which they cannot be awakened; vision has forsaken the
prophet and insight the seer. There is no longer any man who
can interpret the meaning of a vision; it is sealed away in
impenetrable mystery (cf. Dan. 2.4; 5.12, 15; etc.; Rev. 5.1-9;
6.1-3; etc.).

To DRAW NEAR (v. 13) means to worship; the people's worship has now become formal and hypocritical; religion for
them does not mean a living experience but a code of conventional practice which is part of the tradition into which they
have been born. This traditional inheritance, which might have
prepared the people to enter into the realities of religious faith,
has been accepted as something to be formally honoured and
as efficacious in itself—a process which can be illustrated frequently in human history. In these circumstances God will
again work wonders and marvels upon his people which will

be too great for wise men to understand or men of understanding to explain.

THE THIRD WOE

29.15-24

The people who are described as laying deep plans which they hope will not be seen by Yahweh are those spoken of in 28.7-22, 30.1-5 and 31.1-3 who seek security in alliance with Egypt against Assyria. The hope that they will escape notice is utterly vain; a man ought not to imagine that he can both disown his Creator and outwit him (vv. 15 f.). To imagine that is supreme folly, greater even than that of the fool who, in his foolhardiness, says that there is no God (Pss. 14.1; 53.1). 'You turn things upside down!' (v. 16) means: 'The perversity of all your thinking! You the masters of the world, and God, according to your thought of him, blind and unregarding.' (For the figure of the potter and his clay, cf. 45.9; 64.8).

17. Many scholars find in this verse an ascending climax; nature is transformed, Lebanon becoming a garden-land, and the garden-land a forest. But, since Lebanon means the cedars of Lebanon, there cannot possibly be an ascending climax in the clause in which it occurs. It seems necessary to use the translation 'thicket' (cf. Hos. 2.12) rather than 'forest' and understand the verse to mean that Lebanon, glorious with cedars, shall become grassland, and the grassland shall become a thicket; in this case the verse refers to the devastation of the land which precedes the restoration which is spoken of in the following verses.

18-21. Thus punished and humbled, therefore, THE DEAF SHALL HEAR when A BOOK is read to them and THE EYES OF THE BLIND

SHALL SEE (not 'look', as AV) OUT OF (THEIR) DARKNESS and mirk (cf. vv. 10-12). The meek and the poor mentioned in v. 19 are the remnant of the people who survive the judgment; they will once again rejoice in Yahweh. The ruthless tyrant and the scoffer are cut off (v. 20; cf. 25.3 f.; 28.14, 22); those who watch for iniquity are the ill-intentioned and malign (cf. Mark 2.3; 12.13). The clause which is given in AV as THAT MAKE A MAN AN OFFENDER FOR A WORD (v. 21) is legitimately taken so and means that even a simple word, spoken without malice or ill-intent, may be adjudged an offence. But the last part of the clause could be rendered as in RSV as BY A WORD, in which case the reference would be to slanderers, informers, traducers and the like. The remainder of v. 21 speaks of those who lay a trap for the man who prosecutes (or rebukes) them in the assembly of the elders at the gate, and those who deny an innocent man his right without a cause. In other words, the offences mentioned in 20b and 21 are offences against the moral law.

22-24 seem somehow apart from the preceding verses. It is only in late literature that we have references to any experiences which could possibly be described as a redemption of Abraham (cf. Book of Jubilees 12; Targ. on Gen. 11.28); but these passages are too late to have any relevance for a passage in a prophetical book of the Old Testament. There seem to be two possibilities; there may have been some incident in Abraham's life which was termed his redemption but of which no record is found in the Old Testament; alternatively, the name Abraham, as used here, may refer to the people commonly named Israel, but it must be admitted that that is a usage not elsewhere found within Isaiah 1-39.

The translation in AV and RSV of the first part of v. 23 is possible but ill-expressed; it says that when Jacob SEES HIS CHILDREN, THE WORK OF God's HANDS, gathered around him once more, he will acknowledge that the time of God's favour has returned. In consequence, all his arrogance and unbelief will cease (cf. vv. 15 f.) and he will again honour the holy God and recognize his own creatureliness before him. The other possible interpretation is that which regards the pronoun HE and HIS CHILDREN as in apposition, the latter acting as a closer definition of the pronoun; in this case the meaning would be: 'For when he, i.e. his children, see THE WORK OF MY HANDS, THEY WILL SANCTIFY MY NAME'. This makes a smoother translation. In v. 24 the people who erred in their spirit are those who were led astray by a spirit of falsehood (cf. vv. 13, 21) and those who murmured are either the rebellious or the slanderers (cf. vv. 15 f., 20).

ISRAEL AND THE GREAT NATIONS

30.1-33

1-5 tell of a Judaean alliance with Egypt. Such a move is condemned not only politically, since Egypt would make use of such an alliance for her own ends and without regard for the welfare or even the survival of her ally, but also because it is an act of distrust in Yahweh and in his power to care for his own people in all their need. This plan for an Egyptian alliance is not sanctioned by Yahweh (v. 1). The phrase 'cover with a covering' (AV) has no obvious meaning; the RSV rendering MAKE A LEAGUE is derived from a text whose literal rendering is 'pour out a libation', which is then interpreted to mean the libation which sealed the compact or league. It is doubtful if a libation was used for such a purpose, so that it is preferable to take another line of interpretation which is open: 'weave a web', i.e. devise schemes, engage in intrigues. In v. 2 the translation TO TAKE REFUGE IN THE PROTECTION OF PHARAOH (RSV) should be adopted. The fact that the Egyptian princes came to Zoan in Lower Egypt and the ambassadors to Hanes or Anusis in Middle Egypt might simply mean that they met the Judaean envoys there. But it also shows, at least incidentally if no more, that the reigning Ethiopian dynasty in Egypt effectively ruled the delta area and, therefore, must have been powerful.

6-7. The southern part of Palestine, the Negeb, was a parched, inhospitable and hazardous land which was believed to be inhabited by demons and malign powers (for 'flying serpent', cf. 14.29). It was, therefore, through such an area that the beasts of the south had to carry the gifts to Egypt to curry favour there and to procure Egyptian help (v. 6). In v. 6 read ON THE HUMPS OF CAMELS, as in RSV. The opening phrase is uncertain of form but its general meaning is not in doubt. 'Utterance concerning the beasts of the south' does not introduce a condemnation of these beasts, in the manner of the use of comparable phrases in chs. 13-23, but that fact does not mean that emendation must be made in the form of it. Verse 7 shows that the two verses are to be associated with vv. 1-5 in their reference to Egypt. The final phrase of v. 7, as it is in AV, has no meaning; RSV should be followed: RAHAB WHO SITS STILL, a title of Egypt. The name Rahab was used of a mythological monster of the deep (cf. Leviathan in 27.1) but here, and elsewhere, is used of Egypt; since the word etymologically means 'storm' or 'violence', the name RAHAB WHO SITS STILL is incongruous and contradictory; but it is justifiably used of a country which promises but never acts in fulfilment of the promise.

8-17. In quietness and in trust

Ch. 8.16-18 refers to the making of a record of some of Isaiah's utterances; in v. 8 reference is made to another comparable occasion. The record is to be written BEFORE THEM, so that they may be witnesses. The phrases used are WRITE IT ON A TABLET and 'INSCRIBE (or engrave) IT on a document'. In the second phrase the verb often means 'to engrave', as upon rock, but the noun which is related to it means normally a scroll or book. It is difficult to confine the second phrase to the writing of something very brief, as the first phrase would imply; rather we should think of it as a primary collection of some of Isaiah's utterances, most likely part or the whole of what is contained in chs. 28-32. (The use of the undefined 'it' in v. 8 reminds us of a similar use in Amos 1-2.) This record is to be a perpetual testimony (RSV, rightly, A WITNESS FOR EVER) that the people have been disobedient and rebellious (v. 9) and that they have tried to corrupt the prophets, tempting them to give pleasing answers and spurious visions and not the true word from God (vv. 10 f.; cf. Amos 2.12; Micah 3.5 f.). The last clause of v. 11 is not a call to Isaiah to make Yahweh disown his people but to cease proclaiming the Holy One of Israel to people who refuse to heed his judgments.

Because they do not heed God but rely on their own iniquitous ways for support, they will not find it, because their iniquity will be like a bulging wall which threatens imminent disaster (v. 13). Verse 14 seems to say that the wall does not fall in ruin of itself, but is broken down by God; rather follow the manner of translation in RSV, 'the breaking of it is like the breaking of a potter's vessel, shattered unsparingly, so that not one fragment remains large enough to gather ashes from a fire or scoop water from a cistern! '

15-17 seem to supply a second answer. They contrast in memorable language the salvation which comes from trust in God and that which is sought by the plans and contrivings of men. IN RETURNING AND REST means in returning to God in trust and in relying on him, as opposed to running off to Egypt and relying on her military aid. Verse 16 speaks of the fate of those who try to secure their own safety. The second half of the verse is clear; those who try to get away on swift mounts will be pursued by an enemy equally swift or swifter. The first half is not so clear; the attempt has sometimes been made to translate it as 'No, but we will take to (or fly to) horses; but you shall flee (or be put to flight)'. But that is very questionable; it is the same verb 'flee' which is used in both parts (see

o

AV). We may suggest this meaning: 'No, but we shall flee (and escape); therefore, you shall flee (in rout).'

In the day of God's blessing 'a little one shall become a thousand and a small one a great nation' (Isa. 60.22), but now A THOUSAND SHALL FLEE AT THE challenge OF ONE. The next phrase may mean 'and at the challenge of five, [a people as great as] you will flee', until all that remains of you is LIKE A FLAGSTAFF ON THE TOP OF A MOUNTAIN, or like a post on a hill.

18-26. The God who waits to be gracious

Verse 18 speaks of the patience of God in face of the wilfulness and lack of trust described in the preceding verses. It is not that God 'will wait' (AV) in the sense that he will delay to be gracious, but that he waits patiently, in the hope that the people will return (cf. v. 15). The statement that 'God will be exalted, that he may have mercy upon you' is not easy; probably we should consider that the verb rendered here as 'be exalted' has the meaning 'desire, yearn' which is to be found in Arabic; that would provide an excellent parallel to the first clause. If, therefore, God so waits patiently for man, man must learn to wait with trust upon God (vv. 18 f). THE BREAD OF ADVERSITY AND THE WATER OF AFFLICTION (v. 20) may be regarded as prisoners' fare (cf. I Kings 22.27); or the words may remind us simply of such a phrase as 'my tears shall be my meat day and night' (cf. Pss. 42.3; 80.5). The word TEACHERS (v. 20) may refer to the prophets who, once persecuted and silenced, now appear in public once more; but the singular TEACHER (so RSV), meaning God, seems much more suitable. Such a use may seem to contradict the statement found elsewhere in the Old Testament (cf. Ex. 33.20; Isa. 6.5; cf. Rev. 1.17) that man cannot see God's face and live, but the meaning probably is that man will once more see the works of God. Verse 21 gives a beautiful description of the fatherly care of God. When the people return to God, they will deface the silver and gold overlay of their images, despising them, and casting them away (or loathing them) as unclean; the last phrase of the verse can be either 'thou shalt bid it be gone' or 'thou shalt call it filthiness'.

23-24 speak of the return of fruitfulness and of bumper harvests to the fields. The verb 'ear' (AV) is used in an obsolete sense meaning 'plough'; 'clean provender' (AV) should be read SALTED PROVENDER (as RSV). SALTED PROVENDER was the best kind (cf. Job 6.5); presumably the grain crop was so heavy that even the finest of it could be used as feeding for cattle.

25-26 describe the response of nature, the streams on the hills and the enhanced brightness of the sun and moon. It is doubtful if, in this context, these natural manifestations should be regarded as preternatural signs such as are to be found in apocalyptic literature. They are rather intended to describe in somewhat hyperbolical language how the effects of the new day will be found throughout the realm of nature. Nor should it be thought that these verses show a delight in material benefits which betokens a rather low conception of the benefits which God bestows upon his faithful people; rather were they regarded as part of a greater whole, of a complete renewal of man and all creation.

27-33. Judgment on Assyria

The first two verses speak of the anger and indignation of Yahweh as he comes in anger from afar (i.e. Sinai or heaven) to judge nations with the sieve of annihilation and to misguide them to their destruction (contrast Hos. 11.3 f.). That God should misguide men or lead them astray is theologically unacceptable to us; but it can be understood as a way of expressing an inescapable destruction and doom. The expression THE NAME OF YAHWEH (v. 27) has the same value as the divine name by itself, although the day was to come when men, in reverence, were to speak of 'the name' rather than use the divine name. Note that not yet in these verses is Assyria specifically mentioned. Whereas many scholars think that v. 29, which

comes in very suddenly, should be read with v. 32 and refer
to a festival celebration after the destruction of Assyria, it may
be taken where it stands and refer to the jubilation felt by
Judah at the fall of Assyria. What festival is in mind as representing the gladness and rejoicing of the people's deliverance
is not clear; a night festival might suggest the Passover, but it
speaks of deliverance rather than joyfulness; a much more
gladsome occasion was the autumn festival of Ingathering,
when the vintage was gathered in.

Verse 30 continues in the line of 27-28; 'the lighting down
of his arm' (AV) means the alighting or fall of it, to strike,
while 'scattering' should be rendered as 'cloudburst'. Verse
31 speaks specifically of the Assyrian, and it is clear that the
utterance suits the circumstances of the period around 701 BC;
the last phrase of the verse should probably be read as 'struck
down with the rod'. In v. 32, whose meaning is not free from
uncertainty, 'grounded staff' (AV) makes no sense; the change
of one letter in the original yields this meaning: 'Every blow
(lit. passing) of his staff of correction which Yahweh lays upon
him (i.e. Assyria) shall be to the accompaniment of tabrets and
harps.' The final clause of v. 32 is very doubtful; 'and in
battles of shaking will he fight with it' (AV) might signify
convulsive battles, battles which shake the earth. 'In battles of
brandishing' has been suggested; that is legitimate and would
more or less mean 'with brandished weapons', but it does not
seem to say much. The clue to the interpretation may lie in the
fact that the word translated 'shaking' or 'brandishing' is
often used in a ritual sense, signifying a so-called heave-offer-
ing; this is especially relevant in view of the reference to
Topheth in the next verse. An expanded form of the meaning
might be: 'They shall be swung on the altar as offerings in the
war in which he will fight with them.' Abbreviated it might
be: 'In holy war he will fight with them and make them a
sacrifice.' Topheth (v. 33) was the place in the valley of Hinnom where sacrifices were made to Molech or Melek (king).
Both forms, Topheth and Molech, are forms expressing con-

tempt, having been given the vowels of the Hebrew word for shame (*bōsheth*). The meaning of Topheth is 'hearth'. Here therefore, where sacrifices were commonly made to Molech, would the great king of Assyria himself be sacrificed; and the breath of Yahweh would kindle the fire (or keep the fire aflame).

EGYPT'S VAIN AGGRESSION AND ISRAEL'S VAIN HELP: YAHWEH THE ONLY DELIVERER

31.1-9

1-3. The Egyptians are men and not God

Verse 1 speaks again of the old conflict between reliance on armaments and trust in the living God (cf. 30.1-5; 36.8-9). The Canaanite chariots in the days of the Judges had struck terror into the hearts of the Israelites until Deborah and Barak gained a notable victory over them by the banks of the river Kishon (Judg. 5.19 ff.); Solomon had given his great kingdom chariots and horses (I Kings 4.26; 9.19; 10.26); Elijah and Elisha had been described as the chariots and horses of Israel, its true defence (II Kings 2.12; 6.17; 13.14). Yet in Isaiah's own day Ahaz had sought help in an extremity from Assyria (cf. II Kings 16.5-9), and now the cry for help had gone to Egypt.

Such defence and armaments seemed to be practical politics; they were considered the only wise and responsible policy for statesmen to pursue. But Yahweh also is wise (v. 2), and his word of judgment which has gone forth will not be recalled. He is about to take action against the faithless people who could not trust in him and against their helpers. Here Judah and Egypt are joined together in the one condemnation; helper and helped will perish together. Human instruments cannot prevail against the will of God (v. 3); when Yahweh puts forth his hand, he works his will.

4-9 concern chiefly the Assyrians. The interpretation of v. 4 is disputed. To interpret the verse to mean that Yahweh will come down undeterred and unfrightened by the noise of the shepherds who would drive him away, and defend his city and his people, is to make an impossible use of the figure of a ravenous lion which is devouring its prey. Rather the interpretation must be that the lion represents the Assyrians who have devastated Judah and are ready to devour Jerusalem; the shepherds are the Egyptians who have come to aid Judah and have succeeded only in making an ineffectual noise which has not deterred or troubled the Assyrians. In such a situation Yahweh COMES DOWN UPON (*not* against) MOUNT ZION to deliver it. Human help has failed; only Yahweh can save. In v. 5 the figure changes; as birds hover over their nest in a time of danger to care for their young and to defend them, so Yahweh hovers over his city with loving care and will not forsake his people, faithless though they have been (cf. 8.8).

6-7 give a sudden call to Israel to return to him against whom they have so grievously revolted. In response they throw away their idols—not for the first time (Gen. 35.2; Josh. 24.2, 23; Judg. 10.16; I Sam. 7.3; Isa. 2.20; 30.22). The temptation to revolt continually returns and assumes many forms; hence the constant need to return to Yahweh with contrite heart.

8-9 tell of the fall of Assyria. It is not the work of men's hands, nor a victory won in battle. The Assyrians flee ignominiously, the flower of their army being taken prisoner; the proud Assyrian warriors become panic-stricken. The meaning of HIS ROCK (v. 9) is uncertain; probably it is to be understood as having a meaning parallel to HIS OFFICERS in the next clause; 'his god' and 'his leaders' have been proposed. 11.12 (cf. also 30.17) might suggest that the ENSIGN or STANDARD which is mentioned in v. 9 is the one which Yahweh raised for his people, and that it was from it that the Assyrians fled; but there is no evidence that the word 'terror' in the same verse

was used as a title of Yahweh, so that we should follow the
translation in RSV. The FIRE of Yahweh IN JERUSALEM may
refer to the altar fire in the Temple (cf. 6.6 f.); but since Yahweh was believed to reveal his presence in fire (cf. the revelation to Moses on Sinai and to Elijah on Carmel; and see Zech.
2.5), it might signify simply his presence in the city and among
his people. The term FURNACE might seem to suit the latter
interpretation better (cf. Gen. 15.17). The circumstances of the
deliverance of Jerusalem as described here remind us very
much of what took place in 701 BC, when the Assyrians, having
defeated an Egyptian army which was on its way to help
Judah, themselves vanished from before Jerusalem without
having suffered defeat in battle, so that the people of the city
must have seen the event as an act of God.

JUST RULERS IN A JUST AND HONOURABLE COMMUNITY

32.1-20

The chapter is in three sections, of which the second and
third are closely linked together. Verses 1-8 speak of righteousness enthroned; 9.14 describe the women of Jerusalem, com-
placent in their arrogance; and 15-20 tell of the effect of the
Spirit in the new age.

1-8. Righteousness enthroned

Verse 1 states that the foundation of the new age will be
a just government and an honest, fair-dealing ruling class.
Verse 2 may be taken, as in AV, to refer to a re-awakened
sense of social responsibility and of mutual helpfulness in the
community among all the members of it; RSV sees its reference as more befitting the KING . . . AND PRINCES mentioned
in v. 1, so that the meaning is that the rulers will exercise a
benign and protective influence (i.e. ROCK, COVERT, shelter) and

will infuse a new sense of life and vitality (i.e. STREAMS OF WATER).

The effect upon the populace in general will be immediate and positive. There will be a new social concern and thoughtfulness. People will no longer shut their eyes and ears to the needs of their neighbours (v. 3), and the rashly blundering will become considerate and prudently thoughtful (v. 4). The stammerers are not those who suffered from a physical defect of speech, but are the annoying mumblers who hum and haw and will not SPEAK PLAINLY. And quite as important in this new age: there will be a true sense of values; THE FOOL will no longer be treated as if he were a man of noble character, nor will THE KNAVE be called a man of honour (cf. 5.20). The fool spoken of here is not simply the dullard and the dolt, but the impious fool, as is made clear in v. 6.

Verses 6-8 seem somewhat expansive in style after the verses which precede them; they describe some of the characteristics of the fool and the knave, making the former out as one who not only speaks folly, but is actively pernicious and corrupting (v. 6), while the latter has no sense of justice or decency but is prepared to deceive for any selfish end. The liberal is liberal not only in his judgments but in all his actions, and is incorruptibly so.

9-14. The women of Jerusalem

In 3.16–4.1 Isaiah denounces the fastidious, wealthy, wanton women for their pride and arrogance; here women of the same breed are rebuked and bidden forsake their careless, self-assured ways, because IN LITTLE MORE THAN A YEAR (RSV. rightly) their joy will be turned into trembling. The vintage will have failed and no harvest will have been gathered in from the fields. The call to them to tremble and shudder (v. 11) is because their careless routine has been broken; they are to strip themselves and wear sackcloth, not, apparently, to bring shame upon themselves—which might have seemed warranted—but as a sign of mourning. The first phrase of v. 12 is difficult;

'they shall lament for the teats' (AV) seems quite unsuitable
if it has reference to the women; but the verbal form is mas-
culine here, and it has been proposed that a slight vocalic
change should be made in the noun, and the phrase then given
general reference: 'Lamentation shall be made for the fields.'
That makes good sense in terms of the sequel, but it would
undoubtedly be better if the reference could still be specifically
to the women. It is interesting therefore, that the Dead Sea
Scroll, 1Q Isaᵃ, reads the verbal form as a feminine imperative;
that gives the translation which should be followed: 'Beat
(in mourning) upon your breasts.' The rest of v. 12 and v. 13
tell that the lamentation is for the THORNS AND BRIERS which
now grow upon fields formerly fruitful and pleasant; the first
part of v. 13 should be taken as in RSV: FOR THE SOIL OF MY
PEOPLE GROWING UP with THORNS AND BRIERS. Barren fields and
a deserted, desolate city—that is the picture. THE HILL (AV
FORTS) mentioned in v. 14 is Ophel, the southern end of the
ridge on which the Temple of Jerusalem stood; what feature of
the city was designated the WATCHTOWER is now unknown. The
unoccupied city will have WILD ASSES as tenants, and FLOCKS
will feed among the ruins.

15-20. The effect of the Spirit in the new age

This section is in some ways parallel in thought with 29.
18-24, and for occasion is to be associated with vv. 1-8 and
attributed to the final period of the prophet Isaiah's ministry;
the intervening verses 9-14 belong to a much earlier period,
probably to the reign of Ahaz, king of Judah, like several
passages in ch. 5. It is the outpouring of God's Spirit which
produces the conditions of the new age (cf. 44.3; 61.1; Ezek.
39.29; Joel 2.28 f.; Zech. 12.10; Acts 2.1 ff.); it is life-giving,
vitalizing power. The effect of this outpouring of the Spirit is
a new fruitfulness in nature and a new state of well-being and
security in human society. Verse 15 is substantially paralleled
in 29.17, but there are differences. Here it is the wilderness
(Lebanon in 29.17) which is to be transformed into garden-

land. The next clause may mean that in the new conditions the garden-land will be so productive that it will be as valuable as a forest. But the word rendered as 'forest' can mean a bare steppe or heath, so that the rendering can be given: 'and the garden-land will be reckoned as (i.e. no better than) a heath'. That would mean that the whole country is so productive that garden-land has lost its high value.

JUSTICE AND RIGHTEOUSNESS are established once more throughout the land (v. 16); the result is social stability and a quiet repose and trust in God (cf. 8.17; 25.9; 26.8; 30.18). Verse 18 means that the unquiet and troubled times caused by enemy invasions into the country are now at an end. In v. 19 the reference to 'hail' (so AV) seems quite out of place; one ancient version supports the rendering: 'And the forest will utterly fall down', which is a perfect parallel to the following AND THE CITY WILL BE UTTERLY LAID LOW. In the new age no watercourses will run dry; men will be able to sow their seed by all of them and not be disappointed. And they will be able to let THE OX AND THE ASS RANGE FREE; so abundant will be the pastures that there will be no need to herd them.

PRESENT DISTRESS AND FUTURE BLESSEDNESS

33.1–35.10

PROPHECY AND PRAYER: A LITURGY?

33.1-24

There is not, indeed, an alternation of prophetical passage and prayer in this passage, but there is such a combination of them that the whole appears as if it might have been a liturgy for use in the Temple to celebrate the deliverance of the people of Judah from a formidable foe. The chapter may be considered in four sections, although the divisions of it are not clear.

1-6. Yahweh is exalted

The first verse speaks of a savage, treacherous enemy who, when his own perfidious work is finished, will himself be betrayed and destroyed. There is a very uncertain and probably corrupt verbal form in the final clause of the verse, but the Dead Sea Scroll 1Q Isaᵃ now confirms what had been thought to be the sense: 'and when you have worked out all your treacheries, you yourself will be betrayed' (so RSV).

2-4 constitute a prayer for God's help and favour. In v. 2 read 'OUR help' (lit. ARM) as parallel to OUR SALVATION in the following clause. The coming of God is often described as being accompanied with thundering noise (cf. 29.6), and with a majestic and, indeed, terrifying manifestation of the powers of nature (v. 3). It is interesting that 1Q Isaᵃ has 'before thy silence' in place of 'when thou exaltest thyself' in the final clause of v. 3, but that is hardly to be preferred. In v. 4 'like the gathering of the caterpillar' (AV) should be rendered as AS THE CATERPILLAR GATHERS (so RSV), which presumably means leaving nothing ungathered but stripping everything utterly bare. As for the running or leaping of locusts, see Joel 2.9 for a description of an invasion of these insects.

5-6 are a contemplation following the prayer; the people are now spoken of in the second person, or are addressed. Earthly thrones perish and proud conquerors are humbled, but God is eternally exalted, and he has filled ZION WITH JUSTICE AND RIGHTEOUSNESS (v. 5; cf. 28.16 f.; 32.15 f.). There is a certain confusion of expression in v. 6, but the general meaning is not in doubt. It may be that the following rendering comes near to the original:

' Wisdom and knowledge are the stability (or security) of your
    times,
  the saving acts of Yahweh your strength,
  and the fear of Yahweh your treasure.'

7-12. The destruction of the enemy

In v. 7 the rendering VALIANT ONES is probably the best that can be made of a doubtful text; 'priests of the altar', another translation which has been proposed (cf. 29.1), while it is possible, does not appear to fit the context. The verse describes the extremities of the situation caused by the actions of the enemy; its second part and v. 8 refer to the treachery mentioned in v. 1. Verse 8 (read WITNESSES in place of 'cities', as RSV) reminds us of Judg. 5.6; the ruthless enemy has made the people of the land forsake the highways. The desolation of the countryside is graphically described in v. 9 by singling out for specific reference the districts which were especially fruitful and luxuriant; the whole land is dried up (not mourns) AND LANGUISHES. When Yahweh arises the enemy is vanquished. Verse

11 is curiously confused in expression. To CONCEIVE CHAFF and BRING FORTH STUBBLE is a remarkable way of saying that all that the enemy can produce will be readily combustible fuel for Yahweh's fire. But the subsequent statement that the enemy's breath is itself to be as fire seems to imply that he will work his own destruction; therefore read it as in the Targum: 'my breath like a fire will devour you.' THE PEOPLES mentioned in v. 12 are presumably the enemy peoples; there is no need to believe that the reference is to the peoples who are to be overthrown in the last days.

13-16. Who can survive the consuming fire?

Yahweh's mighty power has been manifested; let all tremble before him. THE SINNERS IN ZION now quake with fear (v. 14); who among them can hope to endure such a fiery testing? The answer in v. 15 gives a summary of the moral demands of Isaiah and other prophets; they add up to 'clean hands and a pure heart'. Verse 16 is often understood as a reference to Jerusalem; and, if it is genuinely Isaianic, this verse must have given strength to the belief which Jeremiah in his day had to combat, that the Jerusalem sanctuary was sacrosanct and inviolable (Jer. 7.12-14; 26.6-9). But the verse may simply mean that the man described in v. 15 is in an impregnable position in which no harm will befall him and he will never suffer want.

17-24. Words of promise

The king who is to reign is the king of righteousness of the new era (cf. 32.1). The AV translation 'the land that is very far off' suggests 'the happy land, far, far away', remote from this present world of space and time; but the RSV A LAND THAT STRETCHES FAR conveys the meaning of the original words more truly. The extent of the future kingdom is in contrast with the present confinement of the people by their enemies within the city of Jerusalem (cf. 33.7-9). The people will then look back upon THE TERROR through which they have passed and think again of the enemy officers who made the reckoning of numbers and amounts, WEIGHED THE TRIBUTE money, and COUNTED THE TOWERS. The last phrase is difficult; even if it signifies the commanders who counted the city towers which were the main points of resistance to attack, the phrase is not parallel to the preceding two. It may nevertheless be the correct text, and emendations of the noun to 'precious things' etc. may be quite unwarranted. The enemy, with their foreign, unintelligible tongue, will vanish for ever from the land.

20-22 offer a prayer for the future welfare of Jerusalem, 'THE CITY OF OUR APPOINTED festivals'. Not only is it to be a peaceful habitation, but AN IMMOVABLE TENT which will never be destroyed. Here is expressed the doctrine of the inviolability of Jerusalem (cf. v. 16 above). The first part of v. 21 is not easy to interpret, but its meaning may be: 'But there Yahweh will be glorious for us, in A PLACE OF BROAD RIVERS AND STREAMS.' It is tempting to read, as has sometimes been proposed, 'a fountain' instead of 'in a place', but the minor change necessary to get this very suitable result is not warranted. The rivers and streams are, presumably, those which bear refreshing waters to the peoples (cf. Ezek. 47); they are not the waters on which merchant fleets do their trade, as the second part of v. 22 explicitly states.

23a, which is associated in thought with v. 21 and comes in awkwardly after v. 22, may say that Zion is not equipped for such trade; her life is to be found by Yahweh's life-giving streams and not on the merchant highways by river or sea. But it may be an isolated fragment without any essential connection with its present context.

23b-24 add the final details of the pleasing prospect for Jerusalem in coming days. The spoil of the nations which will come to it will be abundant; sickness will be unknown and the people will be forgiven their iniquity. Thus the answer is given to the question put in v. 14.

This chapter 33 has often been ascribed to a period later than that of Isaiah, by some scholars to the end of the seventh century, when Babylon worked havoc in Judah, and by others to a date as late as the time of the Maccabean struggle in the second century BC, although how it came about in the latter case that the chapter ever found a place in the canon of the prophets is not easily understood. But the time of the deliverance of Jerusalem in the year 701 BC has much to commend it. At this time Judah was utterly devastated, forty-six walled city being destroyed and innumerable villages (see pp. 232 f. below and cf. the desolation described in v. 8). Jerusalem was surrendered and a heavy indemnity was paid (II Kings 18. 13-16). The fact that the Assyrians later returned to besiege the city may well have been interpreted as an act of treachery by the people of Judah, the peace of the city having been bought already (v. 1). It is to be noted that the Assyrian king at this time, Sennacherib, was, according to II Chron. 32.21, treacherously put to death by some of his own family. The Assyrians, equally with the Babylonians and much more than the Greeks of a later age, were fierce enemies who spoke a language which the men of Judah did not understand (v. 19). And, most important, the great deliverance from danger in 701 BC, which was not achieved by the weapons or the strategies of war, must have increased the prestige of Jerusalem, so that the great promise of its future expressed in vv. 20-22 and 24 becomes readily intelligible.

THE DESTRUCTION OF THE ENEMIES
OF GOD: EDOM

34.1-17

The first four verses summon the whole world to witness Yahweh's fury which is directed against all nations and against the host of heaven. But vv. 5 f. speak specifically of Edom (although THE PEOPLE I HAVE DOOMED, v. 5, could have a wider reference); and the great conflagration (vv. 9 f.) and the resultant desolation (vv. 11-15) probably have the same reference. The enmity between Israel and Edom went back to early times, as is evidenced by the fact that it is expressed in the story of Jacob and Esau (Gen. 27); it may have been acute during the reign of Ahaz (cf. II Kings 16.5); it was accentuated very much during the time of the Babylonian exile, when Judah was thinly populated and therefore exposed to the inroads of foreign invaders, among whom Edom was prominent (Obad. 10-12). But it seems proper to assume that Edom in this chapter represents all the enemies of Judah.

The chapter contains a poem of high literary worth. The ideas are often those of the prophet Isaiah, but the style seems more florid and the elaborate description of the desolation of the land which is given in vv. 11-15 does not have the distinctive qualities of Isaiah's way of speech.

1-4. In v. 1 all the nations are bidden to listen and pay heed. The next three verses describe how Yahweh lays all his enemies under a ban and destroys them in his fury; they lie unburied in their shame and their bodies rot upon the ground. The host of heaven also will fall in the same act of divine destruction, either because the sun, moon and stars had been objects of men's worship drawing them away in unfaithfulness from the one, true God (cf. II Kings 17.16), or because the angelic powers or patron deities (cf. 24.21) had enticed men to such unfaithfulness. Then the heavens, which were thought of as stretched out like a curtain (cf. 40.22), will be rolled up like a scroll.

5-7 are gruesome in some of their details. The work of destruction in heaven is accomplished first, so that Yahweh's sword is already dripping with blood when it comes down upon Edom. The people of that land who are now to be sacrificed are compared to rams and lambs and goats. Verse 7 tells how the domestic animals of the land as well as the inhabitants will be slaughtered.

8-10 describe the holocaust which ensues. In hyperbole the poet describes the rivers as running with pitch and the dust as turned into brimstone and the whole bursting out into unquenchable fire whose smoke goes up without ceasing. The result is a land utterly waste and barren, untrodden by the foot of man.

11-15. There are terms in these verses whose meaning is very doubtful. In v. 11 the bittern (AV) is a bird of the marshes and does not fit the context; but it is the name of a bird which the context requires, so that the porcupine of RSV is not in order here; which bird is intended cannot be determined with assurance. The second part of v. 11 is also uncertain. HE SHALL STRETCH A LINE OF CONFUSION OVER IT means that the land cannot now be measured with a measurer's line and so can never be rebuilt. The next part may be taken in one of two ways: (i) including the first word of v. 12, which is commonly rendered as 'its nobles' (cf. RSV), read the whole clause thus: 'and its parched wastes (not 'its nobles'; cf. Jer. 17.6) shall be chaotic heaps of stones'; or (ii) follow the evidence of the Greek version and read: 'and the plummet stone of chaotic waste. Her nobles shall be no more.' In both cases the remainder of v. 12 would read as: 'No kingdom shall be acclaimed there and all her princes shall come to nought.' THORNS, NETTLES AND THISTLES will take possession of her palaces and strong towers; they will be a haunt for JACKALS and OSTRICHES (v. 13). The creatures referred to in vv. 14-15 cannot be identified with certainty; in v. 14 they may be jerboas and hyenas (or jackals), while it is probably the he-goat (not the satyr) which calls to his mate; it is the horned owls (or the demons) which alight there by night. In v. 15 the birds which are said to pair and nest there are owls of some variety or other and kites (or vultures). All the birds and animals men-

P

tioned are of types which haunt uninhabited places and desert
areas; the land of Edom is now recognized by them as a suitable haunt.

16-17. It is not easy to decide here which book is intended.
The Book of Isaiah has been suggested, and even the whole
prophetic canon; neither seems likely. Elsewhere in the Bible
there is mentioned a book of life, in which the host of heaven
are numbered and named (cf. 40.26) and in which the destiny
of every man is recorded (cf. Ps. 139.16; Mal. 3.16; Dan. 7.10;
Rev. 20.12). This must be the meaning in the present context;
it is the book of life, the book of fate. The fate decreed for
Edom, therefore, is finally decreed; it is inevitable; and the
very animals which are specified as about to possess the
devastated land will play their part without fail; not one will
be missing. God apportions to each creature its time and place
and to every people and empire its day.

A HIGHWAY SHALL BE THERE

35.1-10

1-2 introduce a chapter which is in marked contrast with the
preceding one; they sound the note of joy and gladness at
once. The gloom is past; a new day has come; fruitfulness has
returned to the land; the wilderness and the desert are to
blossom and flourish like Carmel and Sharon (contrast 29.17;
33.9). In v. 1 read DRY LAND (RSV) for 'solitary place' (AV)
and with some ancient versions omit the words 'for them'.
The rhythmic form of the passage demands that the last three
words of v. 1 (AV, 'as the rose') should be taken into v. 2
thus: 'It shall blossom with asphodel' (not 'rose').

3-4 describe how the people who had been greatly distressed
and discouraged are now to be renewed in courage and in

vigour, because God is about to COME AND SAVE them, working vengeance on their enemies (cf. 33.14; 34.1-2).

5-6a. Then those who had been blind and obtuse will have insight and understanding again; ears will be opened to God's truth and men will learn once more to praise the Lord (cf. 30.20 f; 32.3; contrast 6.10; 29.10).

6b-10. The subject of these verses is the renewed fertility of the desert and the highway which will be built there. In the final part of v. 6b, 1Q Isaᵃ reads a verb thus: 'and streams shall flow in the desert'; this should probably be accepted. The translation of 7b in AV cannot stand, nor does the rendering 'swamp' of RSV suit the context; a more likely rendering, not, indeed, without uncertainty, would be: 'What was a lair of jackals will become a cattle-range, grass with reeds and rushes' (contrast 33.7, 9). In v. 8 the phrase 'and a way' (AV) obviously breaks the sequence; it may be omitted as an inadvertent repetition (so 1Q Isaᵃ) or, with the Greek version, we may read: 'And an undefiled highway shall be there.' In the later part of the verse, set between two perfectly suitable and, indeed, parallel clauses, THE UNCLEAN SHALL NOT PASS OVER IT and 'and knaves shall not trespass on it', there occurs a series of words whose meaning is very difficult to determine. Their literal rendering is: 'and it shall be theirs; a wayfarer'. Clearly this was not the original text, but unfortunately the versions give little aid in the effort to find out what the original text may have been. A simple and minor adaptation would give the translation: 'And it (i.e. the way) shall be for his people as they journey' (lit. going on the way). This great highway (contrast 30.21; 33.8) is to be for the redeemed of God's people, THE RANSOMED OF THE LORD, to return (cf. 42.16; 43.19); no wild beast will make journeying on it hazardous. It is the highway by which God's people return with joy and gladness to Zion.

As will be seen from the references which are given, this

chapter responds in many ways to much that is said in the
preceding chapters of the book. But it must be admitted that
the highway for the return of God's people is much more
characteristic of Isa. 40-55 than of the earlier part of this book,
even if 19.23 f. has a certain relevance. 25.8 and 30.19 do speak
of joy and gladness and of the end of sorrow and sighing, and
26.2 speaks of the righteous entering by the gates of Jerusalem;
but these verses refer to experiences of the people living in the
land of Judah. In this chapter, in the closing verses at least,
the highway is obviously for the return of God's people to the
land. That could refer, in the days of the prophet Isaiah, to
those of the northern kingdom who had been removed as
captives to Assyria when Samaria the capital city was captured (II Kings 17.5 ff.); but the parallel which it shows with
the thought of parts of Isa. 40-55 is notable and cannot be
denied, so that the chapter may belong to the later period of
the Jewish exile in Babylon in the sixth century BC.

A HISTORICAL RECORD

36.1–39.8

SENNACHERIB'S INVASION OF JUDAH AND THREAT TO JERUSALEM

36.1–37.38

Chs. 36-39 constitute a historical appendix to Chs. 1-35 of the Book of Isaiah. They are very closely paralleled in II Kings, the commentary upon which should be consulted for a fuller treatment of them; to II Kings, it is generally agreed, they belong. The reason for their introduction into the Book of Isaiah is undoubtedly the circumstance that these chapters recount some historical events in Judah in which the prophet was very much concerned. Reference should be made to II Kings 18.13–19.37; II Chron. 32.1-23; Herodotus II 141; and the Taylor Prism[1] for other accounts of the invasion of Judah by Sennacherib which took place in 701 BC and is described, especially with regard to the threat made against Jerusalem, in chs. 36-37 here.

36.1 tells very summarily of the capture by the Assyrians of the walled cities of Judah; the Taylor Prism mentions forty-six such cities and innumerable open villages, as well as a great wealth of plunder.

36.2-21 describe graphically the demand of Sennacherib's Rab-shakeh or Chief Steward (Rab-shakeh is a title, not a proper

[1] D. Winton Thomas, *Documents from Old Testament Times*, pp. 64-69.

name) for the surrender of Jerusalem. His address to the representatives of the king of Judah is an effort of rare skill. He took up position beside the conduit of the upper pool (cf. 7.3), and with words of authorization not unlike in form those which the people of Judah had sometimes heard from the lips of their prophets, he said: THUS SAITH THE GREAT KING, THE KING OF ASSYRIA. The meaning of v. 5 is quite lost in the strangely stuttering translation of it which is given in AV; the RSV makes it clear. Words, however grandiose, can never be a substitute for the strategy of war, nor can boasts take the place of military strength. As for Egypt, in whom the people of Judah are inclined to place reliance, it will promise the world and betray those who take such promises seriously. And what can Yahweh, the God of Israel, be expected to do for a people who have but recently taken down his altars and confined his worship to one central shrine? (cf. II Kings 18.4). These taunts must have stung the citizens of the capital to the quick; Isaiah himself had said the same about Egypt (cf. 30. 1-5; 31.1-3); and many of them had been by no means comfortable about the religious reform to which the Rab-shakeh had made such contemptuous reference. At once, the Rab-shakeh introduces a note of scorn (v. 8). And he finishes by using a very daring line. Have the citizens of Jerusalem never thought of the possibility that, in devastating Judah, the Assyrians are fulfilling a commission from Yahweh himself and are the instrument of his fury? (cf. 10.5).

Panic-stricken, the Judaean representatives ask the Rab-shakeh to say what he has to say in Aramaic, and not in the popular Hebrew which the people speak (v. 11). The request is unceremoniously brushed aside; it is to the people that the Rab-shakeh is speaking, warning them not to trust in Hezekiah or in Yahweh (vv. 14 f.). There is no ground for such trust (vv. 18-20[1]). There is only one sensible course open to

---

[1] Arpad and Hamath were in the north part of Syria, and Sepharvaim was between Hamath and Damascus, so that all three had been on Sennacherib's invasion route.

them, to surrender to the Assyrians and to return to normal conditions of life as soon as possible (v. 16). He nonchalantly adds that they will in due course be removed from their native land; but that should mean no loss to them, for the land to which they will go will be like their own, but a greater and a better (v. 17).

36.22–37.7 The Judean representatives present at this interview reported it to Hezekiah (v. 22). The king had no illusions about the seriousness of the situation and went into the Temple to seek guidance, and, at the same time, sent messengers to the prophet Isaiah to tell him of the crisis and to ask for his prayers for the city and its people (37.1-4). The prophet's answer was encouraging; the danger would soon pass; a rumour of trouble at home would cause Sennacherib to leave Jerusalem and he would meet a violent death in his own land (37.5-7).

37.8-38. Vs. 8-20 recount a second visit of the Assyrians to Jerusalem. The occasion seems to have been the change made in the situation by the arrival of an army under the king of Ethiopia (vv. 8 f.). The messengers who now come to Jerusalem use words remarkably similar to those used by the Rab-shakeh on the preceding occasion (37.10-13; cf. 36.18-20). The document which contained their message Hezekiah took with him into the Temple and SPREAD . . . BEFORE THE LORD and prayed for the destruction of the Assyrian king who had treated their God with contempt and his people with mockery (37.14-20). Verses 21-35 record an elaborate answer from the prophet Isaiah to the king's appeal to him, an answer which is in marked contrast to that given in 37.6 f. Verses 22-29 contain what might be called a taunt-song against the king of Assyria, in which his vain boasting is condemned, the rule of Yahweh is affirmed and intimation is made that the arrogant Assyrian will be turned back home ignominiously. Verses 30-32 then declare that for the current year and the one next following the

land will remain uncultivated; thereafter it will be fruitful
again. Verses 33-35 could themselves follow upon vv. 21-22a,
giving the answer of Isaiah, and would make sense without
the intervening verses; they tell how Jerusalem will not be
captured and that the Assyrians will return by the way by
which they came. Verses 36-38 describe a terrible *débâcle* of
the Assyrian army, presumably before Jerusalem, when an
amazingly large number of men are said to have died. Thereafter Sennacherib left Judah with the remnants of his army,
and was murdered by his own sons on an occasion when he
was at worship in the temple of his god.

There are problems of interpretation in these narratives
which cannot be dealt with fully here. One important question
is this: ' Were there two Assyrian overtures to Jerusalem, seeking the surrender of the city, the one before the arrival in
Palestine of the army of the king of Ethiopia and the other
after its arrival? ' Another is this: ' Is the surrender of Jerusalem, which is recorded in II Kings 18.14-16, to be taken in
conjunction with the visit of the Rab-shakeh to the capital, and
should we refer the visit of the Assyrian messengers (37.8-20)
to a later occasion? One argument against the latter interpretation of the evidence is that between the two narratives
of the Assyrian envoys who appeared before the walls of Jerusalem, to call for the surrender of the city, there are notable
parallels, so that the impression is given that, although, as
they appear now, the second is given a different occasion
(cf. 37.9), yet they should be regarded as two slightly varying
accounts of the same event. A reconstruction of the course of
events might, therefore, be given as follows.

II Kings 18.14-16 records the first threat of Sennacherib to
Jerusalem, when the city was surrendered to him and paid a
heavy indemnity. Some time thereafter the army under the
king of Ethiopia arrived in Palestine; the fact that Tirhakah
did not become king of Egypt until 689 BC does not invalidate
this statement, in which he is named, properly for this time
(701 BC), as king of Ethiopia. It was now that Sennacherib sent

his envoys, probably led by the Rab-shakeh, to Jerusalem, and his speech is recorded in 36.12-20 (cf. 37.10-13). The sequel to that challenge was twofold: Hezekiah sought guidance in the Temple as to what he should do in the circumstances and, at the same time, he sent for advice to Isaiah. The former is recorded very inadequately in 37.1 but in an adequate and satisfying form in 37.14-20. The latter is related in one form in 37.6-7, in which Isaiah states that Sennacherib will depart because of a rumour and will be put to death in his own land, and in another in 37.21-22a, 33-36, in which it is said that Sennacherib will not capture Jerusalem but will return home by the way by which he came. In addition, in association with this second form, there are to be found the taunt song of 37.22b-29 and the prophecy that, after a specified interval, the land will be cultivated again (37.30-32).

The final part of the narrative, in 37.36-39, has in vv. 37 f. a statement which is a fitting sequel to 37.7b. It is doubtful if originally these verses followed upon v. 36, which, when it speaks of an angel working destruction in the Assyrian army, means a thoroughgoing *débâcle*, such as that which Herodotus attributes to the fact that a plague of mice gnawed the bow-strings and the thongs of the shields of the Assyrian army; but the incredible number of the dead makes this verse appear like a later addition to the narrative, or the glorification of an originally simpler statement.

HEZEKIAH'S ILLNESS AND RECOVERY

38.1-22

1-8 tell of the king's illness and recovery. The basic account of the occurrence is in II Kings 20.1-11. The notable difference between the two versions is that the one in II Kings contains after v. 6 two verses which are found in Isaiah at the end of the chapter as vv. 21 f. and are out of place there. These

two verses, therefore, should be read in this chapter after
v. 6.

The king's illness is serious and the prophet tells him to
prepare for death (v. 1). Hezekiah was twenty-five years of
age when he came to the throne (II Kings 18.2); the meaning of
'in those days' (v. 1) is quite uncertain; but if it means the
days of Sennacherib's invasion, that would make it that Hezekiah was now in the fourteenth year of his reign (cf. 36.1) so
that he was thirty-nine. Therefore, the king bemoaned his fate
at so early an age, and prayed to God to remember his life
of faithful and dutiful service—which was an implied entreaty
for his life to be spared (vv. 2 f.). Isaiah now returns to the
king to say that his prayer has been heard and that he is to live
for fifteen years more. Verse 6, which promises the deliverance
of Jerusalem from the Assyrians and so connects these verses
for occasion with chs. 36-37, is probably a later addition in this
context. It may very well be that the date which is given in 36.1
properly belongs to this chapter, since it may be observed that
the fourteenth year of the king's reign which is mentioned
there, when taken with the fifteen additional years now granted,
make up the total of twenty-nine years mentioned in II Kings
18.2.

21-22 are to be taken here. The therapeutic value of a fig
plaster was apparently well known in Isaiah's day (v. 21). It is
not unexpected that Hezekiah should ask for a sign that he
would recover from his illness, since the prophet had so soon
before said that he would die (v. 22); the sign which is specified
in vv. 7 f. is given in a somewhat expanded form in II Kings
20.9-11. Probably it was not on a sundial that the shadow cast
by the declining sun was to be shortened by ten steps, but on
a flight of steps which were so set that they served as a good
reckoner of the hour of the day. Likewise Hezekiah's day was
to be abnormally lengthened in the mercy of God. Why the
sun's shadow was shortened by ten steps, and not by fifteen, is
not clear.

9-20, a so-called writing of Hezekiah, is a psalm of thanks-giving and is not found in II Kings 20; it is, therefore, an insertion here. It may or may not have had a connection with Hezekiah, but is eminently suitable for the purpose for which it was introduced where it now stands. The text of it, especially in vv. 12-16, is uncertain and at several points the AV cannot be accepted; the RSV offers a translation which is much better and should be consulted. In v. 10 the words 'in the cutting off of my days' (AV) must be taken to mean 'when my days cease', i.e. when my life comes to an end—a possible, but unlikely rendering. Rather it should be 'in the quietness of my days' i.e. the noonday quietness (so RSV), i.e. when he was in the midst of life and was looking forward to many more years. The tragedy of it was that death would mean for the king separation from the human community on earth and from God (v. 11). In v. 12 the first phrase should certainly be 'My house is pulled up and REMOVED FROM ME LIKE A SHEPHERD'S TENT', i.e. it is as easily taken down as that. The following phrase is also difficult, and there seems to be a certain confusion of personal references. The meaning is probably something like this: 'I roll up my life, as a weaver rolls up his cloth when he cuts it off from the loom.' Again, the phrase 'from day until night' is of uncertain meaning; the whole clause, of which it is a part, may mean: 'From morning until night thou requitest me,' or 'In the brief interval from morning to night thou givest me up.' The words after that, which are attached in sense to v. 12, probably mean 'I wait for the morning' or 'I cry out until the morning.' The sufferer twitters LIKE A SWALLOW and moans LIKE A DOVE, a sign of failing strength; his EYES ARE WEARY WITH LOOKING UPWARD to God for help and he pleads that God will go surety for him (v. 14). At the beginning of v. 15 we should translate: What word can I speak or what can I say for myself?', or, with the Targum, 'What word can I speak or what am I to say to him?' The remainder of the verse is open to question. The AV rendering means that the sufferer will now go quietly and uncomplainingly for the rest of his

life, which is a suitable, if quite uncertain, rendering; otherwise
the Syriac version gives support to the rendering adopted by
the RSV ALL MY SLEEP HAS FLED BECAUSE OF THE BITTERNESS
OF MY SOUL, i.e. sleep has entirely forsaken me. The first part
of v. 16 (AV and RSV) is highly doubtful; THESE THINGS must
be presumably the words and works of God; but it is very
doubtful. Getting some help from the Greek version, we may
venture the translation of v. 16 and the opening of v. 17 in
this way: ' In spite of this, my heart has hope in thee; let my
spirit have rest. Do thou restore me and revive me again, that
my bitterness may become peace.' The rest of the psalm is
easily intelligible. The psalmist acknowledges that he has been
saved from death (v. 17) so that, being still in the land of the
living, he can give thanks to God, as those who go down to
Sheol cannot do (vv. 18 f.). At the beginning of v. 20 we should
probably read: ' The Lord was pleased to save me.'

HEZEKIAH AND MERODACH BALADAN
OF BABYLON

39.1-8

Just as 38.6 connects that chapter with chs. 36-37, so now
39.1b connects this chapter with ch. 38. We saw reason to
suggest that 38.6 is probably an addition to the context in
which it now stands, so that the invasion of Sennacherib into
Judah in 701 BC, narrated in chs. 36-37, need not be considered to be the time of Hezekiah's sickness, which is re-
counted in ch. 38. But, if the visit of Merodach Baladan to
Jerusalem took place soon after the king of Judah had
recovered from his illness, have we any clue as to the date of
these two closely related events? We know that Merodach
Baladan was king of Babylon for a period of twelve years
(721-709 BC) when Sargon was king of Assyria, and for a period
of six months only near the beginning of the reign of Senna-

cherib which began in 705. The latter period seems too short
for such a visit to Jerusalem as is recorded here; the later
years of the earlier period suit very well.

That the whole purpose of Merodach Baladan's visit was to
congratulate Hezekiah upon his recovery from a very serious
illness is refuted by the fact that Hezekiah showed his visitor
all his national wealth. That leads us to the conclusion that
Merodach was seeking the help of Hezekiah, probably as an
ally against Assyria. The prophet Isaiah was, of course, interested in what seemed a venture on the part of his king into
the field of international politics (vv. 3 f.). The prophet's
answer, as given in vv. 5-8, to the effect that the whole wealth
of the country, together with some of the king's sons, would
be transported to Babylon, is very notable and has induced
many scholars to come to the conclusion that these verses, in
the form in which they stand now, must belong to the time
around 600 BC or a little later, when Judah was in grave danger
from the power of Babylon which had by that time succeeded
Assyria as the dominant power in the whole near-eastern area.
But it remains a possibility that to Isaiah, at this time, Babylon,
under the leadership of Merodach Baladan, may have seemed
a very formidable power indeed and he may have expected it
to oust Assyria. If this can be adjudged a real possibility, then
we have to leave open the question of the authenticity of these
verses, however suitably they may be attributed to 600 BC or
thereabouts. The final word of Hezekiah on this occasion (v. 8),
hoping for a continuation of stable conditions in the kingdom
as long as he lived, is like the heart-felt wish of an old man;
yet he may have been only thirty-nine years of age at the time
(cf. II Kings 18.2 and Isa. 36.1).